Pax Britannica: Tracing Customary War Crimes in the Age of Empire

International Humanitarian Law Series

VOLUME 70

The International Humanitarian Law Series is a series of monograhs and edited volumes which aims to promote scholarly analysis and discussion of both the theory and practice of the international legal regulation of armed conflict.

The series explores substantive issues of International Humanitarian Law, including:

- Protection for victims of armed conflict and regulation of the means and method of warfare
- Questions of application of the various legal regimes for the conduct of armed conflict
- Issues relating to the implementation of International Humanitarian Law obligations
- National and international approaches to the enforcement of the law and
- The interactions between International Humanitarian Law and other related areas of international law such as Human Rights, Refugee Law, Arms Control and Disarmament Law, and Intenational Criminal Law.

The titles published in this series are listed at *brill.com/ihul*

Pax Britannica: Tracing Customary War Crimes in the Age of Empire

By

Samuel White and Ikhwan Fazli

BRILL | NIJHOFF

LEIDEN | BOSTON

Cover illustration: Kevin Gilbert, Colonising Species, 1994, Linocut on paper. Linocut of black and white swan adapted from Canberra's armorial bearings, with red and yellow colouring. Printed with kind permission of Kevin Gilbert's widow.

Library of Congress Cataloging-in-Publication Data

Names: White, Samuel Camden Duckett, author. | Fazli, Ikhwan, author.
Title: Pax britannica: tracing customary war crimes in the age of empire: a critical theory of global society and politics / by Samuel Camden and Ikhwan Fazli.
Description: Leiden; Boston: Brill | Nijhoff, 2025. | Series: International humanitarian law series, 1389–6776 ; vol.70 | Includes bibliographical references. | Summary: "The 'original sin' of the laws of war - its exclusion of non-Europeans from its protection - shapes discussions around criminal liability for conduct during colonial expansion.
Identifiers: LCCN 2024062314 (print) | LCCN 2024062315 (ebook) | ISBN 9789004515970 (hardback) | ISBN 9789004515987 (ebook)
Subjects: LCSH: International crimes–Law and legislation. | Criminal liability (International law) | Crimes against humanity–Law and legislation. | International crimes–Law and legislation. | Imperialism–History. | State crimes–Law and legislation. | Great Britain–Colonies–History. | Colonialism–History.
Classification: LCC KZ7139 .W45 2025 (print) | LCC KZ7139 (ebook) | DDC 341.6/9–dc23/eng/20250108
LC record available at https://lccn.loc.gov/2024062314
LC ebook record available at https://lccn.loc.gov/2024062315

Typeface for the Latin, Greek, and Cyrillic scripts: "Brill". See and download: brill.com/brill-typeface.

ISSN 1389-6776
ISBN 978-90-04-51597-0 (hardback)
ISBN 978-90-04-51598-7 (e-book)
DOI 10.1163/9789004515987

Contents

Acknowledgements

Like anything, these works do not just occur in isolation. Thanks are required to the multiple individuals and teams that worked on the project.

To the University of Adelaide, that financially sponsored the primary author through a Postdoctoral Research Fellowship, and the secondary author through Research Assistance funding — thank you.

Finally, to our respective families — thank you.

Foreword

A foreword is meant to convey something about the significance of the book it precedes. It is meant to have greater weight than a mere advertisement but nonetheless tell potential readers why they should read this book. This book is significant, and anyone who thinks about the legacy of the British Empire and the rule of law should read this book.

Decolonisation is a popular term today but, given it is an essentially negative term, it has a potential to mislead. The consequences of colonialism under the British Empire are not going away any time in the foreseeable future. The legacy of the Roman Empire is still with us more than a millennia after its fall. The British Empire was the largest in history and, given that its peak is still within living memory, it still determines the language, the law, the literature and the lineage of so much of the world today. The good and bad of the British Empire must therefore occupy our critical attention. If we are to consider seriously what the rule of law means in this world, we cannot actually decolonise. We can criticise and evaluate the Empire, and reassert the cultures it dominated, but we cannot decolonise away what has happened.

The rule of law is under serious challenge from revisionist powers such as China, Russia and Iran. Now is the time to think about what underlies the international rule of law. To appreciate that so much of what we might value in that legal order has a basis in the British Empire, and that so much of the excesses of that empire were perceived by some, if not all, as wrong at the time, is of fundamental importance right now.

This book concerns the customary war crimes of the British Empire and it addresses in turn eight specific prohibitions, particularly:

- Summary execution
- Sexual violence
- Perfidy
- Slavery
- Looting
- Brigandry and Piracy
- Forced Dispersal and Deportation
- Private warfare

It draws conclusions on the existence and the strength of each one. These war crimes are amongst the most significant of any age, as they are the essence of disorder, inhumanity and brutality, and quite the opposite of the rule of law. The conclusions on each prohibition are therefore a reflection on the British

Empire itself, both in its propensity to inflict such suffering and in its ability to restrain it, whether inflicted by its own forces or by others.

The book concludes that summary execution was widespread but by the 1880s the practice was to prohibit such killing, and also protest such action by other European powers. Most notably for Australians, Lieutenant Harry 'Breaker' Morant was among those court martialled and shot for the execution of Boer prisoners and civilians in South Africa. The British Government also protested the massacre of Herero-Nama people in South West Africa, now Namibia, pursuant to the orders of the German commander, General Lothar von Trotha. Summary execution is still occurring in conflicts today, but this book reminds us that it has been seen as wrong for a very long time.

In relation to sexual violence, which seems to be a recurring feature of any conflict, the book concludes that there was patchy enforcement of a prohibition depending mostly on the will of the commander of the forces concerned. Clear orders were given in various campaigns to prohibit such conduct and sometimes these were enforced. British sailors and soldiers were flogged or sentenced to death for outrages against American women in the war of 1812. Major Norris also investigated claims of attempted rape by members of the British West India Regiment in Sierra Leone in 1898 and 1899. The current prohibitions on sexual violence in war can be seen then to have part of their origin in the practice of the British Empire. Again, even if sexual violence is pervasive, if it was punishable in 1812 then it should most certainly be punishable now. There is no scope for a *c'est la guerre* argument.

Perfidy is a broader topic and usually involved inviting the trust of an adversary and then breaching that trust, whether through breaches of an oath, the misuse of protected emblems or the use of poison and assassination. This was different to the use of deception, such as by camouflage or ambush, as there was no breach of trust. By its nature this is a diffuse and complicated area of the law, differing in its rules for conflict at sea and on land. The book concludes that by the end of the nineteenth century there was an enforceable prohibition on such conduct against Western powers, as seen in the 1880 *Oxford Manual*, and an emerging prohibition on such conduct against non-Western people. The example given is that of British condemnation of a German breach of trust in inviting Herero chiefs for peace talks, and then murdering most of the group in 1903. Whilst perfidy is more clearly regulated today, it still goes on. Any argument that it is somehow justifiable should find a rebuttal in this book, to the effect that perfidy has long been contrary to custom, as well as being contrary to modern treaties.

The prohibition on slavery stands in contrast to the other prohibitions under discussion as perhaps one of the greatest achievements of the British

Empire, while earlier being one of its greatest sources of shame. Much of the British Empire grew upon the slave trade, if not directly then indirectly through the wealth it generated then enabling expansion into the rest of the world. The abolition of slavery grew from the advocacy of Christian groups, which included notable figures such as William Wilberforce, John Newton and JS Mill. The prohibition on the trade became a key task of the Royal Navy throughout the nineteenth century. Today article 99 of the 1982 *United Nations Convention on the Law of the Sea* (*UNCLOS*) of 1982 has its origin in these developments, stating:

> **Prohibition of the transport of slaves**
> Every State shall take effective measures to prevent and punish the transport of slaves in ships authorized to fly its flag and to prevent the unlawful use of its flag for that purpose. Any slave taking refuge on board any ship, whatever its flag, shall *ipso facto* be free.

The practice of slavery persisted in some parts of the Empire, such as in what is now Malaysia, or in West Africa where it still persists, or in the practice of 'blackbirding' in Queensland. The book concludes that the prohibition was not complete but was nonetheless enforceable and significant in British imperial policy. Slavery remains an issue, with modern slavery legislation appearing in the United Kingdom and Australia, and this book reminds us what an important and hard-won achievement the abolition of slavery was.

Looting of cultural property on the other hand has a less admirable history. The book concludes that while there may have been an enforceable prohibition against the looting of Western cultural property, by the end of the nineteenth century there was no such prohibition in respect of looting of non-Western property. The book describes the Congress of Vienna in 1815 compelling France to restore cultural property looted from Europe during the Napoleonic Wars, whereas there was no requirement for France to return cultural objects taken from Egypt. There are ongoing controversies over the Parthenon Marbles and the Koh-I-Noor diamond as mentioned in the book, and also the return of human remains and cultural objects from museums and universities to indigenous groups around the world. This would suggest that there was no settled customary prohibition on looting the cultural property of non-Western people in the British Empire at the end of the nineteenth century. The important point today is that if looting was prohibited in some cases in 1815 then, if racism is no longer acceptable, it should be prohibited in all cases. Even if imperfectly, the customary prohibition of the nineteenth century provides a basis for such a prohibition now.

Brigandy and piracy had a very different character. As *hostis humani generis*, the enemy of all humankind, pirates may be the first war criminals in international law. Brigands too are described as armed robbers, bandits, pillagers and freebooters. The book is confident in concluding that brigandry on land and piracy at sea was prohibited during the period in question. International law provided no protection for such persons, who were in themselves a threat to the legal order. These people could be attacked and put to death, with this probably occurring in South East Asia against pirates in the early nineteenth century and in Europe against brigands during the Hundred Years War and the English Civil War. Whilst today the prohibition is equally clear, brigands and pirates would now have the legal protections of any criminals, even if they could be attacked whilst engaged in brigandry and piracy. The longstanding nature of these prohibitions nonetheless underscores their importance today. It is relevant to the discussion of private warfare in Chapter 7 below. The concept of illegitimate combatants has also had prominence since the beginning of the United States' 'Global War on Terror' in 2001. This book therefore provides some important perspective on the legitimacy of participation in combat, as well as which combatants are worthy of privileges and protection, with each being issues of both morality and law.

Possibly the worst and most enduring legacy of the British Empire has been what might since the 1990s have been called ethnic cleansing. This includes deporting a population or destroying it through genocide and forced assimilation into a larger culture. There is plenty of evidence of both occurring right up until the end of the nineteenth century. Examples of deportation include moving native North American, Australian Aboriginal or New Zealand Māori populations onto reserves or moving Boer families into concentration camps. Even if these populations were not taken to another country altogether in terms of the Empire, they were clearly taken from their own land and forced to live in much diminished conditions somewhere else. At worst, there was wholesale slaughter. This was the case in Australia. Despite considerable evidence of genocidal campaigns in various parts of the country, many do not accept that this occurred. There was only one notable prosecution in respect of the Myall Creek Massacre in 1838. The effect nonetheless has been an almost complete deprivation of language, law and land for Aboriginal people in most of the more populated parts of the country. The book concludes that by the end of the nineteenth century there was an emerging prohibition on forced dispersal and deportation of Western populations but it was patchy, while there was certainly no prohibition on this conduct towards non-Western populations. Even if in stark contrast to the law as it stands now, this is still not surprising given the ongoing impacts of settler colonialism in parts of the Empire such as Australia. This book should add to the impetus for a sober reckoning on this today.

The final chapter deals with the prohibition on private warfare. For those living in industrialised liberal democracies, the monopoly of the state over warfare is a deep seated assumption. The idea that private actors could wage warfare is virtually inconceivable. In many other parts of the world private warfare is the norm, whether in Myanmar, Lebanon or Papua New Guinea. The presence of tribal warfare, private militias or warlords would be the antithesis of the rule of law, their presence even defining the absence of legal restraints on violence. The conclusion of this book is that, by the end of the nineteenth century, the prohibition against private warfare 'was fully crystallised' in the British Empire. This did not extend to non-Western peoples and this foreword has already mentioned some of the horror that follows from this. Again, if racism is no longer acceptable, then the legacy of the British Empire should be that any private warfare is now contrary to the rule of law. The barely acknowledged assumption that the state has a monopoly on warfare which exists in so many Commonwealth countries is then a legacy of that empire.

Having considered the various prohibitions under discussion, it is possible now to consider the overall significance of this book. There are a number of important points to note in this fascinating collaboration between Associate Professor Sam White and Ikhwan Fazli Bin Adi Bokharee. The first is the collaboration between the authors themselves. White is from a settler society in Australia which is one of the key beneficiaries and inheritors of the British Empire. If ever there was a society which sought to displace and supplant its original inhabitants, then Australia is it. On the other hand, Fazli is from Malaysia, a state which was subject to British rule and excesses but not to settler colonialism to the same extent as Australia. Malaysia has maintained traditional forms of authority alongside British style parliamentary democracy and the rule of law in the form of the common law. The differing but also the shared perspectives of the authors are important. There is little literature on the customary laws of war of the British Empire, nor much co-authorship of legal texts between Malaysians and Australians. The mere fact of this collaboration then is in itself significant in moving to a more mature understanding of the legacy of the British Empire — those living with that legacy need to talk about it together.

The next important point about this book is what it says about the rule of law in the British Empire, particularly at its height in the late nineteenth and early twentieth centuries. There were clearly horrific excesses but the fact that there were occasions when there was legal accountability means that there was restraint. The rule of law did restrain power and arbitrariness, even if only rarely or not at all for some prohibitions and far from perfectly. Whilst the British Empire does not look at all restrained to many today, the beginnings of its rule of law legacy can be found. This is important in assessing culpability at the time. It is not possible to say that this was just the way things were back then. Some people at the time knew that there should be prohibitions, that they were being breached, and that something should be done about it. This opens the way to discussing restitution and acts of contrition today.

The assertion of the rule of law during the height of the British Empire, even in only a small way, should also make for a more sophisticated assessment of the legacy of that Empire. The rule of law we enjoy today, however imperfect, has its origins in this history. The British Empire did bring parliamentary democracy and the common law to many parts of the world. Despite independence, many parts of the Commonwealth still value these attributes of their societies, indeed these are key values in the 2012 Commonwealth Charter, which states:

> Affirming that the special strength of the Commonwealth lies in the combination of our diversity and our shared inheritance in language, culture and the rule of law; and bound together by shared history and tradition; by respect for all states and peoples; by shared values and principles and by concern for the vulnerable.[1]

The shared aspect of this history is as important as the rule of law itself. In addition to the practical benefit of being able to share case law, legal expertise and legal scholarship, just as in this book, the reinforcing effect of numerous countries upholding these traditions is immeasurable but clearly significant given the terms of the Commonwealth Charter. The current threats to the international rules-based order means that this shared legacy may be more important than ever. It may just provide the necessary strength to maintain that order.

This writer has experience travelling through southern Africa and engaging in rule of law discussions in India, Sri Lanka, Bangladesh, Malaysia, Singapore, Brunei, the Philippines, Papua New Guinea, Solomon Islands, Fiji, New Zealand, Canada, the United States and the United Kingdom. The shared common law tradition has made for an invaluable starting point in considering both domestic and international law, as well as national values and interests. This is not just a case of shared knowledge but also a shared way of thinking

1 *Commonwealth Charter*, Preamble, https://thecommonwealth.org/charter.

where law should restrain power, where the common law can develop to meet new challenges and where these values operate as much through private citizens as through government. The common law then is a culture as well as a legal system. This cultural legacy of the British Empire then can always act as a counter to authoritarianism. Whether it is successful in particular instances or not, it has persisted and inspired people to assert the rule of law where they can.

The approach of this book to analysing the practice, as opposed to the theory, of applying customary prohibitions in war also underlies this more sophisticated assessment of the British Empire. Despite the history of international law being Eurocentric and imperial in many respects, the historical evidence provided in the book for the application of different prohibitions at different times illustrates that this history has both a detrimental and beneficial legacy. To say now that the British Empire was a bad thing is just as unsatisfactory as saying simply that it was a good thing. It was not everywhere and always the same.

A further important point is the place of this book in the developing scholarship on customary laws of war across time and space, considering its totality rather than just the British Empire. The religious insight and consideration of natural law in Chapter 1, and the conclusion, is profound. Whilst the substance of the prohibitions may vary between religions and cultures, the presence of restraint in the conduct of warfare tells us much about the human condition. Despite our propensity for violence there is something within in us that says it must somehow be authorised and controlled, even if in practice it is often not. Traditions across the world mourn past violence and yet still seek ways to justify and manage it now. The desire for power creates the propensity for violence. This means that we never seem to be able to overcome our need for violence as a means of control, even though that control can only ever be transitory. On the other hand, the destruction which this violence causes means that humanity is always seeking ways to mitigate it effects. These competing desires forever seem to be in tension.

This book therefore is an important contribution to understanding warfare, war crimes, the British Empire and ourselves. I am grateful to have been asked to write this foreword and commend the book to readers.

Professor Cameron Moore, University of New England

Introduction

> Surely it is a heresy to believe that infidels are not masters of their own property; consequently, to take from them their possessions on account of their religious beliefs is no less theft and robbery than it would be in the case of Christians.
>
> Nor are the East Indians stupid and unthinking; on the contrary they are intelligent and shrewd so that the pretext for subduing them on the ground of their character could not be sustained. Such a pretext on its very face is an injustice. Plutarch said long ago that the civilising of barbarians had been made the pretext for aggression, which is to say that a greedy longing for the property of another often hides behind a pretext. And now that well known pretext of forcing nations into a higher state of civilisation against their will ... is considered by all theologians ... to be unjust and unholy. They [heathens and infidels] are not to be deprived of sovereignty over their possessions because of their unbelief, since sovereignty is a matter of positive law, and unbelief a matter of divine law ... In fact I know of no law against such unbelievers as regards their temporal possessions. Against them no King, no Emperor, not even the Roman Church, can declare war for the purpose of occupying their lands, or of subjecting them to temporal sway.[2]

∴

Sovereignty is a bundle of rights and responsibilities. It allows for control over one's land, one's resources, one's future. It also requires accepting one's past.

We in the former colonies of the British Empire — some that have become Republics, others that have left the Commonwealth, and others yet who remain constitutional monarchies — are often blessed with better, longer and richer lives than any forebears we may have. We are also left with the legal and moral legacies of those of the Iron Age of the British Empire: those decades of

2 Hugo Grotius, *Mare Liberum* [Freedom of the Seas] (Oxford University Press, 1916) 19, as cited by Henry Reynolds, Aboriginal Sovereignty: Reflections on Race, State and Nation (Allen & Unwin, 1996) 44.

 | DOI:10.1163/9789004515987_002

expansion for land, whose flags and symbols and prerogatives expanded across the globe regardless of those systems it found. Those decades of possessing lands were premised upon percieved levels of civilisations. It is important, therefore, to understand in-depth the legal frameworks of the Age of Empire.

A Legal Legacies

One of these legacies is law. As the British Crown extended its holdings, these operations did not occur in a lawless vacuum. There were clear rules, responsibilities, rights and regulations that applied to colonists before, during and after their settlements in new lands.[3] For the most part, these obligations arose from the unique nature of the legal foundation upon which there were built: the Royal Prerogative. The term 'prerogative' is apt to be misunderstood, and is often taken to signify something tyrannical. However, prerogative power is defined and delimited by law, and acts done in purported exercise of the Royal Prerogative are contrary to law if they exceed constitutional boundaries.

As a historical entity, 'the prerogative can only be fully understood in its more recent manifestations through taking a long-term perspective'.[4] Necessarily, this requires a discussion of its etymology.[5] The term comes from Latin, describing a collection of individuals who voted first in matters of state.[6] The English derivate, *prerogative*, took on the meaning of a special right or privilege, possessed by an individual or group. It was equally tied to the feudal concept of *majesty*, linked to those privilege holders.[7] This amalgam can be found in the period of history after the fall of the Western Roman Empire led to its division amongst successive Germanic tribal kingdoms. These kingdoms in turn influenced the legal evolution of prerogative power, combined with customary Germanic law. Feudal law, as this melting pot of legal systems came to be known, took precedence from the 8th century onwards, with 'its

3 See Enid Campbell, 'Prerogative Rule in New South Wales 1788–1823' (1964) 50 *Royal Australian Historical Society Journal* 162, 175–9.

4 Andrew Blick, 'Emergency Powers and the Withering of the Royal Prerogative' (2014) 18(2) *International Journal of Human Rights* 195, 196.

5 Noel Cox, *The Royal Prerogative and Constitutional Law: A Search for the Quintessence of Executive Power* (Taylor & Francis Group, 2020) 21. See also Sebastian Payne, 'The Royal Prerogative' in Maurice Sunkin and Sebastian Payne (eds), *The Nature of the Crown: A Legal and Political Analysis* (Oxford University Press, 1999) 77.

6 William Blackstone, *Commentaries on the Laws of England* (Clarendon Press, 1765–69) vol 1, 239.

7 Thomas Poole, 'Judicial Review at the Margins: Law, Power and Prerogative' (2010) 60 *University of Toronto Law Journal* 81, 95–6.

stress upon personal relations, landed property and lack of written, formal, legislation [which] is related to [Germanic] law rather than Roman law'.[8] The feudal melting pot of Roman and Germanic law is an important, and oft-understudied, part of executive power. It is an important theme that will be consistently referred to throughout this work.

Understandably, the bundle of original prerogative rights in Anglo-Saxon history was related to landholding and from this flows many prerogative powers concerned with land (both its ownership, and its protection) such as the prerogatives of war, peace, annexation and internal security.[9]

In accordance with its linkages to majesty as a concept, the Crown also began to adopt a theological basis, reflecting that the monarch was God's representative on Earth and without peer.[10] As a hierarchy, those underneath the monarch were required to provide service and absolute fealty. This requirement was derived from the Roman tradition of allegiance. In the Roman Republic, no one could lawfully serve in the military without taking the oath which bound him to be faithful and obedient to his general, saving the fidelity he owed to the Roman senate and people. It was absolute, and unconditional.[11] The destruction of the Republic meant that the same oath was taken to the Emperor as commander-in-chief and living deity, and expanded outside the remit of military personnel and to all inhabitants of the Empire.[12]

As the German concept of a human *konig* (king) merged with that of the Roman *August Imperator* (divine king) so too did the Crown evolve from feudal to theocratic. To this theocratic Crown are linked the notions that the king is absolutely perfect[13] and absolutely immortal,[14] is incapable of doing or thinking wrong and has no folly or weakness,[15] and in the eye of the law is present at one and the same instant in every court of justice in the realm.[16] The issue of the Crown, and its powers, being theocratic or feudal is neither novel nor unique; it occupied the minds of medieval Anglo-Saxon jurists when debating the nature of the Crown. For some, the Crown was theocratic, its wearer

8 Maurice Keen, *The Laws of War in the Late Middle Ages* (Routledge, 1965) 72.

9 Samuel White, 'The Late Middle Ages in Northern Europe' in Samuel White (ed), *The Laws of Yesterday's Wars: From Indigenous Australians to the American Civil War* (Brill, 2021) 101, 108.

10 Cox (n 5) 25.

11 Vegetius, *The Military Institutions of the Romans* (Loeb Classical Library, 1902) 22.

12 John Allen, *Inquiry into the Rise and Growth of the Royal Prerogative in England* (Longman, Brown, Green and Longmans, 2nd ed, 1859) 134.

13 Blackstone (n 6) 246.

14 Ibid 249.

15 Ibid 246.

16 Ibid 270.

anointed by God and not subject to human law;[17] for others, the feudal king was simply human and accountable.[18] The current tension between extra-constitutional powers derives from the friction between theocratic and feudal Crowns.

This tension was solved, however, by the Glorious Revolution of 1688. The change in dynasty (from the House of Stuart to William III) saw a change in the Crown, but William and his wife Mary inherited 'a panoply of legal powers as ample as that borne by their two immediate predecessors'.[19] The subsequent 1689 *Bill of Rights* established, beyond doubt, the supremacy of Parliament but was for the most part declaratory. It only abolished two prerogatives — a standing army, and the power to suspend Acts of Parliament. Yet in doing so, it firmly established parliamentary supremacy and is argued to be the date that the powers of the Crown froze.[20] This had occurred earlier under Lord Coke's decision in the 1611 *Case of Proclamations.*[21] The *Bill of Rights*, however, implemented into formal law the political reality of England — the Crown's growing subservience to Parliament.[22] The *Bill of Rights* is therefore an incredibly important moment in legislative history, and provides a conceptual underpinning for the discussion of the royal prerogative within this thesis.

The Glorious Revolution provided that the Crown's powers can only be used in accordance with convention and the principle of responsible government.[23] The King no longer appointed by God but by Parliament, could now do wrong. This is important, for the English courts have accepted that the maximum scope of the royal prerogative is to be ascertained from this date; for 'it is 350 years and a civil war too late for the Queen's court to broaden the prerogative'.[24] The importance of this is reiterated throughout the following

17 Walter Ullmann, *Principles of Government and Politics in the Middle Ages* (Routledge, 4th ed, 1978) 121–3.

18 Ibid. See further FW Maitland, *The Constitutional History of England* (Cambridge University Press, 1908) 181–3, 515–18.

19 David Keir, *Constitutional History of Modern Britain 1485–1937* (A&C Black, 1938) 269.

20 *British Broadcasting Corp v Johns* [1965] Ch 32, 79 (Diplock LJ).

21 *Case of Proclamations* (1611) 12 Co Rep 74.

22 Article 1 specifically limited the royal prerogative, holding that 'the power of suspending the laws or the execution of laws by regal authority without consent of Parliament is illegal': *Bill of Rights 1689*, 1 Wm 3 & Mary 2, c 2.

23 Geoffrey Marshall, *Constitutional Conventions — The Rules and Forms of Political Accountability* (Oxford University Press, 1986).

24 *British Broadcasting Corporation v Johns* [1965] Ch 32, 79 (Diplock LJ). However, in the *Case of Proclamations* in 1611 (prior to the Glorious Revolution) Lord Coke held that the sovereign could only exercise the prerogatives he had, and not create new ones: see *Case of Proclamations* (1611) 12 Co Rep 74, 77 ER 1352 (KB).

chapters, and any discussion of prerogative powers must necessarily cover historical examples prior to 1688.

Whilst the Glorious Revolution saw the Crown firmly established as always being feudal, the prerogative powers have persisted in a residual fashion, reflecting their theocratic origins. This has led to a divergence in what is meant by the term 'prerogative', best epitomised by the positions advocated by Sir William Blackstone and AV Dicey. A comparative discussion of their definitions has become near-ritualistic, 'performed increasingly self-consciously and semi-ironically'.[25]

Sir William Blackstone was not the first to describe the royal prerogative, but he was the first to attempt to do so comprehensively. Blackstone declared:

> By the word prerogative we usually understand that special pre-eminence which the King hath, over and above all other persons, and out of the ordinary course of common law, in right of his regal dignity ... it can only be applied to those rights and capacities which the King enjoys alone, in contradiction to others, and not to those which he enjoys in common with any of his subjects.[26]

Such a position reflects the theocratic nature of the Crown, a power that is exercised by the monarch and the monarch alone. AV Dicey rejected this, and accused Blackstone of 'applying old and inapplicable terms to new institutions, and especially of ascribing in words to a modern and constitutional King the whole, and perhaps more than the whole, of the powers actually possessed and exercised by William the Conqueror'.[27] Dicey proposed alternatively that:

> The prerogative appears to be historically and as a matter of fact nothing else than the residue of discretionary or arbitrary authority which at any given time is legally left in the hands of the crown. The prerogative is the name of the remaining portion of the Crown's original authority ... Every act which the executive government can lawfully do without the authority of an Act of Parliament is done in virtue of the prerogative.[28]

---

25 Thomas Poole, 'United Kingdom: The Royal Prerogative' (2010) 8(1) *International Journal of Constitutional Law* 146, 147.

26 Blackstone (n 6) 232, cited with approval in *Davis v Commonwealth* (1988) 166 CLR 79, 108 (Brennan J); *Plaintiff M68/2015 v Minister for Immigration and Border Protection* (2016) 257 CLR 42, 133 (Gageler J).

27 AV Dicey, *An Introduction to the Study of the Law of the Constitution* (Palgrave Macmillan, 10th ed, 1959) 8.

28 Ibid 424–5.

Dicey's popularity in the United Kingdom,[29] is perhaps undermined by his careless articulation of the power.[30] Dicey fails to acknowledge the concept of the duality of the Crown. In comparison, Blackstone's restrained approach is 'consistent with Australia's legal independence from Britain, the constraints of federalism and the paramountcy of the Commonwealth Parliament'.[31] It will accordingly be adopted here.

There are, of course, alternative ways to categorise the royal prerogative — via the basis of its source; the effect the prerogative power has; or along a Montesquieuan taxonomy.[32] Within Australia, HV Evatt expanded on his earlier seminal doctoral work whilst sitting on the bench, where His Honour suggested the prerogative can fall within three categories.[33] The first category is what was titled 'executive prerogatives', which allowed the Commonwealth to perform *acts* such as declaring war, coining money, acquiring territory and granting pardons.[34] These prerogatives can also be linked to Germanic traditions. The second form of prerogatives that Evatt J titled were 'common law prerogatives', being those prerogative powers linked to the Crown as a person — such as legal immunities and exceptions.[35] The third class of prerogatives were titled 'priority rights', which included rights to royal metals, and land.[36] This division of the

---

29 *Attorney-General v De Keyser's Royal Hotel Ltd* [1920] AC 508, 526 (Lord Dunedin); *Burmah Oil Co Ltd v Lord Advocate* [1965] AC 75, 99 (Lord Reid); *Council of Civil Service Unions v Minister for the Civil Service* [1985] AC 374, 398 (Lord Fraser).

30 Colin R Munro, *Studies in Constitutional Law* (Butterworth, 1987) 160.

31 *Williams [No 1]* (2012) 248 CLR 156, 344 [488] (Crennan J). See further *Federal Commissioner of Taxation v Official Liquidator of EO Farley Ltd* (1940) 63 CLR 278, 320 (Evatt J) (*EO Farley*); *Davis v Commonwealth* (1988) 166 CLR 79, 108 (Brennan J); *Plaintiff M68* (n 26) 133.

32 Cox (n 17) 47–8. Another line of academic thinking divides the prerogative power into two classes — one that is Germanic, and the other Roman. Chief Baron Fleming in *Bates' Case* divided prerogative power into 'the ordinary' and 'the absolute': (1606) 2 St Tr 371, 389. Blackstone (n 6) book 1, ch 4, 239–40 divided them into 'incidental' and 'direct'. Joseph Chitty, *A Treatise on the Law of the Prerogatives of the Crown: And the Relative Duties and Rights of the Subject* (Garland, 1978) divided the powers into what he viewed as local, and others which were fundamental rights on which authority rested and were necessary to maintain it. More recently Sir William Wade divided them into 'simplistic' and 'eccentric' in William Wade, 'Procedure and Prerogative in Public Law' (1985) 101 *Law Quarterly Review* 180.

33 For the doctoral work, see Herbert Vere Evatt, 'The Royal Prerogative' (LLD thesis, University of Sydney, 1924). The thesis has been published as Herbert Vere Evatt, *The Royal Prerogative* (Law Book Co, 1987). For the case law, see *EO Farley* (n 31) 278, 320.

34 *EO Farley* (n 31) 278, 320–1.

35 Ibid 322.

36 Ibid.

royal prerogative was adopted with approval in the United Kingdom,[37] and has advantages in particular with denoting executive prerogatives which are applicable in federal, or unitary, systems.

The difficulty with defining and researching elements of the royal prerogative is identifying the exact scope of their existence and power. Walter Bagehot, in *The English Constitution*, notes that any review of prerogative powers would conclude that the Crown holds many plenary powers which 'waver between reality and desuetude, and which would cause a protracted and very interesting legal argument if ... [the Crown] tried to exercise them'.[38] Yet it was the basis for colonisation, and the legal foundation for many acts by the Crown in creating, then maintaining, *Pax Britannica*. The Royal Prerogative is the authority to grant honours and awards,[39] as well as mercy.[40] The prerogative of war[41] allows for operations to be declared unilaterally in order to conquer land, and is 'the only source of authority to kill or capture an enemy in war'.[42] Equally, under the prerogative of peace any or all part of a territory may be sacrificed to another State or non-state group in order to cease hostilities.[43] The Royal Prerogative exists to protect the State, and in its modern manifestations continues to remain a legal foundation in those areas of statecraft which remain jealously protected from statutory abridgement. Accordingly, it provides the authority to move military forces;[44] as well as a right to ownership of the royal metals.[45] It also extends to prerogative ownership of swans.[46]

B A Tale of Two Swans

Swans — a rather odd creature to be protected by residual powers of the Crown — provides an interesting case study and perfect symbol of the issue

37 House of Commons Public Administration Select Committee, *Taming the Prerogative: Strengthening Ministerial Accountability to Parliament* (Report, 2004) 5–6.

38 Walter Bagehot, *The English Constitution*, ed Paul Smith (Cambridge University Press, 2001) 49.

39 Noel Cox, 'The Royal Prerogative in the Realms' (2007) 33(4) *Commonwealth Law Bulletin* 611.

40 *Attorney-General (Cth) v Ogawa* (2020) 384 ALR 474 (Allsop CJ, Flick and Griffiths JJ).

41 *Shaw Savill & Albion Co Ltd v Commonwealth* (1940) 66 CLR 344.

42 Cameron Moore, 'Military Law and Executive Power' in Robin Creyke, Dale Stephens and Peter Sutherland (eds), *Military Law in Australia* (Federation Press, 2019) 69, 98.

43 *R (Miller) v Secretary of State for Exiting the European Union* [2017] UKSC 5.

44 *China Navigation Co Ltd v Attorney-General* [1932] 2 KB 197, 207 (Scrutton LJ).

45 *Cadia Holdings Pty Ltd v New South Wales* (2010) 242 CLR 195, 210–11.

46 *The Case of Swans* (1592) 7 Co 15b, 16a; 77 ER 435, 436.

at play in this book. *The Case of Swans* is the logical starting point, although prerogative rights to swans had been claimed since 1186 by the British Crown.[47] The *Case of Swans* famously confirms the general principles regarding ownership of wild animals, and confirms the rights of the monarch with regard to unmarked swans. It arose when Dame Joan Young and Thomas Saunger were directed by the sheriff of Dorset to round up 400 loose unmarked swans from the rivers of Dorset because the queen, Elizabeth I, sought possession of them. Young and Saunger sought to argue that the swans belonged to them.

The grandfather of Dame Joan's first husband had assisted in the dissolution of the local monastery, and Henry VIII had allowed him to purchase the estate. The estate had then passed to his grandson and heir (Dame Joan Young's late first husband, Giles Strangeways, named after his grandfather). Young and Saunger said that they had been given the right to the swans for one year by Strangeways. However, the court held as follows:

> It was resolved, that all white swans not marked, which having gained their natural liberty, and are swimming in an open and common river, might be seised to the King's use by his prerogative, because that Volatilia, (quae sunt ferae naturae) alia sunt regalia, alia communia: ['because fowl, which are of a wild nature, are sometimes royal and sometimes common'] and so aquatilium, alia sunt regalia, alia communia: [because water birds are sometimes royal and sometimes common'] as a swan is a royal fowl; and all those, the property whereof is not known, do belong to the King by his prerogative: and so whales and sturgeons are Royal fishes, and belong to the King by his prerogative. And there hath been an ancient Officer of the King's, called Magister deductus cignorum, ['Master of the Game of Swans'] which continueth to this day.[48]

Why swans? Well, in medieval times, swans were luxury goods. The precise reason for this is unclear but it has been hypothesised that it may relate to their beauty, solitary nature, and the difficulty in keeping swans:

> Since ancient times, swans have been associated with tranquility and nobility, featuring in myths and stories around the world. Their high status is likely to have come about because of their perceived beauty and

47 N Ticehurst, *The Mute Swan in England* (Cleaver-Hume Press, 1957) 5–7.

48 *The Case of Swans* (1592) 7 Co 15b, 16a; 77 ER 435, 16a–16b.

> natural behavior; they are solitary birds, strong and aggressively protective of their young but at the same time graceful and elegant on the water ...
>
> Swans were luxury goods in Europe from at least the 12th century onward; the Medieval equivalent of flashing a Rolex or driving a Lamborghini. Owning swans signaled nobility, along with flying a hawk, running hounds or riding a battle-trained destrier. Swans were eaten as a special dish at feasts, served as a centerpiece in their skin and feathers with a lump of blazing incense in the beak. They were particularly associated with Christmas, when they would be served in large numbers at royal feasts; forty swans were ordered for Henry III's Christmas celebrations in 1247 at Winchester, for example.[49]

The prerogative right to swans is one that has been firmly, if not loudly, protected. *The Case of Swans* made clear that the monarch of England only has rights in relation to a particular kind of swan native to Britain, the mute swan (*Cygnus olor*). Other kinds of swan sometimes seen in Britain such as the whooper swan (*Cygnus cygnus*) are not covered by the regal privilege. Yet the 'majesty' of the swan as a symbol is found through the former British Empire; and was a prerogative that evolved with colonisation — as the Australian experience shows when black swans were discovered.[50]

Generally, early references to the royal prerogative were couched in the colour-neutral terms of 'swans' in English, '*cignes*' in Norman French and '*cigni*' in Latin.[51] It is true that at one point in the *Case of Swans*, the Court spoke of a prerogative to 'white swans'.[52] However, in the European worldview in 1592, a white swan was a tautology. The concept of a black swan existed, but only as an oxymoron. As early as the 2nd century, the satirist Juvenal referred to something non-existent as a '*rara avis in terris nigroque simillima cygno*', 'a rare bird, a black swan or the like'.[53] In 1576, the rumoured friend of Shakespeare, Thomas Bedingfield, asked 'What Man is so mad as wil[l] say the swan is

49 Emily Cleaver, 'The Fascinating, Regal History Behind Britain's Swans', *Smithsonian Magazine* (31 July 2017).

50 Ken Blore, 'A Royal Prerogative to Black Swans?' (2019) 93(2) *Australian Law Journal* 104–110.

51 *An Act for Swans 1482* (UK), 22 Edw 4, c 6 (written in Norman French and translated into English); *The Case of Swans* (n 48) (written half in English and half in Latin).

52 *The Case of Swans* (n 48).

53 Juvenal, *The Sixteen Satires* (P Green trans, Penguin Books, 3rd ed, 1998) Satire VI, line 165.

black?'[54] As it turns out, that man was the Dutch explorer Willem de Vlamingh nearly 200 years later. On 8 January 1697, at the mouth of the river that would later be known as Swan River, de Vlamingh recorded the first European account of black swans. His journal entry for that day reads, 'saw two young swans which we followed, ... brought both on board, they are very black'.[55]

De Vlamingh's encounter with black swans exploded the European understanding of the essential characteristics of a swan. The discovery 'reveal[ed] that a characteristic previously associated with it was never really essential ... swans need not be white'.[56] Thus, seen through 16th century eyes, the casual reference of the King's Bench to 'white swans' cannot be read as words of limitation, for in fact those words carried the meaning of all known swans in the world. It follows that, applied to its logical limits, the King's prerogative to unmarked swans on open waters extended to all swans, including black swans, at the time the royal prerogatives transferred to Australia between 1788 and 1836. Given that Australia had both wild swans and 'Colonists [who] at once owed allegiance to the King and so his proprietary rights',[57] it might be thought that the royal prerogative to swans was applicable to local circumstances.[58] Although in 1869, William Forsyth noted, '[w]hether the same prerogative applies to *black* swans the authorities do not inform us'[59] (a claim taken up in *Burge's Commentaries on Colonial and Foreign Laws* in 1914)[60] it clearly does.

The black swan's role in Australian heraldry and culture extends to the first founding of the colonies in the eighteenth century, and the black swan has often been equated with antipodean identity. The black swan is featured on the flag, and is both the state bird and state emblem of Western Australia; it also appears in the coat of arms and other iconography of the state's institutions

---

54 Thomas Bedingfield, *Cardanus' Comfort* (translation of Girolamo Cardano, *De consolatione libri tres*), quoted in JA Simpson and ESC Weiner, *The Oxford English Dictionary* (Clarendon Press, 1989) vol 17, 348.

55 W Robert (ed), *The Explorations, 1696–1697, of Australia by Willem de Vlamingh* (Philo Press, Amsterdam, 1972) 68–70. See also at 72 recording another sighting on 11 January 1697.

56 J Goldsworthy, 'The Constitution and Its Common Law Background' (2014) 25 Public Law Review 265, 277–278. See also HV Evatt, *The Royal Prerogative* (n 33) 140.

57 HV Evatt, *The Royal Prerogative* (n 33) 140.

58 Compare HE Renfree, *The Executive Power of the Commonwealth of Australia* (Legal Books, 1984) 591: 'This prerogative does not seem to be appropriate for Australia'.

59 W Forsyth, *Cases and Opinions on Constitutional Law, and Various Points of English Jurisprudence* (Stevens and Haynes, 1869) 179 (emphasis in original).

60 A Renton and G Phillimore (eds), *Burge's Commentaries on Colonial and Foreign Laws Generally and in Their Conflict with Each Other and with the Law of England* (Sweet and Maxwell, 1914) vol 4, Pt 1, 655.

including the Territorial Flag of the Australian Capital Territory. The black swan is symbolic of Australia, just as the white swan is symbolic of England. This is why Kevin Gilbert's *Colonising Species* — depicted on the front cover of this book — is all the more symbolically powerful, and significant for this book. The white swan, protected by the Royal Prerogative (and hinted at by Crown) imported by colonists across the globe, is seen to break the neck of its brethren black swan. Hinted within the image are themes of colonisation, power and 'the othering' which are all fundamental to those with lived experiences of colonisation (such as Kevin Gilbert, an Indigenous Australian man). Yet unlike fauna, colonists did exist within legal frameworks and had responsibilities. The legacies of these responsibilities continue to this day.

C Colonisation & Responsibility

It matters not if the land was acquired by private means, or by an organ of the State. The case study of the acquisition of India is clearest on this point: a piecemeal expansion and conquest of the sub-continent through private companies and private means does not absolve the British Crown of its ultimate annexure of the land. Sovereignty is, after all, a bundle of rights and responsibilities.

As famously reasoned by Max Huber in the *Island of Palmas* arbitration, judicial facts must be evaluated 'in the light of the law contemporary with it, and not of the law in force at the time when a dispute in regard to it arises or falls to be settled'.[61] This is arguably in line with the non-retroactive character of legal construction (*nova constitutio futuris formam imponere debet, non praeteritis*), as advanced by influential legal writers since at least Lord Coke (Chief Justice of the King's Bench from 1613–1616).[62] As an inquiry focused towards

61 *Island of Palmas (Netherlands v United States of America) (Award) (1928)* 2 RIAA 829, 845. See also: *Land and Maritime Boundary between Cameroon and Nigeria (Cameroon v Nigeria) (Judgment)* [2002] ICJ Rep 303, 404–5 [205]; Alexander Orakhelashvili, 'Treaties and Titles to Territory' (2003) 62(1) *Cambridge Law Journal* 9, 10.

62 Edward Coke, *The Second Part of the Institutes of the Laws of English* (Brooke, 1797) vol 1, 292. See also: Elmer E Smead, 'The Rule Against Retroactive Legislation: A Basic Principle of Jurisprudence' (1936) 20(1) *Minnesota Law Review* 775, 776; Ben Juratowitch, *Retroactivity and the Common Law* (Hart Publishing, 2008) 29; Zhenni Li, 'International Intertemporal Law' (2018) 48(2) *California Western International Law Journal* 341, 388. See generally: BS Chimni, 'Customary International Law: A Third World Perspective' (2018) 112(1) *American Journal of International Law* 1, 1–46; J Patrick Kelly, 'Customary International Law in Historical Context: The Exercise of Power Without General Acceptance' in Brian D Lepard

identifying Imperial customary laws of war, this considers the international law existing throughout the early pre-Modern and colonial periods until the 1899 *Hague Conventions*. These early regulations, although seeking to regulate intra-European warfare, marks a line in the sand with the development of the laws of war (and in part the codification of the laws of war in the colonies). It marks a useful point from which analysis can occur before and after; although of course the law developed in a piecemeal fashion alike to other branches of international law (such as arms control).

What becomes clear is that whilst the othering of international law excluded 'natives' in foreign lands from the protection of the laws of war (Part 1, Chapter 1) the principles of humanity could and did apply if individual commanders wished to (Part 1, Chapter 2). They often did.

A critical question then is the issue of State responsibility for when the laws of war are broken. The issue of State responsibility is clearest when actions are conducted by an organ of the State. It is a cardinal principle of international law that a State does not escape responsibility merely because its organs or agents have exceeded their authority under domestic law. This remains so even if the conduct were overtly or manifestly unlawful. Nevertheless, it is still necessary that the organ or agent acted in an official capacity. A person is acting in an official capacity when they either:

- Hold themselves out as performing official functions, or
- Use powers, methods or means placed at their disposal by virtue of an official capacity.

In either situation, the person's conduct is attributable to the State for the purpose of establishing its responsibility.[63] It is for this reason that those who held *imperium* within the power structures of Europe often issued ordinances to control, direct and punish those subordinate to them. These war ordinances are reflective of *opinio juris* — issued due to a belief of the legal requirement to abide by the laws of war.

It is in these war ordinances that this book is somewhat concerned. War ordinances had been the usual method across the Medieval period for European courts and military tribunals to restate and apply their traditional *jus armorum* or domestic chivalric customs,[64] as developed over hundreds of

(ed), *Reexamining Historical and Theoretical Perspectives on Customary International Law* (Cambridge University Press, 2017) 47, 47–85.

63 *Caire Claim* (*France v Mexico*) (1929) 5 RIAA 516.

64 Samuel White, 'The Late Middle Ages in Northern Europe' in Samuel White (ed), *Laws of Yesterday's Wars* (n 9) 101, 102. See also John Collins, *Martial Law and English Laws, c1500–c1700* (Cambridge University Press, 2016) 22–3.

years.[65] In line with the evolving nature of warfare throughout the pre-Modern period and its ceaseless stream of continental conflicts,[66] adjacent to the rise of nation-States and centralised militaries,[67] Western countries would later codify these regulations into written articles intended for specific campaigns.[68] This was seen in the 1621 Articles of War drafted by the Swedish King Gustavus Adolphus during the Thirty Years War (1618–48).[69] In the British context, prominent examples of these may be seen throughout the English Civil War (1642–51), and the subsequent Cromwellian Conquest of Ireland (1649–53), where both Parliamentarian and Royalist commanders issued their own Articles of War which included guidance for how to engage with enemy soldiers and non-combatants.[70] The legacy of these early regulations, as evidence of initial State practice, becomes pivotal given their influence on the development of eighteenth and nineteenth-century Imperial warfare[71] — as per how later commentators such as Arthur Wellesley (Master-General of the Ordnance from 1819–1827) and Sir Charles Edward Callwell (1859–1928) would cite past instances of English military conduct when issuing their own ordinances.[72]

---

65 David A Schlueter, 'The Court-Martial: A Historical Survey' (1980) 87(1) *Military Law Review* 129, 131–2.

66 See, eg, Warren Chin, 'Technology, War and the State: Past, Present and Future' (2019) 95(4) *International Affairs* 765, 765–83. See also: John Collins, *Martial Law and English Laws, c1500–c1700* (n 64) 30, 91; David Eltis, *The Military Revolution in Sixteenth Century Europe* (IB Tauris, 1995) 6–42.

67 See, eg: Kenneth F McKenzie Jr, 'Elegant Irrelevance: Fourth Generation Warfare' (1993) 23(1) *Parameters* 51, 51–60; William S Lind et al, 'The Changing Face of War: Into the Fourth Generation' (1989) 69 (October) *Military Review* 1, 2–11; Martin Van Creveld, *The Transformation of War* (Free Press, 1991).

68 Timothy McCormack and Gerry Simpson, *The Law of War Crimes: National and International Approaches* (Cambridge University Press, 1998) 41. See also Kenneth Ögren, 'Humanitarian law in the Articles of War decreed in 1621 by King Gustavus II Adolphus of Sweden' (1996) 36(313) *International Review of the Red Cross* 438, 442.

69 See William Winthrop, *Military Law and Precedents* (Government Printing Office, 2nd ed, 1920) 907–18.

70 Barbara Donagan, 'Atrocity, War Crime, and Treason in the English Civil War' (1994) 99(4) *American Historical Review* 1142, 1142. See also John Collins, *Martial Law and English Laws, c1500–c1700* (n 64) 171–2.

71 See, eg, Ala Alyrres, 'War at a Distance: Court-Martial Narratives in the Eighteenth Century' (2008) 41(4) *Eighteenth-Century Studies* 539, 539–42. See also: Timothy McCormack and Gerry Simpson, *The Law of War Crimes: National and International Approaches* (n 68) 41–3; John Collins, *Martial Law and English Laws, c1500–c1700* (n 64) 208–9, citing Alison Games, *The Web of Empire: English Cosmopolitans in an Age of Expansion, 1560–1660* (Oxford University Press, 2008) 255–88.

72 Geoffrey Parker, 'The Etiquette of Atrocity: The Laws of War in Early Modern Europe', in Geoffrey Parker, *Empire, War and Faith in Early Modern Europe* (London, 2003) 155,

Early English ordinances,[73] such as the Lancastrian King Henry V's (of Agincourt fame) 1419 *Mantes Ordinances*, had primarily revolved around punishing desertion among the rank and file, in addition to protecting church property from pillage.[74] However, evidence of later decrees during the pre-Modern period points towards an eventual shift towards the recognition of more universally humanitarian concepts including the safeguarding of civilians[75] — especially as natural reasoning and Christian thought remained the leading influences on legal development,[76] rather than positivist ideals.[77] It has also been contended that this humanitarian shift was caused by the increasing influence of IHL jurists on emerging military traditions and the training of officers,[78] including the Oxford-based academics Alberico Gentili and Richard Zouche.[79] Tuba Inal also suggests that this was a consequence of the exclusive sovereignty granted to States through the treaties signed under the 1648 *Peace of Westphalia*,[80] which allowed nations to focus on justifying wartime conduct or *jus in bello* rather than the reasons for war (*jus ad bellum*).[81]

---

citing Letter from Arthur Wellesely (Master-General of the Ordnance) to George Canning (President of the Board of Control of the British East India Company), 1820.

73 See generally Charles M Clode, *Administration of Justice Under Military and Martial Law* (J Murray, 1872).

74 Andrew Martinez, 'Disciplinary Ordinances for English Armies and Military Change, 1385–1513' (2017) 102 *Journal of the Historical Association* 361, 361–2.

75 Beatrice Heuser, 'Ordinances and Articles of War before the Lieber Code, 866-1863' in Terry Gill et al (eds), *Yearbook of International Humanitarian Law* (Asser Press, 2018) vol 21, 139, 139-64. See also: Christopher Duffy, *The Military Experience in the Age of Reason* (Atheneum, 1988) 10–13; John Collins, *Martial Law and English Laws, c1500–c1700* (n 64) 7–8.

76 See Antony Anghie, 'Francisco De Vitoria and the Colonial Origins of International Law' (1996) 5(3) *Social and Legal Studies* 321, 323, citing Alfred Rubin 'International Law in the Age of Columbus' (1992) 39(1) *Netherlands International Law Review* 5, 5–35.

77 See Alfred P Rubin, 'The Law of Piracy: British Practice in the Nineteenth-Century' (1988) 63(1) *International Law Studies* 201, 270–1.

78 John Collins, *Martial Law and English Laws, c1500–c1700* (n 64) 109, citing Francis Grose, *Military Antiquities Respecting a History of the English Army: From the Conquest to the Present Time* (S Hooper, 1788) vol 2, 54.

79 Andres Wagner, 'Alberico Gentili: Sovereignty, Natural Law, and the System of Roman Civil Law' in Stefan Kadelbach, Thomas Kleinlein and David Roth-Isigkeit (eds), *System, Order, and International Law: The Early History of International Legal Thought from Machiavelli to Hegel* (Oxford University Press, 2017) 92, 104–6.

80 Tuba Inal, *Looting and Rape in Wartime* (University of Pennsylvania Press, 2013) 43.

81 See ibid 43, citing JT Johnson, 'Lieber and the Theory of War' in CR Mack and HH Lesesne (eds), *Francis Lieber and the Culture of the Mind* (University of South Carolina Press, 2005) 61, 62.

According to Mahmoud Bassiouni,[82] a distinct example of this increasing acceptance of humanitarian notions was the English King James II's 'stern' criticism of his Marshall Conrad von Rosen in 1689 for murdering 'innocent non-combatants' during the Williamite War in Ireland (1689–91).[83] Notably, by this point, English wartime ordinances had also begun including clear references to extraterritorial effect. Under the 1640 *Laws and Ordinances of Warre* for instance, issued by King Charles I during the Bishops' Wars against Scotland (1639–40), commanders were instructed to apply customary provisions 'in ... enemies countrey'.[84]

However, these early regulations cannot be summarised as having developed without uncertainties.[85] Beatrice Heuser compellingly points to the applicability of specific ordinances being likely reliant upon the personal will of commanders,[86] which perhaps reflects the unsettled character of English customary law before eventual codification.[87] Hence, assessing the enforceability of specific customs may be challenging during periods where centralised authority was contested. In the pre-Modern context, this was especially seen during the Glorious Revolution (1688–9) when ordinances issued by the deposed King James II were later determined by the Convention Parliament as 'unconstitutional'.[88]

Throughout the colonial period, similar situations arose as Imperial frontiers expanded and more powers were transferred to overseas State agents[89] such as Governors, Superintendents and Residents (an emissary-like position that, in the Malayan context, eventually assumed administerial responsibilities

82 Mahmoud Bassiouni, *Crimes Against Humanity in International Criminal Law* (Martinus Nijhoff, 1999) 154.

83 Timothy McCormack and Gerry Simpson, *The Law of War Crimes: National and International Approaches* (n 10) 39.

84 Theodor Meron, *War Crimes Law Comes of Age* (Clarendon, 1998) 8–10. See also John Collins, *Martial Law and English Laws, c1500–c1700* (n 64) 93.

85 Barbara Shapiro, 'Codification of the Laws in Seventeenth Century England' (1974) 19(2) *Wisconsin Law Review* 428, 431.

86 Beatrice Heuser, 'Ordinances and Articles of War before the Lieber Code, 866–1863' (n 75) 162–4. See also MH Keen, *The Laws of War in the Late Middle Ages* (Taylor & Francis Group, 2015) 190–1.

87 Barbara Shapiro, 'Codification of the Laws in Seventeenth Century England' (n 85) 431.

88 Beatrice Heuser, 'Ordinances and Articles of War before the Lieber Code, 866–1863' (n 75) 39–43. See also: David A Schlueter, 'The Court-Martial: A Historical Survey' (n 65) 143; *Rules and Articles for the Better Government of His Majesties Land Forces in Pay* (1688), discussed in William Winthrop, *Military Law and Precedents* (n 69) 920.

89 See Damian O'Connor, 'Defending Australia: Imperial Expansion and Local Defence' (2009) 6(1) *Journal of Australian Naval History* 5, 14. See also John Collins, *Martial Law and English Laws, c1500–c1700* (n 64) 282–3.

following the Perak War (1875–6).[90] Despite the significant discretion provided to these colonial officers or 'men on the spot'[91] they still faced clear censure by Parliament for complacency — as seen when Sir William FD Jervois (Governor of the Straits Settlements from 1875–7)[92] was criticised in the House of Lords for 'having gone beyond [their] instructions'[93] during the Perak War (1875–6). These internal censures, as well as external comments by various colonial powers, are critical in unpacking the colonial laws of war that applied at the time of Empire, and for which breaches of the laws of war can be measured against.

Some might argue that the conduct of Sir William was that of an individual, and does not (nor should not) bind the relevant colonial power if undertaken *ultra vires.* The general rule of international responsibility is that States are not liable for the acts of private persons i.e. individuals or corporations, which are neither officials nor organs of the State. The exception is where they are either:

- Acting on the State's instructions; or
- Acting under the State's direction or control.

The question of whether a State has exercised sufficient control over the actions of a person or persons is to be determined in each case by looking at the particular conduct in question.

Under modern international law, a State can be responsible for the conduct of persons who exercise governmental authority in circumstances where official authorities are absent but where the exercise of governmental authority is required: art 9 of the Articles on Responsibility of States for Internationally Wrongful Acts (ARSIWA). Such situations arise where private persons perform elements of government functions without a State's authority — such as the annexure of land, the conduct of public order and security operations, or taxation.

In *Yeagar v Islamic Republic of Iran* (1984) 17 Iran-US CTR 92, a US national was forcibly detained after a revolutionary movement overthrew the Iranian

90 Netusha Naidu, '"Sly Civility" and the Myth of the "Lazy Malay": The Discursive Economy of British Colonial Power during the Pahang Civil War, 1891–1895' in Farish A Noor and Peter Carey (eds), *Racial Difference and the Colonial Wars of 19th Century Southeast Asia* (Amsterdam University Press, 2021) 179, 180. See also C Northcote Parkinson, *British Intervention in Malaya 1867–1877* (University of Malaya Press, 1960) 153–4, citing letter from Sir Andrew Clarke (Governor of the Straits Settlements) to Henry Herbert (Secretary of State for the Colonies), 24 February 1874.

91 See, eg, Frédéric Mégret, 'From "Savages" to "Unlawful Combatants": A Postcolonial Look at International Humanitarian Law's "Other"' in Anne Orford (ed), *International Law and its 'Others'* (Cambridge University Press, 2006) 265, 281–2.

92 John S Galbraith, 'The "Turbulent Frontier" as a Factor in British Expansion' (1960) 2(2) *Comparative Studies in Society and History* 150, 161.

93 See United Kingdom, *Parliamentary Debates*, House of Lords, 3 July 1876, vol 230, col 827 (Lord Stanley of Alderly). See also: United Kingdom, *Parliamentary Debates*, House of

government. The Tribunal found that the actions of the 'guards' were acting on behalf of the new government, or at least exercising elements of government authority in the absence of official authorities, in operations which the new government must have had knowledge and to which it did not specifically object. Iran did not establish that it could not control the new guards in this operation. The Tribunal found that the acts of the two men who took the claimant to the hotel were attributable to Iran. So too may States 'acknowledge and adopt' the conduct of another entity (for example, private persons, other States or international organisations) with the consequence that the conduct is attributed to the State[94] — as occurs upon accepting sovereignty of a land.[95]

It is necessary to go through these various scenarios, for the expansion of Imperial borders was never static nor, necessarily, compliant with domestic law. In some areas of the globe, it happened accidentally. In others, it happened with deliberate foreplanning. Yet again, in others it occurred through private means and via private individuals. Sometimes, colonies were marked by redcoats and bluejackets, reflecting the land and naval forces respectively.

This is particularly so within the British Empire, which instilled *Pax Britannica* across an Empire upon which the Sun never Set. The two authors of this monograph hail from different colonies under the same Crown: Australia and Malaysia. We have been both catalysed to write this book as we compared notes and discovered trends across the conflicts as they expanded from British beachheads on foreign soil, and encountered differing cultures and conflicts. Analysing the flow of people, ideals, material, regiments, and values across the Empire highlighted that this was a network where laws were evolving, developing and undergoing a metamorphosis. This was clearest actually in the laws of war. Emerging from the battlefields of Europe, with its strict class structure and the economic imperatives of the Church, these laws of war that were codified for imperial expansion were inherently European and focused on regulating inter-European warfare. There was no thought of it ever applying to 'the other' until circumstances forced a clash of civilisations. Even then, the development of international law in Europe was focused on Europe and its interaction with the world; as colonial powers, rather than equals. The 'savage' was noted in this law; feared, despised and respected; but never equal. As Martens pithily noted:

Lords, 3 July 1876, vol 230, col 839 (Earl of Carnarvon); United Kingdom, *Parliamentary Debates*, House of Lords, 3 July 1876, vol 230, col 844 (Earl of Kimberley).

94 See ARSIWA art 11.

95 South China Sea Arbitration, *Philippines v China*, Award, PCA Case No 2013-19, ICGJ 495 (PCA 2016), 12th July 2016, Permanent Court of Arbitration [PCA].

> It is natural law, not international law, which is applicable to the relations between civilized nations with the nations of Asia ... In Asia, international law transforms itself into natural law.[96]

This is for the hard law; the bi- and multi-lateral treaties. As this research discovered and presents, there was soft (but equal) customary law and development of natural law ideas that developed from each colonial power in its interactions with their subjects, and its European neighbours. For Britain, the rise of humanitarianism and the abolition of slavery saw it begin to question itself both in its own colonies, and in former conduct reflected in others. Although the application of European laws of war were voluntary, they were applied.

It follows, then, that although as a matter of law there was no strict requirement to apply European laws, regulations and approaches to warfare to 'the other' (as per the European, and therefore British, approaches to the laws of war) there is sufficient State practice to demonstrate that 'contracts of conduct' were made in differing regions of the British Empire. What applied in one colony, as a matter of law, applied in another where the Crown was the same.

This book proceeds in two parts. Part 1 covers 'the othering' of international law, so as to explicitly establish the methodology through which Part 2 proceeds. Part 1, Chapter 1 highlights the nature of European laws of war and international law more generally during the period of global colonisation. It does so to provide a fair and sound foundation for the exception introduced in Part 1, Chapter 2: that of State practice exceptionalism. This introduces the methodology that underpins Part 2, of which the majority of this monograph consists of (and from which the novel nature of this monograph is found). Part 2 introduces, through deep doctrinal research into British Imperial practice, eight separate colonial war crimes that applied through the Empire. These include prohibitions on: summary executions, sexual violence, perfidy, slavery and forced movement, unnecessary looting of cultural property, brigandry and dispersal. Each will be discussed in turn. Part 2 specifically does not focus on the crime of aggression — for this research is focused on the *jus in bello* of colonial wars, regardless of their 'justness' (which is a focus on much literature in this

96 Friedrich de Martens, *La Russie et l'Angleterre dans l'Asie Centrale*' (1879) 11 *Revue de Droit International et de Législation Comparée* 227, 241, as quoted by Frédéric Mégret (n 91) 265, 283.

area). This book offers the war crimes identified in Part 2 as non-exhaustive, and further research by others might uncover further examples.

This is, ultimately, a work of legal history. To that end, one actually looks forward to having errors pointed out, in the hope of further clarifying and expanding on the knowledge provided herein.

Samuel Camden Ducket White & Ikhwan Fazli Bin Adi Bokharee

PART 1

The 'Othering' of International Law

CHAPTER 1

The Othering of Non-Western Peoples

Introduction

Western attitudes to war have undergone four major transformations in the modern period.

First, in reaction to the Wars of Religion (1562–98), a consensus emerged that wars should not be fought to spread 'true' religion. Second, the Industrial Revolution led to the invention of more effective weapons and communications, and made possible the deployment of large armies over great areas. The French Revolution (1789–9) and the Napoleonic Wars (1789–1815) were perhaps the first 'total' wars of modern times, involving whole populations in determining their way of life.[97] The new concepts of war were articulated by the nineteenth-century Prussian military strategist Carl von Clausewitz (1780–1831), whose magnus opus *Vom Kriege* first appeared in 1832/4. Clausewitz regarded war as an instrument of policy, designed to disarm the opponent and hence impose one's own political will on him. War is 'only a part of political intercourse, therefore by no means an independent thing in itself'.[98] The conduct of war must be strictly controlled by attainable political objectives. Clausewitz could almost be Samuel rebuking Saul when he writes:

> in such dangerous things as War, the errors which proceed from benevolence are the worst ... it is even against one's own interest, to turn away from consideration of the real nature of the affair because the horror of its elements excites repugnance.[99]

Third, the development of international law from Grotius onwards, and its institutionalisation through the League of Nations and subsequently the United Nations, has established the position that the only permitted wars are defensive wars. Finally, the principle that all nations have a right to self-government has been accepted, and imperialism has been discredited.

---

97 Michelle Gordon, *Extreme Violence and the 'British Way': Colonial Warfare in Perak, Sierra Leone and Sudan* (Bloomsbury, 2020) 202.

98 Book 5, Chapter 6 (Penguin, 1986) 402. See also Book 1, Chapter 24 on War as a continuation of policy by other means.

99 Book 1, Chapter 1, at 102.

 | DOI:10.1163/9789004515987_003

It is important to position these four transformations, in how they intersect and operate with the concept of *Pax Britannica* and the laws of colonial warfare. As Mégret notes, the original sin of the laws of war (now increasingly called international humanitarian law)[100] is that it othered.[101] By this, Mégret means that it comes from a Eurocentric perspective, regulating European States. It is an important position to begin with, as articulated in this Chapter, so as to further expand on the exception in the following chapter (of individual State practice). the first sections of this Chapter address the othering in two limbs: from both a legal doctrine perspective, as well as a critical legal lens. It does so to both challenge and outline the historical underpinnings of the original sin. The second sections then turn to demonstrate how the relevant laws of war at the time of Empire had exceptions for those wars fought against natives. This in turn lays the foundation for the exception — State practice — outlined in the subsequent Chapter.

The Ugly History of International Law

Discussions on Eurocentrism of international law involve a wide spectrum of opinions, where critical legal scholars (including from the Third World Approaches to International Law or 'TWAIL' school) present their grievances. The explicit and unquestionably European character of international law has been powerfully asserted by historians of the discipline, such as JHW Verzijl:

> Now there is one truth that is not open to denial or even to doubt, namely that the actual body of international law, as it stands today, not only is the product of the conscious activity of the European mind, but also has drawn its vital essence from a common source of beliefs, and in both of these aspects it is mainly of Western European origin.[102]

This section navigates the Eurocentric activity of the rise of international law and weaponisation of language. It does so to highlight and confirm as a general

100 Jean Pictet, "Humanitarian Ideas Shared by Different Schools of Thought and Cultural Traditions", in Jean Pictet (ed.) *International Dimensions of Humanitarian Law* (Henry Dunant Institute, M. Nijhoff, 1988) 3, 4.

101 Frédéric Mégret (n 91) 279, 287.

102 *International Law in Historical Perspectives* (AW Sijthoff, 1968) vol 1, 435–6.

rule, under European / international law at the time of colonisation, that there was no general concept that the laws of war applied to 'uncivilized' nations. Chimni notes that:

> The alienation of international law from the peoples of the third world was epitomised in the civilisation/barbarian divide that made them and their territory into objects of international law. If third world peoples ever metamorphosed into subjects of international law, it was only ever to surrender sovereignty to colonial masters. The moment of empowerment was the moment of complete subjection. It was a time of absolute alienation of third world peoples from international law. Death, destruction, pillage, plunder and humiliation are the key words that best capture the relationship between third world peoples and international law in this period.[103]

The history of international law is structured around the idea that different phases of the history of the discipline were characterised by distinctive styles of jurisprudence. This Chapter challenges that, by highlighting how one pervasive idea has flowed throughout.

The Original Sin

With the rise of a monotheistic religion, the idea of divine right (and absolute freedom from sin against 'the other') emerged.[104] It is here that the original sin evolved in the laws of war; and it is here that discussions must begin. One of the earliest examples of divine right is found in biblical history biblical history. The rabbis distinguished between *milḥemet ḥova* (obligatory war) and *milḥemet reshut* (optional war):

> Rava said: All agree that Joshua's war of conquest was *ḥova* (obligatory) and the expansionist wars of David were *reshut* (optional). But they differ with regard to [the status of] a pre-emptive war intended to prevent idolaters from attacking them.[105]

103 BS Chimni, 'The Past, Present and Future of International Law' (2007) 8(2) *Melbourne Journal of International Law*, 504.

104 Rory Cox, *Origins of Just War* (Princeton University Press, 2023).

105 Babylonian Talmud *Sota* 44b.

The 'expansionist wars of David' are seen as more questionable, notwithstanding Psalm 18:48, 'He has subdued nations beneath my feet'.[106] Elsewhere the Talmud insists that the king would need to seek authorisation from the Great Court of 71 justices, as well as divine approval through the oracle[107] of the High Priest, before engaging in such a war.[108] As these institutions have not existed for 2,000 years the definition of 'competent authority' virtually rules out the possibility of non-defensive war; there is no Jewish equivalent to the process by which some seventeenth century English Puritans declared wars to be 'commanded by God' simply because they were deemed by the leadership to be in conformity with God's will.[109]

The Talmudic distinction between *kibbush yaḥid* (individual conquest) and *kibbush rabim* (public conquest) may indicate the need for popular support in addition to the other requirements.[110] War against the Canaanites is based on the *ḥerem*, or holy ban; it is a war of extermination that knows no bounds (verses 15–18). Justification — a sort of *jus ad bellum* — is offered, on the grounds that these nations might teach Israel 'abominations' and lead them to sin (verse 18).[111] No restraints are indicated. It is the first othering.

Homer recognised the dividing line between humans and animals throughout the *Iliad*. Humans, unlike animals, can be both savage and compassionate. Achilles, in his *ariestia,* comments to Hektor:

> I will have no talk of pacts with you, ...
> As between men and lions there are none,
> no concord between wolves and sheep, but all

---

106 That the rabbinic tradition is not entirely anti-imperialist is demonstrated by a midrash such as *Targum Sheni* on Esther (probably 8th century) that wildly exaggerates the extent of the dominions of Solomon and Ahab.

107 The Urim and Tumim (Exodus 28:30), the precise nature of which is a matter of debate. The oracular function assumed by the rabbis is hinted at in Ezra 2:62; Nehemiah 7:65. Compare the Roman practice of seeking guidance from auguries through the fetial priests.

108 Mishna, *Sanhedrin* 1:5.

109 JT Johnson, Ideology, Reason and the Limitation of War: Religious and Secular Concepts 1200–1749 (Princeton University Press, 1977) 104, and 117 f., especially the section on Alexander Leighton 125 f.

110 Inbar 94 refers only to the later comments of Rashi (*Gittin* 8b and *Avoda Zara* 20b) and Maimonides (*Terumot* 1:2) for the consensus requirement.

111 Compare Deuteronomy 9:5. The novelist Dan Jacobson explored the Bible's ambivalence about the conquest in *The Story of the Stories: The Chosen People and its God,* (Harper & Row, 1982). Michael Walzer aptly observes that no biblical author 'undertakes to construct an argument on behalf of the seven Canaanite nations comparable to Abraham's argument on behalf of the Canaanite cities of Sodom and Gomorrah': 'Idea of Holy War in Ancient Israel' (1992) 20(2) *Journal of Religious Ethics* 215, 215.

> hold one another hateful through and through
> so there can be no courtesy between us.[112]

This scene, of Achilles transformed into an animal, is laden with Homer's implied view of what it means to be human: to be willing to parley, to consider self-restraint, to respect others as possible friends.[113] Achilles is not a hero in the story. He is a lesson in Fate, and in the excesses of war. Indeed, the *Iliad* starts with a forewarning of the purpose of the tale:

> Rage — Goddess, sing the rage of Peleus' son Achilles,
> murderous, doomed, that cost the Achaeans countless losses,
> hurling down to the House of Death so many sturdy souls,
> great fighters' souls, but made their bodies carrion,
> feasts for the dogs and birds.[114]

Homer is warning us of what can occur when the laws of war — which, as David Feany noted, were well recorded for the Hellenes — are broken. Yet he also talks to us of the importance of these regulations, lest we end up doomed. This latter concept — of humanising the foe — is critical in international humanitarian law, and the historic laws of war to a certain point. Yet there is a clear dividing point where the foe has transitioned from an equal, to lesser, and it is this degradation of the enemy that modern international humanitarian law has sought to reintroduce and codify.

Specifically, the story of David and Goliath highlights the use of degrading language to dehumanise, and to vilify the enemy. Goliath, vested in the contemporary symbols of wealth and prestige — mail armour, shield bearer, sword and spear — is met with David, a shepherd and armed with a sling. Often the story ends there; but a literary analysis of the language demonstrates the layers that this choice of weapons means to Goliath.

> And David said to Saul, Let no man's heart fail because of him [Goliath]; thy servant will go and fight with this Philistine.
>
> And Saul said to David, Thou art not able to go against this Philistine to fight with him: for thou art but a youth ...

112 *The Iliad* (trans. Robert Fagles, 1990) 22.308ff.

113 Jonathan Shay, *Achilles in Vietnam* (Simon & Schuster, 1995) 83.

114 *The Iliad*,1.1.

> [David answered,] *Thy servant slew both the lion and the bear; and this uncircumcised Philistine shall be as one of them*, seeing he hath defined the armies of the living God
>
> David said moreover, *The LORD that delivered me out of the paw of the lion, and out of the paw of the bear, he will deliver me out of the hand of this Philistine.*

David, who did not need armour to fight animals, dismisses the weapons in lieu of a sling and stave. He approaches Goliath:

> And when the Philistine looked about, and saw David, he disdained him …
>
> And the Philistine said unto David, *Am I a dog, that thouh comest to me with staves?*

Goliath immediately grasps that David defines and intends to treat him sub-human — an animal, to be fought without honour. This Abrahamic origin story — shared by those of the Christian, Jewish and Islamic faith — is perhaps more shaping than is often given credit for. As Jonathan Shay, classicist and combat trauma psychologist notes:

> Twentieth-century nationalism has taken over the biblical tendency to measure loyalty by how vehemently one dehumanizes the enemy. When American soldiers and their commanders in Vietnam debased the enemy, they echoed very ancient proofs of their faith in God and of their own religious merit. … The Judeo-Christian (and Islamic) world view has triumphed … that dishonouring the enemy now seems natural, virtuous, patriotic, pious.[115]

Shay is, with respect, not utterly correct in this statement. Islam has always tried to mitigate the cruelty of wars even against those who are *Dar Al-Harb*. The Prophet Muhammad instructed: 'Observe good treatment towards the prisoners'.[116] Islamic law guarantees that prisoners of war shall be treated humanely and with respect — fed and watered, clothed if necessary, and protected from the heat and the cold and from cruel treatment. Their families

---

115 Shay (n 113) 115.

116 Muhammad ibn Jarīr al-Ṭabarī, *Tārīkh al-Ṭabarī: Tārīkh al-Umam wa al-Mulūk*, (Dār al-Kutub al-ʿIlmiyyah, Beirut, 2001) vol 2, 39.

which include parents, grandparents and children would remain with them, so as to protect family unity.[117]

There is some resonance here with the Roman notion of *bellum justum*; though the rabbinic classification is into obligatory and optional rather than just and unjust.[118] A defensive war is obligatory (just); a pre-emptive war *might* be.[119] Roman warfare was known for the marked absence of restrictions on the categories of persons who were considered legitimate targets of war, so much so that *bellum romanum* has become a synonym for total war. Implied within *bellum justum*, although not often discussed, is its applicability to civilised sovereign States — which necessarily requires a degree of externality. In order to be able to conduct just war, through the *fetiales*, a sedentary population with established borders was necessary. Those who did not fit into this concept of a regular, legally defined enemy (the *hostis justus*) were incompatible with the concept of just war. Accordingly, bandits, pirates and rebels (who primarily were internal threats) were not 'regular' or 'traditional' enemies, and the *jus in bello* could not apply to them.[120]

Such a perspective flowed through into feudal warfare, within the melting pot of Germanic individualism and Roman legalism.[121] Central to medieval public warfare were tactics designed to compel the other party to accept the validity of their claim. Such means and methods included forced contributions, arson, plunder, and injuries against certain individuals, destruction of property, ransom, and use of lethal force. As noted by Girart, Duke of Burgundy (an independent sovereign, therefore capable of public war) discussing the use of burning and plundering around him:

---

117 Muḥammad ibn Aḥmad al-Sarakhsī, *Kitāb al-Mabsūt* (Dār al- Maʻrifah) vol 9, 135, 196; vol 10, 129, 131; vol 16, 145; vol 26, 145.

118 The Puritan Henry Ainsworth, leader of the Separatist congregation in Amsterdam, in his *Annotations upon the Five Books of Moses* (John Bellarmine, 1627), leaning upon Maimonides, makes the same distinction. JT Johnson comments that 'this distinction overrides any that might be attempted between offensive and defensive war'; he is incorrect. See: JT Johnson, *Ideology, Reason and the Limitation of War: Religious and Secular Concepts 1200–1749* (Princeton University Press, 1977) 131.

119 Efraim Inbar points to the distinction between pre-emptive and preventive war: Efraim Inbar, 'War in the Jewish tradition' (1987) 9(2) *Jerusalem Journal of International Relations* 83, 96. He cites *Leem Mishneh* who interprets Maimonides' expression 'war to enlarge the borders of Israel' (*Mishneh Torah: Melakhim* 5:1) as preventive war, to deter potential aggressors. (Inbar wrongly attributes *Leem Mishneh* to Joseph Karo; the author was the Salonika-born rabbi Abraham ben Moses di Boton, 1545?–1588).

120 See, for example, Wouter G Werner, 'From Justus Hostis to Rogue State: The Concept of the Enemy in International Legal Thinking' (2004) 17(2) *International Journal for the Semiotics of Law* 155, 158, 167.

121 See Samuel White, *Keeping the Peace of the Realm* (LexisNexus, 2021) Chapter 3 generally on the development of feudal law.

If my neighbour starts a quarrel with me,
With fire burns my lands to cinders;
And I, his, on all sides;
If he steals my castles or keeps,
Then so it goes until we come to terms,
Or he puts me or I put him in prison.[122]

Procession through hostile territory — to *chevauchee* — demonstrated the justice and moral superiority of one's claim, and further undermined the position of an impotent noble unable to defend what they claimed theirs. Although some tactics evolved that sought to introduce sharp war — such as the *chevauchee* — there were rules that regulated it, such the right of captives to ransom rather than execution.[123] Judeo-Christian rules expanded throughout the medieval period, to begin to crystalise into a very definitive set of rules on class and religion. For inter-European warfare, there were particular restrictions on methods, means and weapon systems. For intra-continental fighting (such as against Enemies of the Faith), there were explicit exceptions to the principles of humanity due to 'the other'.

This is not a particularly novel observation, but goes to highlight the legal historical framework that underpinned the European continent, prior to the advent of colonisations and Empire. It also highlights, in a linked but separate way, how even modern discussions around international law are still framed through the perspective of 'othering'.[124] When modernity wrought significant changes to these institutions, the code of warfare was not thrown out but merely adapted, often with very few changes.

Legal Historical Framing of Eurocentrism

The formation of international law, while boasting a grand historical narrative, is tainted with a less illustrious side. A glaring illustration of this blemished history is, among many other blemishes, the Mandate System, a concept introduced

122 Quoted in Richard W Kaeuper, *Chivalry and Violence in Medieval Europe* (Oxford University Press, 1999) 177.

123 Michael Bryant, *A World History of War Crimes: From Antiquity to the Present* (Bloomsbury, 2016) 58.

124 Samuel White, 'Sharp War Soft War' in *International Committee of the Red Cross* (forthcoming).

by the League of Nations and later perpetuated by the United Nations.[125] The Mandate System here is defined as the 'modified form of internationally lawful superordination'[126] and as the 'normative turning point that embodied a combination of continued colonialism and a foreshadowing of decolonization'.[127] More specifically, the role it took in governing as the 'sacred trust of civilization' in promoting the 'well-being and development' of peoples whom were 'not yet able by themselves under the strenuous conditions of the modern world'.[128]

This 'sacred trust' also went on to classify groups in the order of their relative echelons of civilisation, each requiring more tutelage than the next.[129] The Middle East was assumed a stand-alone position. The Tribal Tropical Africans required 'an infinite number of years or decades of economic or political advancement under European tutelage' whilst the Primitive Pacifics 'would probably remain European subjects at least for a period of centuries, if not forever'.[130] Anghie comments on this where he suggests the League legitimises its endeavours with by establishing their activity as a 'science' in colonial administration, a 'science' that manifested in the 'most intrusive and comprehensive' forms with specialised systems.[131] The 'science' emerged with a centralised system that valued 'census, education … and the modification of legal systems'.[132] The system is legitimised in this sense given *some* liberties and freedoms were offered to European subjects.[133] However, Anghie ought to take it a step further and approach the proposition with similar or more rigor as Lumumba, citing Nkrumah in doing so.[134] Lumumba directs attention to the suggestion that recognises when slavery reduced in value, the European hand scrambled for the continents, when colonialism became too iniquitous, independence

125 Carsten Stahn, *The Law and Practice of International Territorial Administration Versailles to Iraq and Beyond* (Cambridge University Press, 2008).

126 Ruth Gordon, 'Saving Failed States: Sometimes a Neocolonialist Notion' (1997) 12(6) *American University International Law Review* 903, 941.

127 Ibid.

128 *The Covenant of The League of Nations*, signed 28 June 1919 (entered into force 10 January 1920) art 22.

129 William Roger Louis, 'The Era of the Mandates System and Non-European World' in Hedley Bull and Adam Watson (eds), *The Expansion of International Society* (Clarendon Press, 2008) 202.

130 Ibid; Ruth Gordon (n 126) 944.

131 Antony Anghie, 'The Heart of my Home: Colonialism, Environmental Damage and the Nauru Case' (1993) 34(2) *Harvard International Law Journal* 445, 495.

132 Ibid.

133 Ibid.

134 Kwame Nkrumah, *Neo-Colonialism: The Last Stage of Imperialism* (Nelson, 1965) 15–31.

supervened but imperfectly.[135] Pseudo-emancipation emerges and produces the neo-colonial regime of which it is at its most 'diabolical' stage.[136]

The first methodology (*preclusive position*) holds that those without any civilization were unable to enjoy any of its benefits or protections: be it accepted sovereignty, or protection under the laws of war. As Dr Rowan Nicholson has argued, a preclusive approach sets out that allegedly less civilised peoples were unable to enjoy any of the benefits or protections of international law during conflicts with Western powers:[137] whether this is an acceptance of national sovereignty, or protection under the laws of war.[138] He describes three variants of this framework, that emerged at different points throughout the Imperial era.[139]

First, there was the view that the territories inhabited by less civilised peoples were *terra nullius* or unclaimed by a legal entity.[140] As MF Lindley explained in 1926, the consequence of this was that mere occupation was sufficient to allow Western States sovereignty over said land, as opposed to other territories that required a higher threshold of conduct such as 'prescription' or the continuous exercise of sovereign powers.[141] This appears to have been a position shared by Emmerich de Vattel, considered by Imperial historians to be the pre-eminent international lawyer during the early nineteenth-century,[142] who argued that less industrialised peoples who survived 'only by hunting,

135 Ibid.

136 Ibid. Importantly, the reader is invited to draw a parallel between the doings of the Mandate System in the establishment of the Palestinian Protectorate, Palestine today and observe this as direct evidence of the ongoing neo-colonial project. See generally UN Human Rights Office of the High Commissioner, 'UN expert warns of new instance of mass ethnic cleansing of Palestinians, calls for immediate ceasefire' (Press Release, 14 October 2023).

137 Rowan Nicholson, 'Was the Colonisation of Australia an Invasion of Sovereign Territory?' (2019) 20(2) *Melbourne Journal of International Law* 493, 502.

138 Ibid 502–4.

139 Ibid 502.

140 Ibid 502–3.

141 MF Lindley, *The Acquisition and Government of Backward Territory in International Law: Being a Treatise on the Law and Practice Relating to Colonial Expansion* (Longmans, Green and Co, 1926) 1–2. See also Brian Slattery, 'Aboriginal Sovereignty and Imperial Claims' (1991) 29(4) *Osgoode Hall Law Journal* 681, 699.

142 See Robin FA Farbel, 'Laws of War in the 1812 Conflict' (1980) 14(2) *American Studies* 199, 199–218. See generally Donald E Graves, '"Every Horror was Committed with Impunity ... and Not a Man was Punished!" Reflections on British Military Law and the Atrocities at Hampton' (June 2009) *War of 1812 Magazine* <https://www.napoleon-series.org/military-info/Warof1812/2009/Issue11/c_hampton.html>.

and their flocks'[143] merely 'ranged through [rather] than inhabited'[144] their traditional lands. Accordingly, he reasoned that 'though the conquest of the civilised empires of Peru and Mexico was a notorious usurpation, the establishment of many colonies on the continent of North America might, on their confining themselves within just bounds, be extremely lawful'.[145]

The second view suggested by Nicholson is similar to the first but instead suggests a more limited category of what constituted *terra nullius*. As retrospectively described by the International Court of Justice in *Western Sahara*, this adapted test was essentially that semi-civilised peoples could demonstrate effective occupation and that only those who lacked 'social and political organization' were incapable of legally inhabiting territories under international law.[146] Accordingly, as re-expressed later in *Cameroon v Nigeria*, in territories inhabited by people who met this political test, treaties between Western powers and indigenous rulers 'were regarded as derivative roots of title'.[147]

Finally, the third approach ignores any assessment of *terra nullius* and broadly excludes non-Western peoples from contemporary international law.[148] This more extreme stance appears to directly align with Speirs' description of the transcultural view that wartime prohibitions only covered wars 'within Christendom ... or between civilized nations'.[149] Consequently this combined position (henceforth only referred to as 'preclusive') may be summarised as an approach that clearly implements the exclusion of non-Western peoples under the Othering framework.[150] When considering further the religious element favoured by transcultural theorists, the preclusive view is perhaps best encapsulated by the 1607 judgment of Lord Coke (Chief Justice of the Court of Common Pleas at this point) in *Calvin's Case* that all infidels were 'perpetual enemies' as the law held they could not be converted, and 'between them, as with the devil, whose subjects they be, and the Christian, there is

143 Emmerich de Vattel, *The Law of Nations*, (tr Béla Kapossy and Richard Whatmore, Liberty Fund, 2008) 129.

144 Ibid 130.

145 Ibid, discussed in Rowan Nicholson, (n 137) 493, 502–3.

146 *Western Sahara (Advisory Opinion)* [1975] ICJ Rep 12, 39 [80]–[81].

147 *Cameroon v Nigeria (Judgment)* [2002] ICJ Rep 303, 405 [205], citing ibid 39 [80].

148 Rowan Nicholson, 'Was the Colonisation of Australia an Invasion of Sovereign Territory?' (n 137) 506–10.

149 Edward Spiers, 'Surrender in Britain's Small Colonial Wars of the Nineteenth-Century' in Holger Afflerbach and Hew Strachan (eds), *How Fighting Ends* (Oxford University Press, 2012) 253, 253–6.

150 See the previous section.

perpetual hostility'.[151] In 1859, the future member of Parliament (and former British East India Company (BEIC) employee) John Stuart Mill similarly opined in his influential essay titled *A Few Words on Non-Intervention* that:

> To suppose that the same international customs, and the same rules of international morality, can obtain between one civilized nation and another, and between civilized nations and barbarians, is a grave error … the rules of ordinary international morality imply reciprocity. But barbarians will not reciprocate. They cannot be depended on for observing any rules.[152]

Perhaps the clearest representation of this distinction between the civilised and uncivilised under IHL was seen through the arguments of General Sir John Ardagh, the British delegate at the plenary meeting of the 1899 Hague Conference, who argued that the use of dum-dum bullets on 'savage races' was an acceptable departure from the prohibition of explosive bullets under international law.[153] As noted by James Brown Scott, who recorded the proceedings of the conference, Ardagh's contention was that when a '[Western] soldier is wounded by a small projectile, he is taken away in the ambulance, but the savage, although run through two or three times, does not cease to advance'.[154] Fortunately for IHL's development, however, Britain finally complied with the prohibition three years later.[155]

It is often argued that the preclusive approach, whilst out of step with modern sensibilities, was *the* law of the day. The Russian jurist Friedrich De Martens

151 *Calvin's Case* (1608) 77 ER 377, as reprinted in *The Reports of Sir Edward Coke, In Thirteen Parts, A New Edition* (Joseph Butterworth and Son, 1826) vol 4, 29. See also Henry Reynolds, (n 2) 43.

152 John Stuart Mill, 'A Few Words on Non-Intervention' (1859) 60(360) *Fraser's Magazine for Town and Country* 766, 766–76. See also John Stuart Mill, 'A Few Words on Non-Intervention' (1990) 27(3) *New England Review* 252, 259–60.

153 Tuba Inal (n 80) 67, citing James Brown Scott (ed), *The Proceedings of the Hague Peace Conference: Translation of the Official Texts* (Oxford University Press, 1920) 276–8, 286–7. See also Kim A Wagner, 'Savage Warfare: Violence and the Rule of Colonial Difference in Early British Counterinsurgency' (2018) 85(1) *History Workshop Journal* 217, 229, citing note by Lord Lansdowne (Secretary of State for War), 8 December 1899, CAB/37/51/94.

154 James Brown Scott (ed), *The Proceedings of the Hague Peace Conference: Translation of the Official Texts* (n 153) 286.

155 Maartje Abbenhuis, Branka Bogdan and Emma Wordsworth, 'Humanitarian Bullets and Man-Killers: Revisiting the History of Arms Regulation in the Late Nineteenth Century' (2022) 104(920–921) *International Review of the Red Cross* 1684, 1689.

(not to be confused with the German jurist of the preceding generation, Georg Friedrich von Martens) argued in 1879 that:

> It is natural law, not international law, which is applicable to the relations between civilized nations with the nations of Asia ... In Asia, international law transforms itself into natural law.[156]

This was not to say that humanitarian principles and international law could not be extended — it was voluntary. But De Martens argued that there was no strict legal requirement as 'Christian nations are obliged to follow no rule towards savages peoples'.[157] This concept of 'othering' was of course consistent with the non-application of international law or natural law to Enemies of the Faith in the Middle Ages.[158] In 1607, Lord Coke had declared all infidels were 'perpetual enemies' as the law held they could not be converted, and 'between them, as with the devil, whose subjects they be, and the Christian, there is perpetual hostility'.[159]

Was this position widely shared? Emmerich de Vattel (1714–67) was a notable Swiss jurist and philosopher whose contributions to the field of international law have left an enduring legacy. His magnum opus, *The Law of Nations* (1758), has had a profound impact on the development of modern international relations and legal thought. Vattel's work was firmly grounded in the Enlightenment ideals of reason, natural law, and the pursuit of justice in international affairs. Vattel went on to develop several ground-breaking concepts that continue to shape the world of international law. His emphasis on state sovereignty, whereby each nation possesses the inherent right to govern itself without external interference, laid the foundation for the Westphalian system of state sovereignty that still underpins the international order. Vattel's assertion of the equality of nations, regardless of their size or power, challenged prevailing notions of hierarchy among states.

Vattel's emphasis on state sovereignty was not merely an intellectual exercise but a reflection of the profound transformations occurring in the global landscape during his time. His work provided much-needed clarity and guidance

156 Friedrich de Martens, *La Russie et l'Angleterre dans l'Asie Centrale*' (1879) 11 *Revue de Droit International et de Législation Comparée* 227, 240–1, as quoted by Frédéric Mégret (n 91) 283.

157 Ibid.

158 Samuel White, 'The Late Middle Ages in Northern Europe' in Samuel White (ed), *Laws of Yesterday's Wars* (n 9).

159 Henry Reynolds (n 2) 43.

as European nations were increasingly engaging with distant lands through colonization, trade, and diplomacy. In this context, Vattel's articulation of sovereignty as the inherent right of each nation to self-governance and non-interference became a cornerstone of modern international relations. One of Vattel's central assertions was the equality of nations. In an era marked by colonial empires and power imbalances, his insistence that all sovereign states, regardless of their size or might, should be treated as equals had a democratizing effect on international relations. This principle challenged prevailing notions of hierarchy among states and paved the way for a more egalitarian approach to global affairs. Accordingly, he opined that a nation must be sovereign which governs itself 'under whatever form, and which does not depend on any other Nation'.[160]

Moreover, Vattel's ideas on sovereignty extended beyond theoretical musings. They profoundly influenced the development of international law, shaping the norms and standards that guide state conduct in today's interconnected world. His emphasis on sovereignty as a natural right of nations contributed to the consolidation of the Westphalian system, which recognized the autonomy and self-determination of individual states. Vattel's enduring legacy lies not only in his philosophical contributions but also in the practical impact of his ideas on state behavior and the principles that continue to guide nations in their interactions on the global stage. Specifically those societies who avoided labour, who chose 'to live only by hunting, and their flocks'[161] could not legally complain if:

> other nations, more industrious, and too closely confined, come to take possession of a part of [their] lands. Thus, though the conquest of the civilised empires of [Inca] Peru and [the Mexica] was a notorious usurpation, the establishment of many colonies on the continent of North America might, on their confining themselves within just bounds, be extremely lawful. The people of those extensive tracts rather ranged through than inhabited them.[162]

160 Ibid 41.

161 Emmerich de Vattel, *The Law of Nations, or, Principles of the Law of Nature, Applied to the Conduct and Affairs of Nations and Sovereigns* (1797) 129.

162 Ibid 130.

This expansive, preclusive interpretation was carried on late into the 19th century by some fringe academics like William Edward Hall[163] or John Westlake.[164] Edward Speirs describes the views of 'transcultural' jurists at the time,[165] who maintained that these prohibitions only applied to conflicts 'within Christendom … or between civilized nations'.[166] To an extent, this was likely a consequence of the complex tapestry of government models present throughout the late nineteenth-century, in contrast to the current near-worldwide homogeneity of the Western model of nation-statehood.[167] European legal scholars responded to this diversity by 'categorising' these 'decentralised chiefdoms … and various other independent entities' based on their perceived levels of development.[168]

It is worth specifically examining the hierarchical status that different categories of non-Western people fell under, in the decision-making processes of late nineteenth-century British colonial officers. Farish Ahmad Noor, a prominent Southeast Asian scholar of Imperial history, points to the writings of John Crawfurd as particularly influential in this space.[169] Crawfurd was a leading BEIC official who served as the British Resident to Singapore from

163 *A Treaties on International Law* (Clarendon Press, 4th ed, 1895) 106–107.

164 John Westlake, *Chapters on Principles of International Law* (Cambridge University Press, 1894) 141.

165 Edward Spiers, (n 149) 253–6.

166 Ibid.

167 See Rowan Nicholson, *Statehood and the State-Like in International Law* (Oxford University Press, 2019) 51–91.

168 Rowan Nicholson, 'Was the Colonisation of Australia an Invasion of Sovereign Territory?' (n 137) 493, 499, citing Liliana Obregón, 'The Civilized and the Uncivilized' in Bardo Fassbender and Anne Peters (eds), *The Oxford Handbook of the History of International Law* (Oxford University Press, 2012) 917, 917–40. See also: Farish A Noor and Peter Carey, 'Why Race Mattered: Racial Difference, Racialized Colonial Capitalism and the Racialized Wars of Nineteenth-Century Colonial Southeast Asia' in Farish A Noor and Peter Carey (eds), *Racial Difference and the Colonial Wars of 19th Century Southeast Asia Racial Difference and the Colonial Wars of 19th Century Southeast Asia* (Amsterdam University Press, 2021) 9, 19, citing John Crawfurd, 'On the Physical and Mental Characteristics of the European and Asiatic Races of Man' (1867) 5(1) *Transactions of the Ethnological Society of London* 58, 58–81; Lauren Benton and Lisa Ford, *Rage for Order: The British Empire and the Origins of International Law* (Harvard University Press, 2016) 99, 188.

169 Farish A Noor and Peter Carey, 'Why Race Mattered: Racial Difference, Racialized Colonial Capitalism and the Racialized Wars of Nineteenth-Century Colonial Southeast Asia' in Farish A Noor and Peter Carey (eds), *Racial Difference and the Colonial Wars of 19th Century Southeast Asia Racial Difference and the Colonial Wars of 19th Century Southeast Asia* (Amsterdam University Press, 2021) 9, 19–20.

1823 to 1826[170] and later published essays using polygenist race theories to differentiate between non-Western peoples for use in Imperial policymaking.[171] Accordingly, these commentaries would be referenced decades later by subsequent colonial officers based in the region such as Sir Frank Swettenham during the Perak War (1875–6).[172] According to Crawfurd, the native inhabitants of Burma and the Malay States fell into an inferior 'second order of civilisation' that ambiguously conferred partial recognition of their rights under international law,[173] in contrast to the extent afforded to States that specifically followed the Western model,[174] and who were accordingly members of that community of nations on more equal terms.[175] While it is beyond the scope of this book to consider the specific difference in rights under colonial international law between partially recognised peoples and entities without recognition, especially given the lack of robust and settled commentary,[176] it must be noted that this assessment clearly affected the decision-making of commanders such as Sir Charles Edward Callwell (1859–1928) on the field.[177]

Yet there were other, more moderate, legal interpretations. In 1532, Vitoria (more on his jurisprudence and its application to the 'other' in Chapter 2) had opined that Indians in the New World 'had true dominion in both public and private matters, just like Christians'.[178] So too did JG Heineccius, in 1743, observe that 'dominion consists solely in the faculty of excluding others from the use of a thing'.[179] MF Lindley's renowned book *The Acquisition and Government of Backward Territory in International Law* provides an in-depth analysis of this subject on the basis of a comprehensive review of state conventions from over four different centuries and continents, to conclude that land was occupied when

170 John Bastin, 'The Letters of Sir Stamford Raffles to Nathaniel Wallich 1819–1824' (1981) 54(2) *Journal of the Malaysian Branch of the Royal Asiatic Society* 1, 58.

171 See, eg, John Crawfurd (n 168) 58, 58–81.

172 Sir Frank Athelstane Swettenham, *British Malaya: An Account of The Origin and Progress of British Influence in Malaya.* (John Lane, 1907) 166.

173 John Crawfurd (n 168) 58, 74.

174 See, eg, John Westlake (n 164) 81–2. See also Michelle Gordon (n 97) 39, citing 'The Perak Expedition', *The Times* (London, 16 February 1876).

175 See generally Arnulf Becker Lorca, *Mestizo International Law: A Global Intellectual History, 1850–1950* (Cambridge University Press, 2015).

176 See Rowan Nicholson (n 167) 88.

177 Charles Edward Callwell, *Small Wars: Their Principles and Practice* (Harrison and Sons, 1896) 29–30.

178 See Francisco de Vitoria, *De Indis et de Ivre Belli Relectiones*, tr John Pawley Bate (Carnegie Institution of Washington, 1917), as cited in Henry Reynolds (n 2) 43, fn 18.

179 Johann Gottlieb Heineccius, *Elementa Historiae Philosophicae* [A Methodical System of Universal Law], tr George Turnbull (1743), as cited in Henry Reynolds (n 2) 41, fn 19.

> it be inhabited by a political society, that is, by a considerable number of persons who are permanently united by habitual obedience to a certain and common superior, or whose conduct in regard to their mutual relations habitually conforms to recognised standards.[180]

What was 'considerable'? This was a difficult question from an inter-temporal perspective. Samuel Pufendorf in 1688 wrote that 'the just size of a state should be measured by the strength of its neighbours'.[181] So too did Vattel argue through analogy that 'a dwarf is as much a man as a giant is ... and a small Republic no less a sovereign State than the most powerful kingdom'.[182] Wolff argued that size was of no issue — it was, like Lindley, a matter of social cohesion.[183] Jeremy Bentham argued then that social cohesion, and the acceptance of punishments from the social group, was the defining feature between living and leaving the State of Nature.[184]

The conclusion here is that a Eurocentric perspective of the world — as the world conquerors — reflected itself both in the laws they established themselves and the exceptions to the rules they created. Power forged frameworks, and these frameworks dictated who was in, and who was out, through language.[185] Huntington identified seven major civilisations differentiated by religion, history, culture, tradition and/or language; Western, Confucian, Japanese, Islamic, Hindu, Slavic-Orthodox and Latin American, with the existence of an eighth African civilisational bloc tentative.[186]

As clashing societal views are less mutable than divergent ideologies, the replacement of the Iron Curtain of ideology with the Velvet Curtain of culture has resulted in more prolonged and violent conflicts, which have only been exacerbated by globalisation, immigration and racism.[187] Contrastingly, Huntington held that conflicts between states within the same civilisation are

---

180 MF Lindley (n 141) 22–23.

181 Samuel von Pufendorf, *Of the Law of Nature and Nations* (1688). See also Henry Reynolds (n 2) 42.

182 See Francisco de Vitoria (n 178). See also Henry Reynolds (n 2) 42.

183 See Christian Wolff, *The Law of Nations Treated According to a Scientific Method* (1749).

184 See Jeremy Bentham, *The Rationale of Punishment* (Robert Heward, 1830). See also Henry Reynolds (n 2) 45.

185 There are of course, many angles to approach Eurocentrism. However, this is the preferred angle as a precursor of sorts in then going on to appreciate the role and relationship of language and law to non-Western peoples during the late Imperial period.

186 Samuel P Huntington, 'The Clash of Civilizations?' (1993) (Summer) 72(3) *Foreign Affairs* 22, 25.

187 Ibid 25–7, 31–2.

likely to be less intense and less likely to escalate into major or even global wars than conflicts between civilisations.[188]

Huntington's 'West versus the Rest' mentality is not reflective of current events, with increasing economic, military, strategic and diplomatic competition and an emerging multipolar power distribution evident, even in Australia's immediate region.[189] We are bearing witness to the largest military build-up since the Second World War, with China developing their own economic and military power in an effort to modernise, not Westernise.[190] Although the West versus the Rest mentality may no longer hold true, double standards in treatment amongst civilisation blocs, whereby nations apply one standard of warfare to kin-countries and different standards to others, continue to underpin the thinking of many military practitioners The rareness of full restraint in conflicts against barbarians and outsiders (implied by the structure of Grotius' *The Laws of War and Peace*)[191] is evident when considering low compliance with international law in European vs. non-European dyads.[192]

Theoretical Framing of Eurocentrism

Edward Said writes that 'ideas, cultures, and histories cannot seriously be understood or studied without their force, or more precisely their configurations of power, also being studied'.[193] This section seeks to theorise the Eurocentricity of law by firstly examining foundational elements and second it scrutinises the normative Eurocentricity of IHL.

A Eurocentric 'person or enterprise' is one that adopts a specific orientation grounded in European realities.[194] It is the adoption of a particular European center.[195] Eurocentric law in this sense is then is 'European-derived', with a

188 Ibid 38–9, 48.

189 Ibid 39–40, 47; Department of Defence, *Defence Strategic Review 2023* (Report, April 2023) ('Defence Strategic Review') 17, 28 [2.4].

190 Huntington (n 186) 36, 41.

191 Helen M Kinsella, *The Image Before the Weapon: a Critical History of the Distinction between Combatant and Civilian* (Cornell University Press, 2017) 70.

192 Ibid 70; Tanisha M Fazal and Brooke C Greene, 'A Particular Difference: European Identity and Civilian Targeting' (2014) 45(4) *British Journal of Political Science* 829, 830, 832.

193 Edward Said, *Orientalism* (Penguin Books, 2003) 5.

194 Jeffrey Lynn Woodyard, 'Locating Asante: Making Use of the Afrocentric Idea' in Dyhana Ziegler (ed), *Molefi Kete Asante And Afrocentricity* (James C Winston Publishing, 2011) 27, 29–32, 35.

195 Eleni Telda, *Sanofka: African Thought and Education* (Peter Lang Publishers, 1995) 106–107.

centered set of values, morals, and norms to regulate and judge polities.[196] As international law (as it exists today) was originally framed by those concepts of chivalry and shared military experiences outlined by Fazal and Greene, it is of no wonder that the legal frameworks *only* regulate a polity who shares and is of that same history and political reality.[197] A difficult consequence for international law was, therefore, for its posture of universality.[198]

In Merryman's words, the civil law, common law, and socialist law are all products of European thought that make up what we know to be 'the law'.[199] This is *the* 'operation' of legal systems, and they ought to be 'made, applied, studied, perfected and taught' as such.[200] To fathom such a proposition, the normative determinants that feed this rhetoric must be realised which Ani has astutely categorised.[201] The core tenets of the European condition begins with materialism as the first value.[202] That reality, nature and social behaviours are led in material terms which promotes the custom of 'acquisition and narcissism'.[203] That means the greater human condition *is* and *should* be understood as a 'zero-sum game' allowing competition, aggression, individualism and the relentless accumulation of material to flourish.[204] International legal frameworks in the time of Empire were based on this, and sought to maximise competitive advantages in opening markets (hence, gunboat diplomacy) and minimising 'checks' on 'advancement'. Ani offers seven determinants for European perspectives of international law:[205]

1) Dichotomous Reasoning: that is the 'separation of the self from the "other"'.[206] A reality that separates 'the self into various dichotomies'.[207] The dichotomous reasoning strictly results in

196 Kenneth Kunn, 'Law as a Eurocentric Enterprise' (1997) 15(2) *Minnesota Journal of Law & Inequality* 323, 325.
197 Tanisha M Fazal and Brooke C Greene, (n 192) 829, 830.
198 Ibid 326.
199 John Henry Merryman, *The Civil Law Tradition: An Introduction to the Legal Systems of Europe and Latin America* (Stanford University Press, 2007) 2.
200 Ibid.
201 Kunn (n 196) 331.
202 Ibid.
203 Ibid 332.
204 Ibid.
205 Marimba Ani, *Yurugu: An African-centered Critique of European Cultural Thought and Behaviour* (Africa World Press, 2008) 82, 98, 104, 195.
206 Ibid 105, 298.
207 Ibid 105.

concluding with the 'either/or'; non-dinutial reasoning[208] and this is distinguished from the 'diunital' rationality that results in the 'both/and'.[209] The compartmentalisation disregards holistic reasoning entirely.

2) Employment of Hierarchies: dichotomous rationality leads the European to organise reality into hierarchies of 'greater and lesser value'.[210] Beseeched here is the utility of reason over passion.[211] This line of thinking leads the European to observe all as better or worse and is the precursor for power-based relationships.[212]
3) Analytical Thought: through a vehement dissection of matters and exclusive examination of matters, this reasoning style works 'to the exclusion of, and not in addition to'.[213] 'Interrelationships' are disregarded, and reality is fragmented, instead of whole.[214]
4) Objectification: beyond the European self, reality is a 'collection of objects to be controlled' and self-worth is equated with the extent of objects under one's control.[215] When a being or item is objectified, to 'think properly about an object, to gain knowledge of (mastery over) an object, *we must control it*'.[216] The consequence here is then 'oppression' and 'degradation'.[217]
5) Abstraction: interrelated with 'objectification', abstraction refers to a reduced emission of ideas that detaches ideas from their context.[218] The use of abstraction is 'reified to the extent that it becomes separate from and more important than the concrete experiences from which it originates'.[219] To consider matters independent of

208 Ibid 34, 68, 97–98.
209 Ibid 34–35. 'Diunital' reasoning here means observing reality as a complemental duality and not a dichotomous adversary. See also Augustine Nwoye, *African Psychology: The Emergence of Tradition* (Oxford University Press, 2022) 115, 119.
210 Ani (n 205) 106.
211 Ibid 94.
212 Ibid 106; Kimberlé Williams Crenshaw, 'Race, Reform and Retrenchment: Transformation and Legitimation in Antidiscrimination Law' (1988) 101(7) *Harvard Law Review* 1331, 1372–1376, quoting Jacques Derrida, *Dissemination* tr Barbara Johnson (University of Chicago Press, 1981) viii.
213 Ani (n 205) 76–79.
214 Ibid.
215 Ibid 106; Kunn (n 196) 336.
216 Ani (n 205) 37.
217 Ibid 402–404.
218 Ibid 70–72.
219 Ibid 71.

their context removes the ability to question correctness and thus becomes a utensil of power.[220] She cites the example of the European preference for written instead of oral communication which is supposed to carry more legitimacy.[221] Ani in this regard could have taken the proposition further and considered it as a power legitimizing tool, permitting the picking and choosing. A tool that consequently denies morality room to enter the equation.

6) Extreme Rationalism: that the cosmos must be perceived exclusively in rational terms.[222] The obsession with structuring and organising matters in rational terms excludes consideration of the softer matters of the human condition.[223] When the human condition is studied in such rational terms, it gives the European the false impression that everything is known and is then capable of then being controlled.[224]
7) Desacralization: when the universe is observed in objective and rational terms, the European is illuded into accepting a 'despiritualized' world and holy forces are unwelcome.[225] If the sacred world is out of the equation, then one is distinctly and easily capable of dominating.

The above imputations are of course, not the only characteristics present to the European, nor are they exclusive to the European.[226] They merely serve the purpose of understanding the legitimising forces of European thought and as reflected through international legal frameworks at the time of Empire, and in particular the theoretical underpinnings of the 'othering' of colonial laws of war.

Colonial Laws of War

Following the foregoing (both from a doctrinal and theoretical perspective) it is important to note that discussions regarding the interconnections between international law and colonial warfare are limited by a significant

220 Ibid.
221 Ibid 107.
222 Ibid 58–59.
223 Ibid 107; Kunn (n 196) 337.
224 Ibid.
225 Ani (n 205) 83–84, 107.
226 Kunn (n 196) 338.

obstacle: that European customary laws of war did not automatically extend to non-Western peoples in colonial conflicts,[227] and that this was reflected in the 'ultra-violence' that characterised European tactics outside of their home continent.[228] Accordingly, any assessment of the applicability of Imperial laws of war in colonial conflicts must factor in this concept of Othering in order to avoid the 'unrealistic' contextualising of IHL developments.[229] As noted by Doreen Lustig, a recurring criticism of postcolonial scholars from the TWAIL school has been this failure to sufficiently 'capture the porous and contested aspects' of international legal history.[230]

One example of overly simplistic assumptions about the origins of international humanitarian law is that the 1864 *Geneva Convention*, as the first binding multilateral treaty, was the starting point and that subsequent nineteenth Century treaty law consolidated the newly emergent international legal constraints. In one sense the proposition is not fallacious — but it certainly lacks nuance. Twice in the 1868 *St Petersburg Declaration* 'the laws of humanity' are identified as the necessary counterweight to the necessities of war. Similarly, the 1899 and 1907 *Hague Conventions and Declarations* are replete with the call to acknowledge and respect the overarching protection of 'the principles of international law, as they result from the usages established between civilized nations, from the laws of humanity, and the requirements of the public conscience'. The Preamble to the 1868 *St Petersburg Declaration* explains that States gathered in the then Russian capital to consider 'forbidding the use of certain projectiles in time of war between civilized nations' and that 'the progress of civilization should have the effect of alleviating as much as possible the calamities of war'. Whilst these conventions — and others that sought to

227 Rowan Nicholson, 'Was the Colonisation of Australia an Invasion of Sovereign Territory?' (n 137) 493, 498. See also Frédéric Mégret (n 91) 265, 278–80.

228 See, eg, Robert Gerwarth, 'The Central European Counter-Revolution: Paramilitary Violence in Germany, Austria and Hungary after the Great War' (2008) 200(1) *Past and Present* 175, 197. See also: Michelle Gordon, *Extreme Violence and the 'British Way': Colonial Warfare in Perak, Sierra Leone and Sudan* (Bloomsbury, 2020) 6, 11; Eric D Weitz, 'The Modernity of Genocides: War, Race and Revolution in the Twentieth Century' in Robert Gellately and Ben Kiernan (eds), *The Spectre of Genocide: Mass Murder in Historical Perspective* (Cambridge University Press, 2003) 53, 55; Tom Lawson, *The Last Man: A British Genocide in Tasmania* (IB Tauris, 2014) 51.

229 See, eg, Ingo Venzke, 'The Path Not Taken: On Legal Change and its Context' in Nico Krisch and Ezgi Yildiz (eds), *The Many Paths of Change in International Law* (Oxford University Press, 2023) 309, 309.

230 Doreen Lustig, 'Governance Histories of International Law' in Markus D Dubber and Christopher Tomlins (eds), *The Oxford Handbook of Legal History* (Oxford University Press, 2018) 859, 859–882.

regulate arms (such as expanding bullets, or strategic bombers — provided clear exceptions for use in colonial warfare on the basis of racist assumptions of 'native strength',[231] there was still an underpinning of the acceptance of the rules of humanity.

Fazal and Greene argue 'the law of war was born of intra-European brutality and designed to regulate it'.[232] But what are these 'European' nations? Fazal and Greene, through in-depth statistical analysis, show that:

> the states that should be considered 'European' for the purposes of this article are those that (1) participated in the initial codification of the law of war in the late nineteenth century and (2) were generally perceived by European states as members of the European community at the time of codification. Because the identity argument depends on recognition by the deciding state of a target state's in-group or out-group status, European states' perceptions of the target state as European or not is the deciding factor when there is a discrepancy between the two criteria delineated above. Our definition excludes the Eastern European countries and Turkey, and includes Russia as well as the United States, Australia, Canada and New Zealand.[233]

They continue that a stronger correlation of sharp war/soft war rhetoric is found in the original signatories of the second 1899 *Hague Convention*. These signatories:

> generated even stronger results on our key independent variable than our preferred coding of Europeans, suggesting that a historical relationship with *jus in bello* may indeed be a key component of identity in predicting civilian targeting[234]

The substantive effect of this variable rivals or exceeds that of other key control variables. The authors show that when a European state fights a non-European state, the probability of civilian targeting increases by over 250 per

---

231 Mark Mazower, *Governing the World: The History of an Idea* (Allen Lane, 2012) 78–79; Jennifer Welsh, 'Empire and Fragmentation' in Tim Dunne and Christian Reus-Smit (eds), *The Globalisation of International Society* (Oxford: Oxford University Press, 2017) 155.

232 Tanisha M Fazal and Brooke C Greene (n 192) 829, 849.

233 Ibid 841.

234 Ibid 841.

cent. Accordingly, whilst Huntington's view is fallible, confirmed by his disproven belief that intra-Slavic conflict between Russia and Ukraine would be unlikely, there is clear evidence that the sharp war philosophy is seen clearest in 'the other'.[235]

Dierk Walter has noted that it was commonplace for late nineteenth-century Imperial actors and men on the spot to reason that the traditional European laws of war (as developed over hundreds of years of continental warfare) be abandoned when faced against 'savage' peoples whose apparently unchangeable violent nature perhaps mandated the preclusion of wartime restraints.[236]

Frédéric Mégret (as outlined above) explains how this contrast between civilised and barbaric peoples, which he summarises as the notion of Othering in IHL,[237] turned primarily on cultural differences regarding the nature of warfare — perceived by colonial commentators as indicative of fundamental differences in the character of non-Western ethnicities.[238] Mégret refers to the belief that non-Western groups 'waged war as complete tribes' to 'take advantage ... and effect ruses ... and massacres'.[239] Perhaps reflecting the religious underpinnings of early IHL developments throughout the Medieval and pre-Modern periods,[240] differences in religion with various non-Western groups have also been suggested as a factor towards this practice of Othering under international law.[241] In the specific context of the Perak War (1875–6), this was highlighted by the contemporary Malaya-based jurist (and former Chief Justice of the Straits Settlements) Sir Peter Benson Maxwell — who wrote following a failed Imperial assault on the Perak Malay village of Pasir Salak in 1876 that

235 Huntington (n 186) 38.

236 Dierk Walter, *Symmetry and Asymmetry in Colonial Warfare ca. 1500–2000: The Uses of a Concept* (Forsvarsstudier, 2005) 18–21.

237 Frédéric Mégret (n 91) 265, 265. See generally Pablo Kalmanovitz, *The Laws of War in International Thought* (Oxford University Press, 2020).

238 See, eg: Frédéric Mégret (n 91) 265 267–8, 289; Partha Chatterjee, *The Nation and its Fragments: Colonial and Postcolonial Histories* (Princeton University Press, 1994) 10, 19.

239 Frédéric Mégret (n 91) 265 291, citing John Fuller, *The Reformation of War* (Hutchinson, 1923). See also Elbridge Colby, 'How to Fight Savage Tribes' (1927) 21(2) *American Journal of International Law* 279, 279.

240 See also: Antony Anghie, 'Francisco De Vitoria and the Colonial Origins of International Law' (n 76) 321; Dale Stephens and Michael W Lewis, 'The Law of Armed Conflict' (2005) 6(1) *Melbourne Journal of International Law* 55, 58, citing Judith Gardam, 'Proportionality and Force in International Law' (1993) 87(3) *American Journal of International Law* 391, 395.

241 See, eg, Frédéric Mégret (n 91) 265, 279, 287. See also Michelle Gordon, *Extreme Violence and the 'British Way': Colonial Warfare in Perak, Sierra Leone and Sudan* (Bloomsbury, 2022) 14.

> a season of panic set in [amongst the British officials]. Rumours of a great Mahometan 'revival', and of a general rising of all the Malay Peninsula arose in the Colony, and spread like wildfire to this country, where we were told that the ferocious and fanatical Malays were about to kindle a religious war against hated foreigners, traders and Christians.[242]

According to the twentieth-century Imperial Major-General John Fuller, the inability of 'savages' to reciprocate traditional wartime customs meant that Western commanders had to be 'more brutal' in contrast to the methods usually pursued against 'civilized nation[s]'.[243] In a contemporary article criticising Imperial nostalgia amongst modern historians, Kim A Wagner highlights the way that savage warfare or racialised violence ubiquitously informed the Imperial project similar to how it shaped other European empires:

> British knowledge and understanding of the people they fought throughout the Empire was invariably shaped by the colonial ideologies and racial hierarchies implicit in the 'civilizing mission' and central to the imperial experience. Construction of the enemy as 'un-civilized', 'savage', or 'fanatic' had severe implications for the conduct of what became known as savage warfare; it dictated and justified techniques of violence that were by the same token considered unacceptable in conflicts between so-called 'civilized' nations.[244]

The British Commander Callwell — whose nineteenth-century writings on colonial warfare were integrated into textbooks on 'warfare in uncivilized countries' at the Royal Military Academy Sandhurst[245] and also adapted by American and French army manuals[246] — is likely the most authoritative

---

242 Sir P Benson Maxwell, *Our Malay Conquests* (PS King, 1878) 59–60, citing United Kingdom, *Further Correspondence Relating to the Affairs of Certain Native States in the Malay Peninsula in the Neighbourhood of the Straits Settlements* (C 1505, 1876) 109. See also Michelle Gordon (n 97) 48.

243 John Fuller (n 239) 191.

244 Kim A Wagner (n 153) 217, 231. See also Michelle Gordon (n 97) 25, citing Volker Barth and Roland Cvetkovski, 'Encounters of Empire: Methodological Approaches' in Volker Barth and Roland Cvetkovski (eds), *Imperial Co-operation and Transfer, 1870–1930: Empires and Encounters* (Bloomsbury, 2015) 3, 10.

245 Tom Menger, '"Press the Thumb onto the Eye": Moral Effect, Extreme Violence, and the Transimperial Notions of British, German, and Dutch Colonial Warfare, ca. 1890–1914' (2022) 46(1) *Itinerario* 84, 91.

246 See generally Daniel Whittingham, *Charles E Callwell and the British Way in Warfare* (Cambridge University Press, 2019).

supporter of this transcultural view.[247] In his 1896 commentary on past European colonial conflicts,[248] he asserted that 'when fighting savages, regular forces are compelled ... to conform to the savage method of battle'.[249] Arguing that non-Western peoples did not have comparable formal institutions that could instead be targeted under traditional wartime customs,[250] Callwell emphasised that Imperial commanders were 'forced to resort to ... village burning and [other] operations ... which the laws of warfare do not sanction'.[251]

A full-throated explanation of Imperial policies surrounding village-burning is perhaps best presented by Winston Churchill, who examined its legitimacy in *The Story of the Malakand Field Force*—where he described his personal experiences as a Second Lieutenant during the Imperial Tirah Campaign (1897–8) in Afghanistan:

> I feel this is a fitting moment to discuss the questions which village-burning raises. Many misconceptions exist on this subject in England. One member of the House of Commons asked the Secretary of State whether, in the punishment of villages, care was taken that only the houses of the guilty parties should be destroyed. He was gravely told that great care was taken. The spectacle of troops, who have perhaps carried a village with the bayonet and are holding it against a vigorous counter-attack, when every moment means loss of life and increase of danger, going round and carefully discriminating which houses are occupied by 'guilty parties', and which by unoffending people, is ridiculous.
>
> ...
>
> What is the actual fact? All along the Afghan border every man's home is his castle. The villages are fortifications, the fortifications the villages.
>
> ...
>
> The assailants retire to the hills. Thither it is impossible to follow them. They cannot be caught. They cannot be punished. Only one remedy remains — their property must be destroyed ... Of course, it is cruel and barbarous, as is much else in war, but it is only an unphilosophic mind

247 Bruce Vandervort, 'War in the Non-European World' in Matthew Hughes and William J Philpott (eds), *Palgrave Advances in Modern Military History* (Palgrave Macmillan, 2007) 195, 195–6. See also Michelle Gordon (n 97) 15.

248 See Charles Edward Callwell (n 177).

249 Ibid 30.

250 Kim A Wagner (n 153) 222–4.

251 Charles Edward Callwell (n 177) 40–2. See also Michelle Gordon (n 97) 18.

> that will hold it legitimate, to take a man's life, and illegitimate to destroy his property.[252]

Accordingly, any intertemporal framework used to identify the Imperial customary laws of war enforced in Malaya (1831–76) must be reconcilable with the clear influence of Othering on the development of international law at this time. Although ordinances issued by Imperial commanders during the Perak War (1875–6) point to pre-*Hague* prohibitions nevertheless being applied in conflicts against non-Western peoples during the late 1890s, an overzealous application would evidently not be reflective of actual State practice.[253]

Conclusion

This Chapter has sought to outline the fundamental basis upon which international laws of war, during the colonial era and that applied during the period of *Pax Britannica.* It did so through the set temporal period outlined at the beginning of this monograph, although the tension felt throughout the Chapter was only resolved with the implementation of the 1977 *Additional Protocol 1* (API) to the *Geneva Conventions.* There, for the first time, the nature of wars of liberation were debated and reformed. As Amanda Alexander notes, API

> was important both for ideological and practical reasons, since API refuted the traditional claim that colonial wars were a domestic matter in which the Imperial power was almost unfettered by international law.[254]

As this Chapter has highlighted, excluding the 'other' was for multiple reasons: pragmatic, ideological and even aesthetic. The authors suggest, however, that historical foundations shaped international law as it grew. The laws of war

252 Winston Churchill, *The Story of the Malakand Field Force: An Episode of Frontier War* (Longmans Green, 1898) 272–4. See also Helen Bradford, 'Gentlemen and Boers: Afrikaner Nationalism, Gender and Colonial Warfare in the South African War' in Greg Cuthbertson, Albert Grundlingh and Mary-Lynn Suttie (eds), *Writing a Wider War: Rethinking Gender, Race, and Identity in the South African War, 1899–1902* (Ohio University Press, 2002) 37, 39; Frank Emery, *Marching Over Africa: Letters from Victorian Soldiers* (Hodder & Stoughton, 1896) 26; Lewis Gann and Peter Duignan, *The Rulers of British Africa, 1870–1914* (Croom Helm, 1978) 143–4.

253 See generally Ingo Venzke, 'The Path Not Taken: On Legal Change and its Context' (n 229).

254 Amanda Alexander, 'International Humanitarian Law Postcolonialism and the 1977 *Geneva Protocol I*' (2016) 17 *Melbourne Journal of International Law* 422, 424.

were a legal doctrine of Europe that applied to Europeans, and through the control of legal frameworks that came with Empire, instilled in international legal frameworks the concept of 'other'. This, according to Mégret, is the original sin of the laws of war. This 'inevitable' colonial expansion seems to have influenced legal historical thinking. In the 8th Edition of *Brownlie's Principles*, there is a paragraph that reads:

> In terms of intellectual history international law was thus European in history. Thence it travelled with the colonizers to the Americas, to Asia, to Africa and eventually to Oceania.[255]

There is a lot to unpack in these two sentences. The argument in *Brownlie's Principles* falls prey to the 'straight line history of eternal progression',[256] where a Great White Man (Grotius, Vitoria, Augustine) discovered international law and it was developed progressively into the modern era. For many parts of European law, this is without a doubt correct — see the progression of Roman,[257] Medieval,[258] and Renaissance[259] laws of war. But it is clear that, outside of Europe, intricate and detailed customs of war existed that perfectly reflected the environment that they evolved in. The cultural norms and customs that developed in many communities outside of Europe actually reflect a more nuanced approach to mitigating war's effects than the customs and codes developed in Europe. Take, for example, the change in traditional Japanese laws of war is particularly pointed, noting many of the cultural norms lost in the post-isolationist reforms of the eighteenth century. Specifically, utilising the European laws of war were a way that Japan could protect itself by claiming quasi-Western statehood status.

Fukuzawa Yukichi, in his 1875 *Outline of the Theory of Civilization,* encouraged Japan to embrace 'European civilization' not because of its superiority but as a means to an end. Indeed, European culture had 'many defects'

255 Ian Brownlie and James Crawford, *Brownlie's Principles of Public International Law* (8th edn, Oxford University Press, 2012) 4.

256 Alonso Dunkelberg, 'It's a Trap! Re-Thinking Samuel Moyn's *Humane* Beyond the North Atlantic' (2021) 12 *Journal of International Humanitarian Legal Studies* 345–360.

257 Samuel White, 'Roman Laws of War' in Samuel White (ed) *Laws of Yesterday's Wars: From Ancient India to East Africa* (Brill Nijhoff, 2021) vol 2.

258 Samuel White, 'The Late Middle Ages' in Samuel White (ed), *Laws of Yesterday's Wars* (n 9) 101–127.

259 Kyle Walker, 'The Renaissance' in Samuel White (ed), *Laws of Yesterday's Wars* (n 9) 127–150.

including the fact that 'war is the worst thing in this world but Western states always go to war'.[260] It was for this reason that Japanese law professors were embedded with Imperial troops, and reports were published in English[261] and French.[262] This form of lawfare was perhaps clearest in the words of Professor Ariga Nagao, legally embeded with the Japanese Imperial Army during the late twentieth century:

> The Chinese, from the point of view of the [European] laws of war, can be compared to the Turks, the Arabs, the Red Skins. However, the Japanese Empire, in its war against one such nation, sought to comply with the laws of war that it would have followed with regards to France, England or Germany. But without sacrificing its military interests. Therefore, in my opinion, it is of great scientific interest to examine to what degree and through which procedures could it put these laws in practice. In fact, the Japanese nation is not the only one that, possessing a civilized army, can find itself in the necessity to engage in hostilities against a Far East people, not used to the customs of war. In the future, a European or American power may find itself in the same situation and then, the precedent of Japan in 1894–1895 will certainly be of great use.[263]

Here, Japan has rejected its pre-European laws of war and adopted those of Europe as a security measure, cementing its 'civilised' status. Yet the claim by Professor Nagao that the cultures of the Far East were not used to the customs of war is curious (particularly noting the Code of Bushido). As Dr Špicová's novel and ground-breaking work demonstrates, there is a demonstrable history in the 'Far East' of customs of war. Indeed, outside of the analysis of the Australian continent, the *Mahābhārata* represents some of the earliest written works on the laws of war.[264]

This Chapter has demonstrated however that both from a European legal perspective, and philosophical perspective, there was very limited room as a general principle to allow for others. The 'othering' of international law resulted

260 Susumu Yamauchi, 'Civilization and International Law in Japan During the Meiji Era (1868–1912) (1996) 24 *Hitotsubashi Journal of Law and Politics* 7.

261 Sakuye Takahasi, *Cases on International Law during the Chino-Japanese War* (1899).

262 Ariga Nagao, *La Guerre Sino-Japonaise Au Point de Vue Du Droit International, Par Nagao Ariga* (1896).

263 Ibid 9.

264 Zuzana Spicova, 'Ancient Indian Laws of War' in Samuel White (ed), *Laws of Yesterday's Wars* vol 2 (n 257) 1, 1–33.

in a mess of theory and practice when it came to the application of international law. Primarily, international law was argued to fully apply to nation states in proportion to their 'civilisation'.[265] Civilisation, in turn, was measured by their similarity to Western nations. For this reason, a few States established outside of Europe — such as the United States, the Latin American Republics, Liberia and the Boer Republics — were viewed as civilised.[266] Indeed, it could be argued that America's approach to 'sharp war' (as seen throughout its 21st century operations) is one grounded in a Eurocentric approach to international law.[267]

Yet, there were instances where the basic principles of humanity were applied to colonial frontiers, even in the face of 'fanatic savages', those superhumans who were alternately too strong to be stopped by conventional bullets or too uncivilised to reciprocate the laws of war. The following Chapter will outline how State practice demonstrates how the exception to the rule came to be.

265 James Lorimer, *The Institutes of the Law of Nations: A Treatise of the Jural Relations of Separate Political Communities* (William Blackwood & Sons, 1883–84) vol 1, 101–2.

266 John Westlake (n 164) 81–2. Maps of the supposedly 'civilised' world as defined by scholars between 1882 and 1949 can be found in Arnulf Becker Lorca (n 175) 356, 362.

267 Samuel White, 'War Without Limits: How Sharp War Theory is a Historical Anomaly' (2024) *International Review of the Red Cross* 1, 20.

CHAPTER 2

State/Imperial Practice as the Exception

Introduction

Chapter 1 established the rule — that the laws of war at the time of colonisation applied between Europeans, for Europeans. This chapter expands on the exception. Specifically, it seeks to show how individual State practice, of individual colonial powers, could create colonial laws of war within their dominion. To that end, the othering of international law as the general rule is found to only apply, insofar as the Empire did not permit principle of humanity. Discussions regarding the interconnections between international law and colonial warfare are limited by a significant obstacle: that European customary laws of war did not automatically extend to non-Western peoples in colonial conflicts,[268] and that this was reflected in the 'ultra-violence' that characterised European tactics outside of their home continent.[269]

However, where agents of Empire did make allowances under the principle of humanity, and applied constraints to warfare; or where colonial powers made diplomatic reservations or sought other colonial powers to moderate their behaviours against 'natives' that they thought unseemly, that particular conduct can be assessed to have become crystalised as a customary prohibition. These prohibitions are expanded in Part 2. This Chapter, however, seeks to outline the methodology by which this exception is arrived at.

This Chapter argues that within the era of colonisation, customary laws of war had crystallised sufficiently for there to be clear expectations of what was, and was not, lawful. This position must immediately be caveated by the restriction that these laws of war were unique to each colonial power, and were based upon individual State practice. To that end, the customary laws of war of Britain were different to the customary laws of war of Spain, Portugal or the Netherlands (as non-exhaustive examples). To save confusion and conflation between modern international legal concepts, this monograph calls such practice 'Imperial practice' (to denote it is limited to just the practice of one Empire) rather that 'State practice'. Some might argue over the normative value of the

268 Rowan Nicholson, 'Was the Colonisation of Australia an Invasion of Sovereign Territory?' (n 137) 498. See also Frédéric Mégret (n 91) 265, 278–80.

269 See, eg, Robert Gerwarth (n 228) 175, 197. See also: Michelle Gordon (n 97) 6, 11; Eric D Weitz (n 228) 53, 55; Tom Lawson (n 228) 51.

 | DOI:10.1163/9789004515987_004

practice of a single State. What can British (Imperial) practice tell us about the state of international law at the time? Quite a lot within set frameworks.

Theodor Meron,[270] Timothy McCormack and Gerry Simpson,[271] have pointed to how the development of international humanitarian law ('IHL')[272] arose long before the multilateral treaties raised in the 1899 *Hague Convention*. Although there was a lack of pre-*Hague* codified international instruments governing how States could conduct armed conflicts outside their own territories,[273] an examination of Imperial practices during the colonial period indicates an acceptance amongst Imperial powers (through instructions to their commanders) of specific prohibitions regarding wartime conduct.[274] These prohibitions were not binding on other States, but on the Imperial powers themselves. It is these conventions that are the basis for Imperial practice.

As famously reasoned by Max Huber in the 1928 *Island of Palmas (or Miangas) (The Netherlands v the United States of America)* ('*Island of Palmas*') arbitration, judicial facts must be evaluated 'in the light of the law contemporary with it, and not of the law in force at the time when a dispute in regard to it arises or falls to be settled'.[275] This is arguably in line with the non-retroactive character of legal construction (*nova constitutio futuris formam imponere debet, non praeteritis*), as advanced by influential legal writers since at least Lord Coke.[276] As an inquiry focused towards identifying Imperial customary laws of war, this paper will consider the international law existing throughout the

---

270 See, eg, Theodor Meron, *War Crimes Law Comes of Age* (n 84) 1–3.

271 See, eg, Timothy McCormack and Gerry Simpson, *The Law of War Crimes: National and International Approaches* (n 68) 41.

272 See Emily Crawford, Annabelle Lukin and Jacqueline Mowbray, 'The Terminology of the Law of Warfare: A Linguistic Analysis of State Practice' (2023) 14(2) *Journal of International Humanitarian Legal Studies* 197, 198.

273 Theodor Meron, *War Crimes Law Comes of Age* (n 84) 1–3.

274 C Northcote Parkinson, *British Intervention in Malaya 1867–1877* (n 90) 309.

275 *Island of Palmas (Netherlands v United States of America) (Award) (1928)* 2 RIAA 829, 845. See also: *Land and Maritime Boundary between Cameroon and Nigeria (Cameroon v Nigeria) (Judgment)* [2002] ICJ Rep 303, 404–5 [205]; Alexander Orakhelashvili, 'Treaties and Titles to Territory' (n 61) 9, 10.

276 See Edward Coke (n 61) 292. See also: Elmer E Smead, 'The Rule Against Retroactive Legislation: A Basic Principle of Jurisprudence' (1936) 20(1) *Minnesota Law Review* 775, 776; Ben Juratowitch, *Retroactivity and the Common Law* (Hart Publishing, 2008) 29; Zhenni Li, 'International Intertemporal Law' (2018) 48(2) *California Western International Law Journal* 341, 388. See generally: BS Chimni, 'Customary International Law: A Third World Perspective' (2018) 112(1) *American Journal of International Law* 1, 1–46; J Patrick Kelly, 'Customary International Law in Historical Context: The Exercise of Power Without General Acceptance' in Brian D Lepard (ed), *Reexamining Historical and Theoretical Perspectives on Customary International Law* (Cambridge University Press, 2017) 47, 47–85.

early pre-Modern and colonial periods until the 1899 first *Hague Convention*. The disputed[277] other principle outlined by Huber in *Island of Palmas*,[278] that changes in applicable law over time should be appraised,[279] will not be assessed in this paper.

Given these difficulties in extending customary prohibitions to non-Western peoples, compounded by the inconsistent English enforcement of pre-Modern general wartime customs, it is apparent that a comprehensive framework is needed to identify Imperial customary laws of war or prohibitions.

With reference to the wording of colonial ordinances, in addition to the writing of both Imperial commanders and jurists, two different intertemporal approaches to international law from that provided in the preceding chapter may be established in line with the previous and more detailed conclusions reached by Lauren Benton,[280] Lisa Ford,[281] Rowan Nicholson,[282] Jacob Katz Cogan,[283] Will Hanley,[284] and Inge Van Hulle[285] — each of whom also appeared to have individually advanced practice-oriented approaches to international law based on case-by-case instances of customs being enforced.[286] This Chapter summarises these approaches, while discussing how the merits of the practice-oriented methodology address the weaknesses of both the preclusive (from Chapter 1) and natural reasoning views. In attempting to frame the advantages of the practice-oriented methodology — especially as a way

277 Philip C Jessup, 'The Palmas Island Arbitration' (1928) 22(4) *American Journal of International Law* 735, 740.

278 Steven Wheatley, 'Revisiting the Doctrine of Intertemporal Law' (2021) 41(2) *Oxford Journal of Legal Studies* 484, 487–8, citing *Island of Palmas* (n 275) 829, 845–6. See also Hersch Lauterpacht, *The Function of Law in the International Community* (Clarendon Press, 1933) 292.

279 *Island of Palmas* (n 275) 845–6.

280 See, eg: Lauren Benton and Lisa Ford, *Rage for Order: The British Empire and the Origins of International Law* (n 168) 21; Lauren Benton, *A Search for Sovereignty: Law and Geography in European Empires, 1400–1900* (Cambridge University Press, 2010).

281 See, eg, Lauren Benton and Lisa Ford, *Rage for Order: The British Empire and the Origins of International Law* (n 168) 21.

282 See, eg, Rowan Nicholson, 'Was the Colonisation of Australia an Invasion of Sovereign Territory?' (n 137) 493, 502–18.

283 See, eg, Jacob Katz Cogan, 'A History of International Law in the Vernacular' (2020) (2–3) *Journal of the History of International Law* 205–17.

284 See, eg, Will Hanley, 'International Lawyers Without Public International Law: The Case of Late Ottoman Egypt' (2016) 18(1) *Journal of the History of International Law* 98, 113.

285 Inge Van Hulle, *Britain and International Law in West Africa: The Practice of Empire* (Oxford University Press, 2020) 19–26.

286 Ibid.

for post-colonial scholars to address recurring past criticisms regarding perceived failures to sufficiently 'capture the porous and contested aspects' of international legal history.[287] This Chapter concludes that adopting a practice-orientated methodology is the only correct approach to interpreting international law in an inter-temporal perspective. This establishes the framework through which Part 2 expands upon through deep doctrinal research.

1 Natural Reasoning

In contradistinction to the preclusive approach provided in Chapter 1, it might be that a natural reasoning (or natural law) perspective of international law can demonstrate that the 'othering' of international law was not as strict a position as it might first seem. Dr Rowan Nicholson referred to this position as 'naturalist-legislative',[288] combining both an expansive *natural reasoning* approach to colonial international law[289] and also a *legislative* view that customary international law could cover all non-Western peoples once it was extended to one non-Western grouping.[290] In doing so, he refers to the ruling of the ICJ in the *North Sea Continental Shelf* cases that the nature of customary norms meant that they 'must have equal force for all members of the international community'.[291] Noting the ambiguity of the legislative view however, particularly in the context of the uncertain positioning of non-Western peoples within the community of nations under nineteenth-century international law, this Chapter will instead focus more on the naturalist line of argument.

The history of natural law theory is a multifaceted journey spanning millennia, encompassing various philosophical, theological, and cultural epochs. Its origins can be traced to ancient Greece, where thinkers like Heraclitus and Socrates explored the idea that there were inherent moral principles governing human conduct.

In the Roman world, Stoic philosophers, particularly Epictetus, and later Cicero, further developed natural law theory. They argued that human beings possessed an innate moral compass, and the laws of the state should align with

287 Doreen Lustig, 'Governance Histories of International Law' (n 230) 859, 859–882.

288 Rowan Nicholson, 'Was the Colonisation of Australia an Invasion of Sovereign Territory?' (n 137) 493, 513.

289 Ibid 510–12.

290 Ibid 513–14.

291 Ibid 513, citing *North Sea Continental Shelf (Federal Republic of Germany v Denmark) (Judgment)* [1969] ICJ Rep 3, 38–9 [63].

these intrinsic principles. This Roman influence on natural law thought is evident in the works of jurists like Ulpian and Gaius, who integrated these concepts into Roman law, leaving a lasting impact on legal traditions. However, it was with the rise of Christianity that natural law theory underwent a profound transformation. Saint Augustine, a prominent Christian theologian, merged Christian beliefs with natural law principles in his theological writings. He contended that God had instilled moral principles within human nature, and individuals should seek to align their actions with these divine principles. Augustine's synthesis of Christianity and natural law significantly shaped Christian ethics and theological thought.

The pinnacle of natural law theory in the Middle Ages came with the work of Thomas Aquinas, a theologian and philosopher. In the thirteenth century, Aquinas synthesized Christian theology with Aristotelian philosophy, creating a comprehensive natural law theory. He argued that human reason could discern moral truths that were in harmony with divine law. Aquinas's *Summa Theologica* remains a cornerstone of natural law theory, profoundly influencing Catholic moral theology and providing a robust framework for ethical reasoning. The history of natural law theory is a testament to its adaptability and enduring relevance as it continued to evolve and shape human thought and ethical considerations through different historical periods.

Of the European, pre-Modern scholars of international law, Hugo Grotius (1583–1645) may be categorised as a supporter of a naturalist intertemporal framework, which posits that certain norms could be applied to both Western and Non-Western peoples through a process of natural reasoning:[292]

> Surely it is a heresy to believe that infidels are not masters of their own property; consequently, to take from them their possessions on account of their religious beliefs is no less theft and robbery than it would be in the case of Christians.
>
> …
>
> They [uncivilised peoples] are not to be deprived of sovereignty over their possessions because of their unbelief, since sovereignty is a matter of positive law, and unbelief a matter of divine law.[293]

A similar view was also taken up by Grotius' predecessor, the Spanish jurist Francisco de Vitoria (1483–1546), who asserted that international legal norms

292 See also Francisco de Vitoria, *De Indis et de Ivre Belli Relectiones* (n 178) 151.

293 Hugo Grotius, *Mare Liberum* (n 2) 19, as cited in Henry Reynolds, *Aboriginal Sovereignty: Reflections on Race, State and Nation* (n 2) 44.

were applicable between Spain and the native populations of the Americas on the basis that they had 'according to their kind, the use of reason'.[294] The conquest, occupation and settlement of the Americas were the first large-scale European colonial ventures since the fall of the Roman Empire. They were also, importantly, the first European colonial endeavours to engage with a completely geographically disconnected culture — unlike the experiences of engagement with the 'Tartars' (Mongols) or the Saracens (to whom they were compared to).[295]

The conquest of the New World brought an extensive re-examination, and sometimes reworking, of whole areas of the legal systems of early-modern Europe: the idea of inheritance and race; land ownership and class; and the laws of war. Under the methodology offered at the start of this paper, it is assessed that the clash of cultures in the first colonial case study is an example of European laws of war demonstrating *ecological resilience* (that being, a capacity to absorb the effects of disturbances through adaption). However, history seems to show that whilst Mexica laws of war were initially ecologically resilient, they ultimately were not able to absorb the effects. This merits expansion.

The clash of Mexica and Spanish brought forth the first attempt from European thinkers of transforming Roman law of nations into something of international law. The issue that colonisation brought forth was not between two States; but to create a system of law that could bridge the gap between two very different cultural orders — hence, *jus gentium*. Like his mentor figure Vitoria, the Salamanca-based theologian Domingo de Soto (1494–1560) made clear that divine law could not apply as 'neither the name nor fame of the Roman Caesars reached the Antipodes and the islands discovered by us'.[296] The whole notion of a universal rule — that applied to war — was 'a silly notion'.[297] Initially the *ius gentum* had been the law used by Romans to deal with the *gentes* — non-Roman citizens. It was based on the concept of the *mos maiorum* or the customs of the majority — Cicero had held that 'there is a fellowship that is extremely widespread shared by all with all'.[298] The jurist Gaius is widely

294 Francisco de Vitoria, *De Indis et de Ivre Belli Relectiones* (n 178) 127.

295 Ibid 181.

296 Domingo de Soto, *De Iustitia et Iure Libri Decem* (1556) 304.

297 Hugo Grotius, *The Rights of War and Peace*, tr AC Campbell (M Walter Dunne, 1905) II, XII, 13; See Peter Fibiger Bang and Dariusz Kołodziejczyk, '"Elephant of India": Universal Empire Through Time and Across Cultures' in Peter Fibiger Bang and Dariusz Kołodziejczyk (eds), *Universal Empire: A Comparative Approach to Imperial Culture and Representation in Eurasian History* (Cambridge University Press, 2012) 7.

298 Cicero, *De Officiis* [On Duties, On Obligations, or On Moral Responsibilities] II, 69.

accredited with having made it into a general law, which 'natural reason established amongst all men and is observed by all peoples alike [this] is called the *ius gentium,* as being the *ius* which all nations employ'.[299]

Pre-colonial, divine law posed an issue to Vitoria's attempt to highlight the savagery of the Mexica: there was no prohibition under human law on cannibalism, but as it is 'held in abomination by all nations who have a civil and humane life' then it was contrary to the *ius gentium.*[300] Divine examples (of Abraham or Jephthah) showed it was acceptable and even pleasing to God to sacrifice humans. The end result of Vitoria's work was that the divine examples highlighted God owned a body; one could not consent to one's own sacrifice.[301] For the Mexica, how could the natural law of Europe somehow apply to those whose natural understanding of the world was reflected in their customs? Soto captured the tension when they held 'that which nature teaches is not within the reach of everyone, but only those who have serene reason and are free from all obscurity".[302] Natural law was therefore universal — and therefore applicable to the Mexica. It just was unfortunate that the Mexica did not have 'serene reason' to understand it. Vitoria thus held that 'it makes no difference that all the barbarians consent to these kinds of laws and sacrifices, or that they refuse to accept the Spaniards as their liberators in this matter'.[303] Natural law — not divine law — made clear that outside of the Bible there existed some basic concepts of humanity which must apply as a matter of legal reasoning in conflict.

Vitoria was then required to engage with whether there were any *natural* laws of war. Vitoria is understandably silent on the matter. The law of hospitality provides, through implication, one form of non-combatant — ambassadors, who 'are by the law of nations inviolable'.[304] The underlying foundation of the law of hospitality — reciprocity — would somehow permit a Mexica natural law right to trade freely in Spain. So too should have Mexica ambassadors been inviolable — although they were not. The inapplicability of divine laws of war resulted in a legal vacuum. Roman natural law was relied upon, with a particular reliance on Cicero (which brings, in a circular way, the preclusive position back into natural law):

299 Gaius, *Institutiones* [Institutes] II, 1.1.

300 Francisco de Vitoria, *De Usu Ciborum* 1.3. See also Francisco de Vitoria, *Political Writings,* tr Jeremy Lawrance (Cambridge University Press, 2010) 209.

301 Ibid 1.4, 215.

302 Domingo de Soto (n 296) III I II, 195.

303 Francisco de Vitoria, *De Indis et de Ivre Belli Relectiones* (n 178) 156.

304 Ibid.

> reason has taught to the wise: necessity to the barbarians, custom to the *gentes* and nature to brute beasts that they should repulse on every occasion by every means all violence to their bodies, their heads and their lives.[305]

Thus, held Vitoria:

> the indiscriminate spoliation of all enemy-subjects alike and the seizure of all their goods [as] justifiable, then it is also justifiable to carry all enemy-subjects off into captivity, whether they be guilty or guiltless. And insomuch as war with pagans is of this type, seeing that this is perpetual and that they can never make amends for the wrongs and damage, it is indubitably lawful to carry off both the children and women of the Saracens into captivity and slavery.[306]

Articulating the norms of natural law were difficult to quantify. Prohibited weapons in warfare seems to fall under specific schemes that civilised nations could agree upon; sovereign recognition however fell under natural law. Bonfils and Fauchille opined that:

> Men of all races, white or black, red or yellow, however unequal they may be in knowledge, in wealth, in industry, must be considered as equal in law. … To deny to tribes or clans who freely occupy the soil, for thousands and thousands of years, the right to independence, to sovereignty, is unacceptable. That these tribes do not have sovereignty as it is conceived of by the peoples of Europe: that is certain. But they have nonetheless a certain notion of it; and the proof is in their treaties, their truces, their alliances, in the protection actually granted by these petty kings or sultans to peaceful explorers.[307]

As highlighted by Nicholson though, it seems as though this naturalist position had reached its peak acceptance in the sixteenth-to-seventeenth centuries and was then eclipsed by more positivist and institutional views of international

305 Cicero, Pro Milone, XI, 30.

306 Francisco de Vitoria, *De Indis et de Ivre Belli Relectiones* (n 178) 181.

307 Henri Bonfils and Paul Fauchille, *Manuel de droit international public* (*Droit des gens*) [Manual of Public International Law (Law of Nations)] (Arthur Rousseau, 4th ed, 1905) 310–311.

law by the nineteenth-century.[308] Although certain post-colonial scholars such as Zhang have evidently embraced this early approach to international law,[309] in the face of the 'ad hoc' commentary from the later Imperial period[310] and the controversies surrounding the eurocentrism that surrounds the 'emerging global history of international law',[311] this chapter contends that the naturalist method does not reconcile with the actual practices of State actors on the Imperial frontiers. While their tradition of entering into treaties with non-Western peoples could suggest the deficiencies of the preclusive approach, commentary by Imperial commanders also clearly rejects an unrealistically extensive application of customary prohibitions to non-Western peoples.[312]

This is especially clear when we consider the writings of later Imperial frontier commanders or men on the spot, such as Callwell,[313] Fuller,[314] and the Singapore-based Crawfurd[315] — the first two of whom clearly supported racialist hierarchies that excluded 'savage' peoples from international law, and the latter who narrowly suggested that native Malayan and other Asian races might fall into a semi-uncivilised category with limited international rights. Accordingly, while a naturalist perspective cannot conclusively be ruled out when assessing colonial military conduct (especially perhaps during the early years of Imperial expansion), it arguably remains necessary to identify an alternative methodology that realistically factors in centuries of British or Imperial State practice.

---

308 Rowan Nicholson, 'Was the Colonisation of Australia an Invasion of Sovereign Territory?' (n 137) 493, 511, citing Stephen C Neff, *Justice among Nations: A History of International Law* (Harvard University Press, 2014) at ch 6.

309 See, eg: Yue Zhang, 'The Right to Restitution of Cultural Property Removed as Spoils of War during Nineteenth-Century International Warfare' (2021) 42(4) *University of Pennsylvania Journal of International Law* 1097, 1097; Yue Zhang, 'Customary International Law and the Rule Against Taking Cultural Property as Spoils of War' (2018) 17(4) *Chinese Journal of International Law* 943, 946.

310 Antony Anghie, *Imperialism, Sovereignty and the Making of International Law* (Cambridge University Press, 2004) 81.

311 Will Hanley, 'International Lawyers Without Public International Law: The Case of Late Ottoman Egypt' (n 284) 98, 118. See generally Julia Emtseva, '"Unveiling the "Legal Conscience of the Civilized World:" A Critical Look at the Institut de Droit International' (Conference Paper, Symposium on 150 Years of the Institut de Droit International and the International Law Association, 2023) 221–5.

312 Frédéric Mégret (n 91) 265, 279, 287.

313 See, eg, Charles Edward Callwell (n 177) 30.

314 See, eg, John Fuller (n 239) 119.

315 See, eg, John Crawfurd (n 168) 58, 58–81.

2 Practice-Oriented Approach

The apogee of Imperial expansion, in the nineteenth century, saw an ideological shift away from natural law reasoning. Unlike natural law — which argues that all States were bound by some higher universal law — positivism argued that the State was the exclusive creator of law, and could not be bound by any law without its consent. Nominally, natural law bound both European and non-European law to some baseline of conduct (in times of peace, and for the purposes of this monograph, in times of war). Positivist jurists, however, devised a series of formal doctrines that excluded the other (as articulated in Chapter 1). Yet positivism bound the State itself, by its own practice.

As noted by Van Hulle, who is similar to Cogan[316] in that she also endorsed Benton and Ford's conception of a vernacular approach,[317] a practice-oriented methodology is useful given the 'confusingly' inconsistent discourse adopted by late nineteenth-century international lawyers.[318] The purpose of a practice-oriented approach here is to reliably appraise State practice regarding customary wartime prohibitions by Imperial commanders, while still acknowledging the different usages of war applied against non-Western peoples in colonial conflicts. This provides the framework for Part 2.

In this sense, it represents something of a compromise struck between the aforementioned preclusive and naturalist approaches — at least in terms of allowing the viability of this extension while still recognising the racial underpinnings of colonial warfare — through a case-by-case appraisal of the application of specific customs of warfare, based on longitudinal State practice. It must be emphasised, however, that this position still posits that non-Western peoples were assumed to be excluded from international law in the nineteenth-century.[319] Instead, the distinctive element of a practice-oriented approach is that it accepts that this exclusion could be overcome through this evidence of State conduct — and that accordingly specific customary prohibitions on wartime conduct could eventually extend to non-Western peoples based on

316 Ibid 212–3.

317 Inge Van Hulle, *Britain and International Law in West Africa: The Practice of Empire* (n 285) 21, citing Lauren Benton and Lisa Ford, *Rage for Order: The British Empire and the Origins of International Law* (n 44) 21. See also Inge Van Hulle, *Britain and International Law in West Africa: The Practice of Empire* (Oxford University Press, 2020) 19.

318 Inge Van Hulle, *Britain and International Law in West Africa: The Practice of Empire* (n 285) 23.

319 See, eg, Rowan Nicholson, 'Was the Colonisation of Australia an Invasion of Sovereign Territory?' (n 137) 493, 499.

consistent application, to the extent that Imperial commanders could potentially be bound by these prohibitions.

Historically, the nineteenth-century British lawyer William Edward Hall may be seen as supporting the practice-oriented model,[320] when we consider his published view that European countries are:

> obliged partly by their sense of honour [and] interests, to be guided by their own artificial rules in dealing with semi-civilised states … long before a reciprocal obedience to those rules can be reasonably expected.[321]

Even in advocating for different rules, writing in 1927, did US Army Captain Elbridge Colby recognise that 'savage tribes' could not be subject to total war:

> It is good to be decent. It is good to use proper discretion. It is good to observe the decencies of international law. But it is a fact that against uncivilized people who do not know international law and do not observe it, and would take advantage of one who did, there must be something else. The 'something else' should not be a relaxation of all bonds of restraint. But it should be [a] clear understanding that this is a different kind of war, this which is waged by native tribes, than that which might be waged between advanced nations of western culture. Ferocity and ruthlessness are not essential; but it is essential to recognize the different character of the people.[322]

This is arguably in line with what Cogan describes as the need for contemporaneous approaches to consider 'international law in action',[323] or the law as it 'was used and contested' by State actors with decision-making capacity, as opposed to 'the law as it appear[ed] in the books'.[324] Pointing to the difficulties in adopting more rigid assumptions of contemporary international law,[325] which this paper contends as including a full exclusion of international rights for non-Western peoples or an extension through natural reasoning, Van Hulle

320 Frédéric Mégret (n 91)' 265, 284.
321 William Edward Hall (n 163) 44.
322 Elbridge Colby (n 239) 279, 287.
323 Jacob Katz Cogan (n 283) 205, 206.
324 Ibid 211.
325 Inge Van Hulle, *Britain and International Law in West Africa: The Practice of Empire* (n 285) 23.

similarly argues that the 'confusingly different' blanket statements used by late nineteenth-century lawyers should be contrasted with State practice.[326]

As highlighted in Chapter 1, the preclusion of traditional wartime prohibitions in colonial conflicts was rationalised by Imperial commanders on the basis that 'uncivilised' peoples were naturally predisposed to irrational violence.[327] This reasoning was especially advanced by Major-General Callwell[328] — who served in the Second Anglo-Afghan War (1878–80) as a Lieutenant.[329] In his *Small Wars*,[330] which Wagner describes as a 'reiterat[ion] of pre-existing ideas among colonial officers ... in various campaigns throughout the British Empire',[331] Callwell contended that there was a 'clear distinction'[332] between civilised opponents — with whom 'principles of modern strategy and tactics were largely if not wholly applicable'[333] — and 'mere gatherings of savages'[334] whose

> hostile tactics are essentially aggressive, and inasmuch as they involve substitution of shock action for fire action, the regular forces are compelled, whether they like it or not, to conform to the savage method of battle.[335]

Michelle Gordon notes how the Imperial Perak Expeditionary Force applied strategies in accordance with Callwell's 'bold and resolute' method of war against non-Western peoples.[336] In line with this, Lewis Gann and Peter Duignan also noted how this practice of irregular or savage warfare

326 Ibid.

327 See also Dierk Walter (n 236) 18–21.

328 Kim A Wagner (n 153) 217, 223.

329 Steven Balbirnie, 'Small War on a Violent Frontier: Colonial Warfare and British Intervention in Northern Russia, 1918–1919' in Gearóid Barry, Enrico Dal Lago, and Róisín Healy (eds), *Small Nations and Colonial Peripheries in World War I* (Brill, 2016) 194, 194.

330 Charles Edward Callwell (n 177) 30.

331 Ibid 220.

332 Ibid 30.

333 Ibid 29.

334 Ibid 30.

335 Ibid.

336 Michelle Gordon (n 97) 81.

> was how the Imperial army waged wars of colonial conquest in Africa. Firing homes, looting stock, and destroying crops was the standard way of suppressing resistance. Similar patterns were evident in Asia.[337]

In isolation, these texts would suggest that the prohibitions on wartime conduct under Imperial laws of war were entirely exempt from application to non-Western peoples who fell under the category of 'uncivilised' nations. However, as noted by Benton and Ford, international law throughout this period sat 'in unusual places'[338] and accordingly alternative mediums of IHL must be considered, including the ordinances issued by colonial officers, and their correspondence with each other. In the Malayan context, despite the writings of influential military manuals such as Callwell's *Small Wars*, Gordon highlights the ordinances conveyed by Governor Jervois during the Perak War (1875–6) — which instructed that the 'indiscriminate' killing of Malay non-combatants was 'forbidden'.[339] By itself, this suggests that the preclusive approach might not be reconcilable with State practice, at least during the Perak War (1875–6), and that consequently a more practice-oriented approach might be meaningful.

As per Bruce Vandervort,[340] the vast number of pre-twentieth century Imperial treaties entered with African and Asian sovereigns potentially demonstrated a partial acknowledgement of the latter's 'personality' under international law. Nico Krisch has similarly argued that, even as the objective of these treaties shifted from symbiotic trade instruments to more unequal concessions, British interactions with said sovereigns were 'governed by law'[341] — albeit

337 Lewis Gann and Peter Duignan, *The Rulers of British Africa, 1870–1914* (Croom Helm, 1978) 144, quoted in Helen Bradford, 'Gentlemen and Boers: Afrikaner Nationalism, Gender and Colonial Warfare in the South African War' in Greg Cuthbertson, Albert Grundlingh and Mary-Lynn Suttie (eds), *Writing a Wider War: Rethinking Gender, Race, and Identity in the South African War, 1899–1902* (Ohio University Press, 2002) 37, 38. See also Graham Dawson, *Soldier Heroes* (London, 1994) 1.

338 Lauren Benton and Lisa Ford, *Rage for Order: The British Empire and the Origins of International Law* (n 168) 21.

339 Michelle Gordon (n 97) 59, quoting letter from Sir William FD Jervois (Governor of the Straits Settlements) to Samuel Dunlop (Captain and Inspector-General of Police of the Straits Settlements) and John FA McNair (Major of the Madras Native Artillery), 22 November 1875, reproduced in United Kingdom, *Further Correspondence Relating to the Affairs of Certain Native States in the Malay Peninsula in the Neighbourhood of the Straits Settlements* (C 1505, 1876) 137.

340 Bruce Vandervort, *Wars of Imperial Conquest in Africa, 1830–1914* (Routledge, 1998) 98–105.

341 Nico Krisch, 'International Law in Times of Hegemony: Unequal Power and the Shaping of the International Legal Order' (2005) 16(3) *European Journal of International Law* (2005) 369, 395–6.

within a hierarchical system that prioritised Imperial interests.[342] In Malaya, as pointed out by Sir Richard Winstedt (1878–1966), examples of the treaties signed between British government agents and Malay polities include:[343] (1) the 1790 treaty between Captain Francis Light and the Sultan of Kedah to lease Penang in return for an annual payment;[344] (2) the 1819 *Treaty of Friendship and Alliance* between the BEIC and the Johor Sultanate that allowed the former to occupy Singapore;[345] and (3) of course, the 1874 *Treaty of Pangkor* that preceded the eventual Perak War (1875–6) and appointed a British Resident to the Perak Sultan.[346] While these texts have been described as 'quintessential legal instrument[s] of European Imperialism'[347] — Van Hulle, in particular, summarises them as 'coerced ... fabricated or purposefully ill-translated and ill-defined'[348] — they also reflect how colonial treaties were often regarded by Imperial actors as binding under international law, albeit sometimes in order to justify acquisitions of land by cession.[349]

---

342 Ibid. See also Inge Van Hulle, *Britain and International Law in West Africa: The Practice of Empire* (n 285) 21.

343 Richard Winstedt, *Britain and Malaya, 1786–1941* (Longmans, Green and Co, 1944) 26.

344 Ibid 13; See also AJ Stockwell, J de V Allen and Leigh R Wright (eds), *A Collection of Treaties and Other Documents Affecting the States of Malaysia, 1761–1963* (Oceana Publications, 1981) vol 1, 134–5.

345 Richard Winstedt, *Britain and Malaya, 1786–1941* (Longmans, Green and Co, 1944) 18. See also AJ Stockwell, J de V Allen and Leigh R Wright (eds), *A Collection of Treaties and Other Documents Affecting the States of Malaysia, 1761–1963* (Oceana Publications, 1981) vol 1, 28–9.

346 Richard Winstedt, *Britain and Malaya, 1786–1941* ((Longmans, Green and Co, 1944) 29. See also: Rupert Emerson, *Malaysia: A Study in Direct and Indirect Rule* (University of Malaya Press, 3rd ed, 1964) 120–1; C Northcote Parkinson, *British Intervention in Malaya 1867–1877* (n 90) 324–5; AJ Stockwell, J de V Allen and Leigh R Wright (eds), *A Collection of Treaties and Other Documents Affecting the States of Malaysia, 1761–1963* (Oceana Publications, 1981) vol 1, 390–2; Mervyn Llewelyn Wynne, *Triad and Tabut: A Survey of the Origin and Diffusion of Chinese and Mohamedan Secret Societies in the Malay Peninsula* A.D. *1800–1935* (US Government Printing Office, 1941) 289–90; Sir Archibald Edward Harbord Anson, *About Others And Myself: 1745 to 1920* (John Murray, 1920) 320.

347 See Inge Van Hulle, 'African Lawyers and the Strategic Uses of Legal Entanglements: The Case of the Gold Coast and Lagos (1880–1920)' (2022) 1(1) *Forum Historiae Iuris* 1,1.

348 Ibid. See also Rowan Nicholson, 'Was the Colonisation of Australia an Invasion of Sovereign Territory?' (n 48) 509, citing DP O'Connell, 'International Law and Boundary Disputes' (1960) 54(1) *American Society of International Law Proceedings* 77, 81.

349 See, eg, DP O'Connell, 'International Law and Boundary Disputes' (1960) 54(1) *American Society of International Law Proceedings* 77, 81. See also *Land and Maritime Boundary between Cameroon and Nigeria (Cameroon v Nigeria) (Judgment)* [2002] ICJ Rep 303, 405 [206].

In 2002, the International Court of Justice in *Cameroon v Nigeria* drew upon Huber's earlier reasoning in *Island of Palmas*[350] and appraised a range of late nineteenth-century international 'treaties of protection' signed between colonial powers and non-Western people.[351] In doing so, the Court sought to determine what characteristics reflected recognitions of sovereignty under international law 'at that time';[352] in the absence of both 'evidence of a central federal power'[353] and any factual 'certainty'[354] regarding their subsequent survival, it was found that the 1884 treaty signed with Great Britain did not confer the chieftains of Old Calabar in modern-day Nigeria any intertemporal legal personality.[355] Contrastingly, and with reference to 'the case of Bahrain and Qatar',[356] the ICJ suggested that 'treaties of protection' which met these two criteria could be capable of conferring non-Western entities the 'ret[ention] thereunder [of] a previously existing sovereignty under international law'.[357]

In the British colony of Malaya, the most prominent example of such a treaty is again likely the 1874 *Treaty of Pangkor* signed between Sultan Abdullah II, the 'head of an independent'[358] Perak and Sir Andrew Clarke, the Governor of the Straits Settlements at the time.[359] Notably, the British view towards this treaty, as reiterated by a former Chief Justice of the Straits Settlements at the time, was that it was signed between 'two nations ... [although] the right of interpreting it falls to the stronger'.[360] Amidst the ambiguities of Imperial discourse however, it remains clear that an effective application of a practice-oriented

350 *Land and Maritime Boundary between Cameroon and Nigeria (Cameroon v Nigeria) (Judgment)* [2002] ICJ Rep 303, 405 [205], quoting *Island of Palmas (Netherlands v United States of America) (Award)* (1928) 2 RIAA 829, 858–9.

351 *Land and Maritime Boundary between Cameroon and Nigeria (Cameroon v Nigeria) (Judgment)* [2002] ICJ Rep 303, 405 [205].

352 Ibid.

353 Ibid 405 [207].

354 Ibid 405–6 [207]–[208].

355 Ibid 405–6 [207].

356 Ibid 404–5 [205].

357 Ibid.

358 Sir P Benson Maxwell (n 242) 51, citing United Kingdom, *Further Correspondence Relating to the Affairs of Certain Native States in the Malay Peninsula in the Neighbourhood of the Straits Settlements* (C 1709, 1877) 67, 82.

359 AJ Stockwell, J de V Allen and Leigh R Wright (eds), *A Collection of Treaties and Other Documents Affecting the States of Malaysia, 1761–1963* (Oceana Publications, 1981) vol 1, 390–2. See also: Khoo Kay Kim and Andrew Clarke, 'The Pangkor Engagement of 1874' (1974) 47(1) *Journal of the Malaysian Branch of the Royal Asiatic Society* 1, 1–12; C Northcote Parkinson, *British Intervention in Malaya 1867–1877* (University of Malaya Press, 1960) 107, 136–8.

360 Sir P Benson Maxwell (n 242) 27.

approach requires an actual appraisal of contemporary laws of war as they were enforced by Imperial commanders.

3 Conclusion

This is all to say that it is clear that, whilst under the preclusive approach to international law non-European states held no legal rights, this was often negated by State practice which conferred status (by its own perspective) through negotiations and treaties. This applies just as much to the acquisition of land and diplomatic negotiations as it does to the rules of warfare within conflict and can be evinced through explicit negotiations with non-European polities; statements by an Imperial power to another about what is or is not acceptable in its relations with non-European persons; individual treaties (verbal or written) by those who held the authority to do so on colonial frontiers; and domestic reprimands, trials and courts-martial for breaches of war ordinances.

Part 2, which follows this Chapter, utilising the above methodology expands on eight identified means or methods of warfare that were prohibited in British colonial laws of war. These include prohibitions on: summary executions, sexual violence, perfidy, slavery and forced movement, unnecessary looting of cultural property; brigandry and dispersal. Each will be discussed in turn.

PART 2

Categories of Colonial Prohibitions or Early War Crimes

CHAPTER 3

Prohibition on Summary Executions

The possibility of a colonial custom establishing the 'right to safe quarter' for enemy prisoners has received significant attention by international law scholars, and merits the primacy of possible colonial war crimes.[361] It was a prohibition that applied to both 'civilised' and 'uncivilised' combatants, and was grounded in a wider, natural law interpretation of honour and transparency in dealing with foes. In particular, proscriptions against killing '[enemies] who yeeld and throw down [arms]' were relatively well-established in late medieval English ordinances such as the aforementioned 1640 *Laws and Ordinances of Warre* published by the Earl of Essex for Charles I during the Second Bishop's War (1640).[362]

The prohibition on summary execution was not absolute throughout the development of European warfare, and it requires a historical analysis to expand upon the moment the prohibition crystallised. As noted by de Libero, the execution of prisoners was initially acceptable under pre-medieval Roman law.[363] Specifically, the ancient practice of *deditio* (act of surrender) gave broad discretion to Roman commanders as to whether their prisoners could be subjected to 'violent acts of humiliation'.[364] As a general rule, it was expected in private and public war, on the Continent, that members of the class to which the chivalric code applied — those of the knights — were to be captured, not executed. The specification of the Continent is important. Reflecting the fractured nature and implementation of *ius militarie,* on the Continent knights were captured, but in Wales and Ireland they were decapitated.[365]

It is important to note that these protections, consistent with the highly stratified society of medieval Europe, were extended under customary chivalric

361 Meron, *War Crimes Law Comes of Age* (n 84) 9.

362 Grose (n 78) 57–69, quoting Robert Devereux, *Laws and Ordinances of Warre, Extablished for the Better Conduct of the Army by His Excellency the Earl of Essex, Lord Generall of the Forces Raised by the Authority of the Parliament for the Defence of King and Kingdom: and Now Inlarged by Command of His Excellency* (1643). See also Meron, *War Crimes Law Comes of Age* (n 84) 9.

363 Loretana de Libero, 'Surrender in Ancient Rome' in Holger Afflerbach and Hew Strachan (eds), *How Fighting Ends: A History of Surrender* (Oxford University Press 2012) 29, 34–5..

364 Ibid 36.

365 Michael Prestwich, *Armies and Warfare in the Middle Ages: The English Experience* (Yale University Press, 1996) 237.

 | DOI:10.1163/9789004515987_005

law only to those of the knightly class; members of the 'vulgar mob' who constituted the infantry and archers on the battlefield, were offered no protection. Coming from the upper echelons of society, a knight was presumably wealthy and thus quite literally worth more alive than dead.[366] Axiomatically, a peasant was simply a mouth to feed. The legal status of a medieval prisoner — especially one who was a knight — is a fascinating example of legal double-think within the class-conscious mind of the Late Middle Ages. Following Roman law, a person taken in a just war became a slave; yet, the rule of *postliminium* — as this Roman Law concept was called — did not apply between Christians.[367] Accordingly, the relationship between the captor and the captive was one of *contract*.

This contractual relationship was not unilateral, but required certain conduct on behalf of the captor, and the captive. Because a ransom was a valuable asset, a captor was anxious to establish his right incontrovertibly, and absolutely, for a ransom could be shared by a co-captor, or a brother-in-arms.[368] It was thereby no surprise to see, in the closing moments of the Battle of Poitiers in 1356, 'the French scattered, and the English running and making prisoners'.[369] From surviving accounts, it truly sounds like a game of tag in the schoolyard.

Yet, it took more than a simple tap to take charge of a captive. To stop confusion, it was an established custom that to claim a ransom, the captive must offer his right gauntlet, and the ransom and contractual obligations were accepted by the captor by placing his right hand into the captive's gauntlet.[370] The contractual obligation included safe escort to a safe place behind the lines, either personally or in the carriage of an individual who could do so, before returning to the battlefield to take another captive.

Moreover, although the obligation was one of contract, the right was one of absolute property. This disconnect between obligation and rights is the primary source of legal dissonance in the law of ransom. A man who killed another's prisoner must pay the ransom[371] — this was unfortunate for the goaler of the prison of La Ferte, who after executing 43 prisoners who were rioting, found

366 Robert C Stacey, 'The Age of Chivalry' in Michael Howard et al, *The Laws of War: Constraints on Warfare in the Western World* (Yale University Press, 1994) 36.

367 John of Legnano, *Tractatus*, Chap 9.

368 Maurice Keen, 'Brotherhood-In-Arms' (1962) 47 *History* 1–17.

369 Chandos Herald, *Le Prince Noice*, (Roxburghe Club, 1842) 108.

370 Richard II, *Durham Ordinances*; see further *Black Book of the Admiralty*, vol 1, 4457.

371 So ruled Archibald Douglas, Warden of the Scottish March — see Archibald Douglas Ordinances s 8 (*Acts of the Parliament of Scotland*, vol I, Appendix IV) 351a.

himself being sued by their captors for their share in the relevant ransoms.[372] This right in a ransom, moreover, was argued to be inheritable, as happened with Edward III's rights in ransom that occurred in the 1350s and 1370s.[373] Like many succession laws, they were complicated; a brother-in-arms of the deceased had a right to a half share in all the gains of war of his companion,[374] and to inherit on his death any booty made in their common enterprise.[375]

Although a captor could do anything, however, which might be deemed necessary to obtain the payment (such as placing him under lock and key; or even in irons)[376] he could not threaten him with death[377] — nor demand that the prisoner do anything that would breach secular or chivalric law or his own honour.[378] If such request was made, then theoretically, this constituted a *delicutm turpis quaestus,* and the prisoner was freed of his obligations, including ransom.[379]

Over time however, it is clear that the rules of medieval chivalry started to expand the concept of who was a non-combatant and who was protected. Donald Wells, for instance, has previously described how early Roman Catholic Church Synods towards the end of the First Millennium had issued 'declarations concerning proper weapons, proper strategies, and proper targets' which reflected the 'combatant/non-combatant distinction' seen in modern laws of warfare.[380] While it would take centuries for this distinction to re-emerge following the European Medieval period, it may be argued that later humanitarian sentiments were a re-assertion of these early Church directives, as a custom developed to check the excess of warfare (and also one that arose from the economic drivers of ransom).

Guerre mortelle — or war to the death — could be declared in select circumstances. Medieval armies announced they were fighting a war to the death by displaying a red flag or banner. For the French this was the *Oriflamme* and for the English, the *Red Dragon*. The former had written on *pavillion nomme sansquartier* and implied that the mercy of the French had been consumed and that no-one's life would be spared; just as a flaming oil destroys everything that can be burnt.[381] The latter, a Anglo-Saxon semiotic depiction, can be traced

372 See the case of *Yvo du Puy v E. du Plessis,* Arch. Nat., X1a 4801, fo 398vo-9.
373 Maurice Keen, *The Laws of War in the Late Middle Ages* (n 8) 159.
374 Maurice Keen, 'Brotherhood-In-Arms' (n 368) 8–9.
375 Maurice Keen, *The Laws of War in the Late Middle Ages* (n 8) 152.
376 Honore Bonet, *Tree of Battles* tr GW Coopland (Liverpool University Press, 1949) 4: 56.
377 Ibid at chapter 6.
378 Paris of Pozzo, *De Duello, vel De Re Militari in Singulari Certamine*, 9:2:33.
379 Bartholomew of Saliceto, Super VIII Cod, Tit 51, 1.7.
380 Donald Wells, *War Crimes and Laws of War* (University Press of America, 2nd ed, 1991) 17.
381 Alexander Gillespie, *A History of the Laws of War — Volume 1* (Hart Publishing, 2011) 121.

to at least 752, where it was used by the King of Wessex in a battle against the King of Mercia.[382] and in the Bayeux Tapestry, held by the man standing beside Harold Godwinson as he is struck in the eye. It is interesting to note that the Anglo-Saxon depiction more closely resembles a windsock than a flag; the metal head of the dragon was aimed towards the wind, and the red fabric attached would move and writhe.

Wars to the Death were most legally valid when fighting against Enemies of the Faith. This reflected a wider convention of differing legal statuses between Christian and non-Christian enemies (as covered in Chapter 1). The inevitable violence required to administer an Imperial, or feudal, state created a body of men whose bellicosity caused constant tension for rulers. Holy Wars offered immediate relief, as any war waged against those who were not Christian, by its very nature, was one that was just.

Yet, *guerre mortelle* could also occur between Christian armies, although when it did occur as between the Armagnacs and the Artoisians in 1414, contemporary witnesses expressed surprise that they were fighting 'as if against the Saracens'.[383] The *Oriflamme* was carried by the French against the English at the Battles of Potiers (1356) and the Battle of Agincourt (1415), where it was captured by English after their victories.[384] Although it did not preclude the possibility of taking prisoners, the intent was no mercy.

The 1415 Battle of Agincourt highlights this well. During the Hundred Year's War fought intermittently between France and England, Henry V ordered the slaughter of an estimated several thousand French captives who had been captured in the battle. The victorious young King only spared those who came from the highest rank of nobility denial of quarter and were accordingly covered by the medieval custom of ransom.[385] As noted by Stacey, this was evidently in line with the commonplace nature of summary executions at the

382 Ibid, 122.

383 See Chris Given-Wilson, 'Edward III's Prisoners of War' (2001) 116 *The English Historical Review* 802–833.

384 Winston Churchill, *A History of the English-Speaking People* (Bloomsbury Publishing, 1965), 319.

385 Justine Firnhaber-Baker, 'Techniques of Seigneurial War in the Fourteenth Century' (2010) 36(1) *Journal of Medieval History* 90, 100. See also: Andy King, '"Then a Great Misfortune Befell Them": the Laws of War on Surrender and the Killing of Prisoners on The Battlefield in the Hundred Years War' (2017) 43(1) *Journal of Medieval History* 106, 114; Theodor Meron, 'International Humanitarian Law from Agincourt to Rome' in Michael N Schmitt (ed), *International Law Across the Spectrum of Conflict: Essays in Honour of Professor LC Green on the Occasion of his Eightieth Birthday* (Naval War College, 2000) 301, 304.

time.[386] For many commanders, only the prospect of profit from ransoming members of the aristocracy was sufficient to incentivise orders to not kill those associated with the other side.[387] Where profit could not be drawn from the other side therefore, 'nonnoble soldiers [had] few compunctions about killing their [captives], as they did at Agincourt'.[388] Stacey emphasises that this was 'expected of them' and that contemporary criticism of the practice had not yet emerged.[389]

Siege warfare also blurred the prohibition on summary executions. In some respects, the law around siege warfare was *lex specialis*. Although it could occur under private warfare, public warfare or Holy Wars, the chivalric code held special rules for the conduct, and consequences, of siege warfare.

Siege warfare was, until the advent and utilisation of gunpowder, rather archaic. It occurred via two methods — by assault (escalade or ambush) or by treaty. Assault by escalade required the besieging party to either breach the walls through the use of siege weapons, or to starve the inhabitants out. Assault by ambush required use of internal dissidents to open the gates.

Siege warfare could also occur via treaty. The position of a defender in a siege was one of discomfort. The besieged leader was in an almost impossible position whereby they could either break an oath to a lord, or resist the attacker and thus risk the charge of rebellion.[390] It was common for a treaty to be made, specifying a certain number of days required for a besieged's lord to arrive and make battle, at a specific location decided upon in advance.[391] If no relief force arrived, then the rights were effectively forfeit, and surrender was a viable option. In some instances, these agreements were established with intricate detail; one such example is the siege by the English of the Scottish town of Berwick in 1333. A written truce was agreed upon, whereby the Scots would not make any improvement in their defence nor resupply the town, whilst the

386 Robert C Stacey, 'The Age of Chivalry' (n 366) 27, 36–8. See also Rory Cox, 'Asymmetric Warfare and Military Conduct in the Middle Ages' (2012) 38(1) *Journal of Medieval History* 100, 110.

387 Justine Firnhaber-Baker, 'Techniques of Seigneurial War in the Fourteenth Century' (n 385) 101. See also Meron, 'International Humanitarian Law from Agincourt to Rome' (n 180) 304.

388 'Robert C Stacey, 'The Age of Chivalry' (n 366) 36.

389 Ibid. See also: Andy King, '"Then a Great Misfortune Befell Them": the Laws of War on Surrender and the Killing of Prisoners on The Battlefield in the Hundred Years War' (2017) 43(1) *Journal of Medieval History* 106, 114; Anthony A Contrada, 'Law and the Morality of War Today in Henry V' (2020) 3(2) *Army Lawyer* 17, 20.

390 See Samuel White, 'The Late Middle Ages' (n 9) 106.

391 Maurice Keen, *The Laws of War in the Late Middle Ages* (n 8) 129.

English agreed not to harm the defenders. If a relieving force did not arrive by a specified date, then the castle would be forfeit but no harm would come to the inhabitants; those who chose to stay would receive protection from the English Crown, and those who chose to leave were given time to dispose of their property and were given a letter of safe conduct.[392]

The chivalric code differed between both methods of siege warfare. If taken by assault, there were no protections to non-combatants; rape, pillage and murder were all condoned and, in fact, promoted; first, because it reinforced the victor's claim in the feud; and second because it was the primary method of payment for the soldiers. If a settlement was taken via assault, there also was no temporal nexus on when the victor could take control; hence, when Luxembourg was taken by Philip the Good of Burgundy, it was only after he had been to the Church of Notre Dame to pray and give thanks that the town was systematically plundered.[393] This followed earlier European traditions around bounty collection.

A broad examination of the general perspectives in this space appears to support Stacey's view. While Desmond Seward has argued that 'by fifteenth-century standards ... captive, unarmed noblemen ... according to the universally recognized international laws of chivalry, had every reason to expect to be ransomed if they surrendered formally',[394] James Hamilton Wylie has speculated that the 'French would have done the same themselves had they been in so perilous a case'.[395] Maurice Keen, in particular, has more pragmatically contended that '[w]hat is important is not that the law of arms tolerated outrages (which it did not do); but that it was not effectively enforced throughout most of the Hundred Years War'.[396]

At the same time however, it is arguable that 1415 is likely the watershed moment for the development of this custom in Imperial history. Although the English conduct itself at Agincourt seems to have not been denounced by the contemporaries of Henry V for going beyond the norms of warfare,[397] it

392 Clifford J Rogers (ed), *The Wards of Edward III: Sources and Interpretation* (Boydell Press, 1999) 67; See also Gillespie (n 381) 124.

393 *Memories d'Olivier de la March,* (Societiey de l'historie de France, 1883) Tome II, 42–43 per Maurice Keen, *The Laws of War in the Late Middle Ages* (n 8) 180.

394 Desmond Seward, *Henry V: The Scourge of God* (Viking, 1988) 81.

395 James Hamilton Wylie, *The Reign of Henry the Fifth* (Cambridge University Press, 1914) 175. See also Theodor Meron, *War Crimes Law Comes of Age* (n 84) 58.

396 Maurice Keen, *The Laws of War in the Late Middle Ages* (n 8) 92.

397 See, eg: Theodor Meron, *Henry's Wars and Shakespeare's Laws: Perspectives on the Law of War in the Later Middle Ages* (Oxford University Press, 1993) 154–71; Anthony A Contrada, 'Law and the Morality of War Today in Henry V' (n 389) 20. See also Christopher Hibbert, *Agincourt* (Severn House, 1964) 129.

became a commonly cited event among influential legal commentators such as Alberico Gentili (1552–1608) for the next few hundred years[398] — who specifically described the incident as a 'hateful and inhuman deed:'

> I cannot praise the English who, in that famous battle in which they overthrew the power of France, having taken more prisoners than the number of their victorious army and fearing danger from them by night, set aside those of high rank and slew the rest. A hateful and inhuman deed … and the battle was not so bloody as the victory.[399]

In the absence of previous discussions before the Battle of Agincourt, the fact that this debate about the legality of the English killings even occurred more holistically points to the beginning of this prohibition's emergence under international law.

As noted by Theodor Meron, Gentili's contributions to the early development of humanitarianism had gone further than merely criticising Henry V's conduct at Agincourt — the pioneering Protestant lawyer also contended that 'children should always be spared and so should women'.[400] By way of analogy, his argument was that their clergy-like inability to 'handle arms'[401] meant that women and children should fall into a wider class of protected non-combatants (*innocentes*) that also included 'peaceful peasants, foreign merchants, and the mentally ill'.[402] Were anyone in this category (including clergymen) to take up arms in active combat, however, then Gentili's view was that this *prima facie* immunity would then be lost.[403] According to Donald

398 See, eg, Theodor Meron, 'International Humanitarian Law from Agincourt to Rome' (n 385) 304. See also Barbara Donagan, 'Atrocity, War Crime, and Treason in the English Civil War' (n 70) 1150, citing Alberico Gentili, *De Jure Belli Libri Tres* [Three Books on the Law of War], tr John Rolfe (Clarendon Press, 1933) 211–12. This is particularly interesting when considering the connection between just and honourable war theories proposed by Gentili and the writings of Shakespeare: Cristiano Ragni, 'Shakespeare's 'Quarrel Honourable' and Gentili's "Iusta Contentio": Henry V and the Forging of the Nation' (2016) 16(2) *Studies in Ethnicity and Nationalism* 218–230.

399 Alberico Gentili, *Three Books on the Law of War*, tr John Rolfe (Clarendon Press, 1933) 211–12.

400 Gentili, *De Iure Belli*, Book ii, Chapter 21, 251, as cited by Theodor Meron, 'Shakespeare's Henry the Fifth and the Law of War' (1992) 86(1) *American Journal of International Law* 1, 25.

401 Ibid.

402 Valentina Vadi, War and Peace: Alberico Gentili and the Early Modern Law of Nations (Brill, 2020) 237–8, citing Gentili, *De Iure Belli*, Book ii, Chapter 20, 250. See also Meron, 'Shakespeare's Henry the Fifth and the Law of War' at 25.

403 Meron, 'Shakespeare's Henry the Fifth and the Law of War' at 25, citing Gentili, *De Iure Belli*, Book ii, Chapter 20, 251–4.

Wells, this was a view ultimately shared by international lawyers from the generation directly succeeding Gentili, including the similarly Oxford-based Richard Zouch (1590–1661).[404] An appraisal of the perspectives of near contemporary European scholars without any ties to England, such as the Spanish theologian Francisco Suarez (1548–1617), also suggests that Gentili's view would not have been entirely out of pace with his peers:

> It is implicit in natural law that the innocent include children, women, and all unable to bear arms; by the jus gentium, ambassadors, and among Christians, by positive (canon) law ... religious persons, priests ... All other persons are considered guilty; for human judgment looks upon those able to take up arms as actually having done so.[405]

By the late seventeenth-century, there is clearer evidence of disciplinary action being enforced against summary executions carried out by English soldiers. On the one hand, overwhelmingly throughout the Cromwellian Conquest of Ireland (1649–53), summary executions of civilians were still practiced during the Parliamentarian sieges at Drogheda, Wexford and Limerick.[406] On the other hand, a customary prohibition against the killing of captive enemies outside of siege warfare was beginning to emerge here, as seen initially through the explicit mention of the right to safe quarter in the aforementioned 1640 *Laws and Ordinances of Warre* published by the Earl of Essex for Charles I during the Second Bishop's War (1640): 'None shall kill an enemy who yeelds and throws down his arms, upon pain of death'.[407]

Towards the end of the English Civil War, there was also the suspension of Parliamentarian commanders such as Colonel Daniel Axtell for executing civilians who had surrendered and initially been granted quarter by said

404 Donald Wells, War Crimes and Laws of War (University Press of America, 2nd ed, 1991) 37.

405 Richard Shelly Hartigan, *The Forgotten Victim: A History of the Civilian* (Precedent Publishing, 1982) 94, citing JB Scott (ed), *Selection from Three Works of Francisco Suárez* (Clarendon Press, 1944) vol 2, 843. See also Paulo Emilio Vauthier Borges de Macedo, 'The Law of War in Francisco Suarez: The Civilizing Project of Spanish Scholasticism' (2012) 22(1) Revista da Faculdade de Direito 1, 22–3.

406 See, eg: James Burke, 'The New Model Army and the Problems of Siege Warfare, 1648–51' (1990) 27(105) *Irish Historical Studies* 1, 1; Micheál Ó Siochrú, 'Atrocity, Codes of Conduct and the Irish in the British Civil Wars 1641–1653' (2007) 195(1) *Past & Present* 55, 55.

407 Grose (n 78) 57–69, quoting Robert Devereux, *Laws and Ordinances of Warre, Extablished for the Better Conduct of the Army by His Excellency the Earl of Essex, Lord Generall of the Forces Raised by the Authority of the Parliament for the Defence of King and Kingdom: and Now Inlarged by Command of His Excellency* (1643). See also Theodor Meron, *War Crimes Law Comes of Age* (n 84) 9.

commanders.[408] A clear contrast may be drawn here against the lack of action taken against commanders found to have executed Irish people who refused to surrender entirely, as was the case with Cromwell's mass execution of the population of Drogheda following a prolonged siege in 1649.[409]

In particular, there is evidence that Ireton used the discretion of his position as head of the Parliamentarian army in Ireland to punish inferior commanders who he considered as having excessively practiced summary execution in disregard of this test of surrender. especially against Irish combatants who had in fact surrendered on terms (a clear contrast to the population of Drogheda, whose commanders had refused to surrender to Cromwell). As further described by Ó. Siochrú:[410]

> Ireton also demanded strict compliance with the conventions of war from his own commanders. He suspended Colonel Axtell, governor of Kilkenny, for executing innocent civilians in retaliation for the death of parliamentary troops, 'by arbitrary power without trial or conviction'. An unrepentant Axtell soon returned to military service, and later argued that 'God did use me as an instrument [in Ireland] ... for the suppressing of that bloody enemy'. Ireton also summoned a council of war to examine charges that Colonel Tothill had ordered the execution of troops who had surrendered on terms. The council stripped Tothill of his command, but Ireton worried that the punishment 'fell short of the justice God required therein to the acquitting of the army from the guilt of so foul a sin'. He notified the royalists of what had taken place, and released other prisoners without exchange or ransom.[411]

The scale of these violations throughout the English Civil War and subsequent Cromwellian period might have paved the way for the emergence of a prevalent norm in the late seventeenth century that considered the summary execution of non-combatants as uncivilised conduct. By 1689, for instance,

408 See, eg, Ó Siochrú (n 406) 76–81.

409 Ibid 55, 57. See also Robin Clifton, 'An Indiscriminate Blackness? Massacre, Counter-Massacre and Ethnic Cleansing in Ireland', in Mark Levene and Penny Roberts (eds), *The Massacre in History* (Berghahn Books, 1999) 107, 107.

410 Ó Siochrú (n 406) 76–81. See also *Sad Newes from Ireland: How the Lord Hath Been Pleased to Chastize the Parliament's Forces by a Losse from the Rebels* (London, 1651), <https://quod.lib.umich.edu/e/eebo2/A87207.0001.001/1:2?rgn=div1;view=fulltext>. As noted by Ó Siochrú, this was a contemporary pamphlet describing the accusations of unlawful killing against Tothill in particular.

411 Ibid.

we have evidence of King James II's distinctly 'stern' criticism of his marshal Conrad von Rosen in 1689 for murdering 'innocent non-combatants' during the Williamite War in Ireland (1689–91).[412] As per Mahmoud Bassiouni,[413] this was part of a drift in English military jurisprudence towards the recognition of more universally humanitarian concepts including the safeguarding of civilians, as inspired by the increasing influence of IHL jurists on emerging military traditions and the training of officers.[414]

It is clear however that these early developments merely applied to external wars between European powers. Mégret contends that the denial of quarter was commonplace in conflicts against Muslims and non-Western peoples after the Crusades (1095–1410), to the extent that the European system of ransom was not customarily extended to non-Western aristocrats.[415] As outlined by Rory Cox, an early instance of this was seen in the 1209 Siege of Beziers during the Albigensian Crusade against the followers of the condemned Cathar sect of Christianity in southern France (1209–1229).[416] Viewed as unprotected by the bounds of of *jus armorum* on account of their heretical beliefs, the Crusader Army (which included a considerable number of volunteers from England)[417] 'spared no one, irrespective of rank, sex or age, and put to the sword almost 20,000 people'.[418]

Rights to safe quarter were precluded sometimes even for Christians who followed more orthodox practices — as prominently seen 'in 1644, when Parliament temporarily passed an article of war forbidding grant of quarter to Irish soldiers captured in England'.[419] However, both Parliamentarian and Royalist commanders during the English Civil War (1642–51) criticised this 1644 ordinance.[420] The Royalist commander Prince Rupert argued that Parliament's

---

412 Timothy McCormack and Gerry Simpson, *The Law of War Crimes: National and International Approaches* n (68) at 39.

413 Mahmoud Bassiouni, *Crimes Against Humanity in International Criminal Law* (n 82) 154.

414 See also John Collins, *Martial Law and English Laws, c1500–c1700* n 64 at 109, citing Francis Grose, *Military Antiquities Respecting a History of the English Army: From the Conquest to the Present Time* (S Hooper, 1788) vol 2, 54.

415 Frédéric Mégret (n 91) 279.

416 Rory Cox (n 386) 118–9.

417 Daniel Power, 'Who Went on the Albigensian Crusade?' (2013) 128(534) *The English Historical Review*, 1047–85.

418 Rory Cox (n 386) 118–9, citing Letter from Amalric and Milo to Pope Innocent III (1209).

419 Charles Firth and Robert Rait, *Acts and Ordinances of the Interregnum, 1642–1660* (HMSO, 1911) 554–5.

420 See, eg, Barbara Donagan, 'Atrocity, War Crime, and Treason in the English Civil War' (n 70) 1148.

decision was 'contrary to the law of nature and nations, [in breach of] the rules and customs of war'.[421] Several lawmakers in the House of Commons also celebrated the refusal of certain Parliamentarian commanders to enforce the ordinance[422] due to its 'irregularitie'.[423]

By the beginning of the High Imperial era (from 1850 onwards),[424] military commanders on the frontier of the British Empire began challenging the enforceability of this emerging customary prohibition on the grounds of military necessity, and by reference to the separate regime previously seen in siege warfare[425] — even as humanist commentary became increasingly accepted by the British public.[426] In 1820, for instance, the Duke of Wellington wrote the following in a letter to the British East India Company as part of his capacity as Master-General of the Ordnance: 'it has always been understood that the defenders of a fortress stormed have no claim to quarter'[427] According to Michelle Gordon, this former view was tied to the increasing emphasis on 'total' warfare amongst European commanders following the Napoleonic Wars (1803–1815),[428] which made the 'suffering of the non-combatant population inevitable'.

At the same time however, Imperial officers during this period often cited the killing of non-combatants by non-Western powers as violations of international law, such that reciprocity was then justifiable through wars of conquest or annexation. As summarised by Alan Lester,[429] British commanders

421 Ibid.

422 Ibid, quoting Edmund Staunton, *Phinehas' Zeal in Execution of Judgment* (1645) 5.

423 See Robert Dore, *Letter Books of Sir William Brereton* (Record Society of Lancashire and Cheshire, 1984) 199–200.

424 See Anthony Reid, 'A New Phase of Commercial Expansion in Southeast Asia, 1760–1850' in Anthony Reid (ed), *The Last Stand of Asian Autonomies: Responses to Modernity in the Diverse States of Southeast Asia and Korea, 1750–1900* (Macmillan Press, 1997) 57, 57–82.

425 Frédéric Mégret (n 91) 279.

426 See James Heartfield, *The Aborigines' Protection Society: Humanitarian Imperialism in Australia, New Zealand, Fiji, Canada, South Africa, and the Congo, 1836–1909* (Hurst, 2011). Cf Stuart Bedford, 'Archives, Oral Traditions and Archaeology: Dissonant Narratives Concerning Punitive Expeditions on Malakula Island, Vanuatu' in Geoffrey Clark and Mirani Litster (eds), *Archaeological Perspectives on Conflict and Warfare in Australia and the Pacific* (Australian National University Press, 2022) 211, 211.

427 Geoffrey Parker (n 72) 155, citing Letter from Arthur Wellesely (Master-General of the Ordnance) to George Canning (President of the Board of Control of the British East India Company), 1820.

428 Michelle Gordon (n 97) at 202.

429 See, eg, Alan Lester, *Imperial Networks: Creating Identities in Nineteenth Century South Africa and Britain* (Psychology Press, 2001).

during the Cape Frontier or Kaffir Wars (1779–1879) against the Xhosa peoples in South Africa consistently referred to the killing of Jesuit preachers by local warriors as 'heinous' contraventions of wartime customs.[430]

When considering a practice-oriented approach however, evidence of State practice points to Imperial commanders not reciprocating when it came to their own violations of this custom. Throughout the late Kaffir Wars (1779–1879), which were contemporaneous with the Perak War (1875–6)[431] and the early Australian Frontier Wars (1788–1888), recent commentary has emphasised how Imperial agents directly supported indiscriminate settler violence against Xhosa-speaking communities.[432] Notably, Susan Blackbeard has also pointed to how British administrators 'concealed' evidence of these atrocities to avoid penalising agitators.[433] During the Third Kaffir War (1799–1803), this was particularly seen where British soldiers were alleged to have killed both Khoekhoe (who are native to Southern Africa) and Boer fighters who had surrendered peacefully. Robert Ross notably points to this event to suggest that British State practice across the early Xhosa Wars did not extend any prohibition on killing non-combatants to non-Europeans:

> Not at that meeting, but at a number of other moments, the Khoekhoe demonstrated that they were very well acquainted with colonial history and compared what they were doing to previous attacks on British power. The actions of Dutch farmers in the Graaff-Reinet rebellion in 1799, or at Slagter's Nek (described as Rooywal), were perhaps not such good examples of the leniency of the British towards rebels; indeed, there were those who pointed to British perfidy in hanging the rebels after they had surrendered under an amnesty.[434]

Similar incidents were also seen in New Zealand, most namely during the 1869 Te Kooti's War. As described in great detail by Gillespie, 120 Tūranga Māori were imprisoned at Ngātapa in January 1869 and summarily executed by British

430 Ibid 63.

431 David M Crowe, *War Crimes, Genocide, and Justice* (Palgrave Macmillan, 2014) 73–4.

432 Michelle Gordon (n 97) 43.

433 Susan Blackbeard, 'Acts of Severity: Colonial Settler Massacre of amaXhosa and abaThembu on the Eastern Frontier of the Cape Colony, c.1826–47' (2015) 17(2) *Journal of Genocide Research* 107, 107–32.

434 Robert Ross, *The Borders of Race in Colonial South Africa: The Kat River Settlement, 1829–1856* (Cambridge University Press, 2013) 209, citing Hermann Giliomee, 'The Burgher Rebellions on the Eastern Frontier, 1795–1815', in Richard Elphick and Hermann Giliomee (eds), *The Shaping of South African Society, 1652–1820* (Longmans, 1979), 338–58.

forces and their Māori auxiliaries, as part of their attempt to capture the Maori leader Te Kooti.[435] Most strikingly, the 'scale of these executions was unprecedented in New Zealand history'.[436] It is perhaps notable that this occurred a year after Te Kooti's raid on Matawhero, where '54 men, women and children were killed, including 20 Māori'.[437] Colonel George Stoddart Whitmore, who was the Commanding Officer at Ngatapa, later argued that Te Kooti's executions were committed 'in fair war and did not contravene Māori custom in war'.[438] While merely relating to an internal uprising as opposed to an external war, it is also notable that the British East India Company's use of extrajudicial summary executions in its harsh response to the Indian Rebellion of 1857 did not result in much backlash from contemporary international lawyers.[439]

When reflecting on how warfare was conducted in the British Empire's external wars by the late nineteenth century, a specific prohibition against the killing of women and children may be more easily established.[440] Article 23 of the 1863 American *Lieber Code* for instance, which was said to largely align with customs and laws of warfare at this time,[441] outlines that '[p]rivate citizens are no longer murdered'.[442] Furthermore, despite the aforementioned difficulties elsewhere, contemporary State practice in Malaya during the late Imperial period seemed to indicate that certain commanders attempted to punish contraventions of this custom.[443] Throughout the 1870s in particular, ordinances issued by Governor Jervois during the Perak War (1875–6) demonstrates how British soldiers were 'forbidden' from the 'indiscriminate' killing of

435 Alexander Gillespie, 'Māori Warfare and the New Zealand Wars — Atrocities, Chivalry and Apologies' in Samuel White (ed), *The Laws of Yesterday's Wars: From Indigenous Australians to the American Civil War* (n 9) 44, 64.

436 Ibid.

437 Ibid.

438 *Rongowhakaata Claims Settlement Act 2012* (NZ) s 9(6).

439 See Michelle Gordon (n 97) at 63.

440 Timothy McCormack and Gerry Simpson, *The Law of War Crimes: National and International Approaches* (n 68) 41–3.

441 Dietrich Schindler and Jiří Toman (eds), *The Laws of Armed Conflicts: A Collection of Conventions, Resolutions, and Other Documents* (Martinus Nijhoff, 4th ed, 2004) 3–23.

442 Francis Lieber et al, *General Orders No 100: Adjutant-General's Office, Instructions for the Government of Armies of the United States in the Field* (D Van Nostrand, 1863) art 23 ('*Lieber Code*'). See also Victoria Colvin and Phil Orchard, 'A Forgotten History: Forcible Transfers and Deportations in International Criminal Law' (2021) 32(1) *Criminal Law Forum* 51, 59.

443 William McIntyre, *The Imperial Frontier in the Tropics, 1865–75* (Palgrave Macmillan, 1967) 300.

Malay women and children.[444] Mohamad Rashidi Pakri highlights an atrocity where a captive Malay teenager named 'Panjang Meru' was hung without trial by soldiers under the command of Brigadier-General John Ross.[445] While Ross ultimately 'escaped a court-martial' or any explicit penalty other than being temporarily excluded from promotions,[446] the War Office published an apology to showcase the Imperial government's 'deep regret' for this 'summary execution':

> His Royal Highness feels compelled to express his deep regret at the course that was adopted in peremptorily ordering the summary execution of this Malay without any sort of trial.[447]

Notably however, actual evidence of how else this customary prohibition was enforced during the Perak War remains unfortunately elusive. As lamented by Wesseling,[448] more often than not, no effort was made by the Colonial Office to record non-British casualties in wartime.

From 1899 onwards, British State practice following the 1899 *Hague Convention* evidently points to an acceptance of this prohibition in its codified form.[449] By 1902, we have significant evidence of domestic prosecutions taken against British soldiers accused of killing non-combatants during the Boer Wars in South Africa. The most famous example of this was the Anglo-Australian officer Harry 'Breaker' Morant, who was prosecuted and executed

444 Michelle Gordon (n 97) 59, quoting letter from Sir William FD Jervois (Governor of the Straits Settlements) to Samuel Dunlop (Captain and Inspector-General of Police of the Straits Settlements) and John FA McNair (Major of the Madras Native Artillery), 22 November 1875.

445 Mohamad Rashidi Pakri, 'An Imperial or a Personal Legacy? The Rivalry of W.E. Maxwell and F.A. Swettenham in British Malaya' (2011) 84(2) *Journal of the Malaysian Branch of the Royal Asiatic Society* 33, 36–42. See also: Frank Swettenham, *The Real Malay* (John Lane, 1900) 210–23; Northcote Parkinson (n 90) 309; JM Gullick, 'William Maxwell and the Study of Malay Society' (1991) 64(2) *Journal of the Malaysian Branch of the Royal Asiatic Society* 7, 31.

446 Mohamad Rashidi Pakri, 'An Imperial or a Personal Legacy? The Rivalry of W.E. Maxwell and F.A. Swettenham in British Malaya' (n 219) 36–42. See also Northcote Parkinson (n 90) 309.

447 Michelle Gordon (n 97) 68, citing Enclosure: Armstrong to John Ross (Brigadier General of the Bengal Army), 27 October 1876, TNA CO882/3.

448 Henk Wesseling, 'Colonial Wars and Armed Peace, 1870–1914: A Reconnaissance' (1981) 5(2) *Itinerario* 59.

449 *Hague Convention I* arts 61–3.

by a British military tribunal for summarily killing Boer prisoners who had surrendered.[450]

This is also visible through the British reaction to excessive violence practised by other European powers in colonial frontiers. For instance, both Frédéric Mégret and Albert Grey emphasises how the British government publicly characterised the 1903 German massacres of Herero-Nama prisoners in Southwest Africa as 'breach[es] of the laws of war'.[451]

As noted by Kreienbaum in his article on 'Colonial Policy before 1914',[452] settler colonies such as 'Rhodesia or German South-West Africa' had featured significant conflicts between growing colonial communities and native populations over sparse land. He also points to the Herero-Nama-War as particular example of this, on account of the widescale brutal practices adopted by the German settler community at the time against the Herero and Nama peoples.

Accordingly, with its roots beginning in the 1600s as the internal English Civil War raged on, it is clear that a customary prohibition on summary executions of unarmed combatants, and non-combatants generally, had likely started to crystallise by the late nineteenth century. Again, while uncertainties surrounding its application to non-Western peoples would point to difficulties in universal enforcement before 1899 under both the preclusive and practice-oriented perspectives, a reading under the latter would highlight that it had become customarily enforceable by the 1880s in overseas Imperial wars even before the first *Hague Convention*.

---

450 Martine Piquet, 'Shoot Straight, You Bastards! Australians in the Boer War: The Breaker Morant Case' (2007) 66(1) *Victorian Representations of War* 273–87.

451 Albert Gray, 'The German Colonies of Africa' (1919) 1(25) *Journal of Comparative Legislation and International Law* 33.

452 Jonas Kreienbaum, 'Colonial Policy, Colonial Conflicts and War before 1914', (Blog Post, 14 February 2022) <https://encyclopedia.1914-1918-online.net/article/colonial_policy_colonial_conflicts_and_war_before_1914>.

CHAPTER 4

The Prohibition on Sexual Violence

While proscription against sexual violence have been included in early English military jurisprudence such as the Royalist Articles of War issued during the English Civil War (1642–51),[453] it has been suggested that 'the actors necessary to help the development' of this emerging prohibition during the eighteenth and early nineteenth centuries 'were not effective on the international stage'.[454] Accordingly, while a holistic reading of British conduct in external wars suggests that this prohibition was enforceable under the practice-oriented perspective by the decade preceding the *Hague Conventions* (including in wars against non-Western peoples), it took considerable time for British Imperial practice among military commanders to actually reflect written conventions here.

There are two particular factors relevant to the crystallisation of this prohibition which seem amplified when compared to the others discussed in this text. First, the fact that even the enforcement of domestic prosecutions for crimes against sexual violence was hindered by sexist attitudes among British Imperial commanders until approximately the nineteenth century with the rising influence of feminist activism on Imperial policies.[455] And second, the exacerbating impact of the limitations of records from the Colonial Office regarding non-British victims.[456] As also highlighted by Heuser, 'if the perpetrators are aware of criminality of the offence they have committed and the punishment awaiting them, they may be inclined to destroy the evidence, by killing the victims of rape or plunder or any non-fatal assault, thereby exacerbating their actions'.[457] These issues will be explored further in this chapter.

---

453 See, eg, Barbara Donagan, 'Atrocity, War Crime, and Treason in the English Civil War' in Gary Sheffield (ed), *War Studies Reader: From the Seventeenth Century to the Present Day and Beyond* (Bloomsbury Academic, 2010) 158, 176.

454 Tuba Inal (n 80) 172.

455 See, eg, Anthony Simpson, *Masculinity and Control: The Prosecution of Sex Offenses in Eighteenth-Century London* (New York University Press, 1984) 204. See also Bill McCarthy and Rosemary Gartner (eds), *The Oxford Handbook of Gender, Sex, and Crime* (Oxford University Press, 2014) 211.

456 Henk Wesseling, 'Colonial Wars and Armed Peace, 1870–1914: A Reconnaissance' (n 448) 53, 59.

457 Beatrice Heuser, 'Atrocities in Theory and Practice: An Introduction' (2012) 14(1) *Civil Wars* 2, 21.

 | DOI:10.1163/9789004515987_006

It will be useful to take a step back and go through the wider history of how this prohibition developed over time. Historically, prohibitions against sexual violence were clearly not applied against non-Christian peoples during the Crusades. According to the early medieval historian Rory Cox, canon lawyers during the time of the Crusades tended to identify religious wars and conflicts with the category of just war known as 'Roman war' or 'hostile war'. Specifically, these were conflicts involving 'incontrovertible legal justification and accompanied by almost no obligation of restraint'.[458] Foremostly it must be acknowledged that holy wars were conceptualised as struggles of morality against a common evil, and this overwhelmingly 'influence[d] how opponents were treated, and thus conflicts based fundamentally on religious differences would seem to conform to a concept of religious asymmetry'.[459]

Cox, in particular, highlights the Siege of Jerusalem (1099) during the First Crusade (1096–1099) to support this religious asymmetry argument:

> The infamous massacre of Jerusalem in 1099 by the army of the First Crusade is perhaps the most obvious example of religious asymmetry encouraging military brutality. Contemporary chronicles give gruesomely detailed reports of how the Muslim and Jewish populations were put to the sword, so that crusaders waded up to their ankles in rivers of blood, with the limbs of the fallen floating around on the surface.[460]

In line with this, the American historiographer Finucane also notes how the sexual abuse of both male and female prisoners was 'common enough' during the First Crusade — in particular by the *Tafur* Crusaders who later became infamous in contemporary literature for their supposed propensity for cannibalism and depravity.[461] According to the eleventh century Frankish historian

458 Rory Cox, 'Asymmetric Warfare and Military Conduct in the Middle Ages' (n 386) 100, 110, citing JA Brundage, 'Holy War and the Medieval Lawyers', in TP Murphy (ed), *The Holy War* (Ohio State University Press, 1976) 118, 122–5; See also FH Russell, *The Just War in the Middle Ages* (Cambridge University Press, 1975). It must be acknowledged however that Russell does not analyse the nature of 'just warfare' beyond the thirteenth century.

459 Rory Cox, 'Asymmetric Warfare and Military Conduct in the Middle Ages' (n 386) 100, 116–8.

460 Ibid 118, citing Rosalind Hill (ed), *The Deeds of the Franks and the Other Pilgrims to Jerusalem* (T Nelson, 1962).

461 Ronald C Finucane, *Soldiers of the Faith: Crusaders and Moslems at War* (St. Martin's Press, 1983) 176.

Guibert of Nogent (1055–1124), the *Tafurs* were a company of Crusaders who were 'unattached to any of the [Christian] princes' and instead sworn to poverty.[462] As a result, they would not have been bound by the traditional *jus armorum* or domestic chivalric customs applicable to the men-at-arms sworn to Western European princes and re-stated and enforced by their courts and military tribunals. As considered elsewhere in this book,[463] the wider convention in this time period of differing legal statuses between Christian and non-Christian enemies meant that these customs had been loosened anyways for even the attached Crusaders.

When appraising this space, Cox also refers to the retrospective commentary of Ambroise of Normandy, the eleventh century court minstrel to King Richard I the Lionheart (1157–99). In particular, Ambroise is known to us now for having provided entertainment to the English Court during the later Third Crusade (1189–1192) through his compiled poetry and chronicles regarding the events of the First Crusade and Kingdom of Jerusalem:

> The fact that these deeds were committed against infidels found clear approval in the chronicle sources, and no qualms or reservations were voiced about the legitimacy of such killings. Similarly, Ambroise applauded the mass execution of 2700 Muslim prisoners — including women and children — by Richard I of England at Acre in 1191, further indicating that a different code of military conduct for Christian soldiers was deemed acceptable when treating with non-Christian enemies.[464]

This celebration of violence against non-Christians at the Jerusalem could potentially be contrasted against the horrified Papal accounts during the 1202 Siege of Zara (otherwise known as Zadar), where the Venetian-funded soldiers of the infamous Fourth Crusade (1202–1204) against the Byzantine Empire were excommunicated by Pope Innocent III for committing violence on other Catholics:

> In comparison, when the armies of the Fourth Crusade sacked the Christian city of Zara (a far less bloody affair than that of Jerusalem or

462 Conor Kostick, *The Social Structure of the First Crusade* (Brill, 2008) 116.

463 See, eg, pt I ch I.

464 Marianne Ailes and Malcolm Barber (eds), *The History of the Holy War: Ambroise's Estoire de la Guerre Sainte* (Boydell Press, 2003) 5524–35, cited by Rory Cox, 'Asymmetric Warfare and Military Conduct in the Middle Ages' (n 386) 100, 118–9.

> Acre), the crusaders were excommunicated by Pope Innocent III and faced considerable censure from Christian commentators.[465]

It is also clear that prohibitions on sexual violence were not practiced during the 1209 Albigensian Crusade against Cathar heretics in southern France. In response to Malcolm Barber's interpretation that 'the Albigensian crusades went far beyond the normal conventions of early thirteenth-century warfare', Rory Cox argues that religious asymmetry 'must stand out as the determining cause'.[466] As written by the Papal legates Amalric and Milo to Innocent III regarding the sack of Béziers:

> Our men spared no one, irrespective of rank, sex or age, and put to the sword almost 20,000 people. After this great slaughter the whole city was despoiled and burnt, as divine vengeance raged miraculously.[467]

More broadly this is aligned with the common prevalence in private warfare during the early medieval period of unpunished sexual violence against non-combatants, with Firnhaber-Baker noting that '[a]lmost all seigneurial wars, particularly from the second quarter of the fourteenth century on, generated at least one allegation of *raptus, stupro, violencia carnaliter cognoscere*, or the like'.[468] At the same time however, despite the glaring lack of effective enforcement before the fourteenth century, prohibitions against sexual violence appeared in early English military commentaries such as John of Salisbury's *Policraticus* (1159) during the reign of Henry II of England (1133–89).[469] Undoubtedly, this was part of the eventual shift in the law of armed conflict towards the recognition of more universally humanitarian concepts including the safeguarding of civilians[470] — particularly as natural reasoning and

465 Rory Cox, 'Asymmetric Warfare and Military Conduct in the Middle Ages' (n 386) 100, 119.

466 Ibid 120, citing from Malcolm Barber, 'The Albigensian Crusades: Wars Like Any Other?' in Michel Balard, Benjamin Z Kedar and Jonathan Riley-Smith (eds), *Dei Gesta per Francos: Crusade Studies in Honour of Jean Richard* (Ashgate Publishing, 2001) 45–55.

467 WA Sibly and MD Sibly, *The History of the Albigensian Crusade: Peter of les Vaux-de-Cernay's Historia Albigensis* (Boydell Press, 1998) 289–90.

468 Justine Firnhaber-Baker, 'Techniques of Seigneurial War in the Fourteenth Century' (n 385) 90, 98.

469 See Donald Wells, *War Crimes and Laws of War* (University Press of America, 2nd ed, 1991) 19, citing John Dickenson (ed), *The Statesman's Book of John of Salisbury* (Russell and Russell, 1963) 213.

470 Beatrice Heuser, 'Ordinances and Articles of War before the Lieber Code, 866–1863' (n 75) 10–13; John Collins, *Martial Law and English Laws, c.1500–c.1700* (n 64) 7–8.

Christian principles remained the leading influences on legal development,[471] instead of positivist ideals.[472]

As a more striking compromise, the start of the Hundred Years War in 1337 may stand out as the first instance in English history where English commanders began enforcing proscriptions against the violation of (presumably French) civilians by their soldiers.[473] The writings of Sir John Froissart, who served as a chronicler to the court of King Edward III, are particularly of note. As emphasised by Professor Corinne Saunders of Durham University, Sir Froissart recorded that 'the shameful treatment of women [was] a powerful emblem of enemy dishonour and immorality' in contrast to English chivalry'.[474]

A specific example of the enforcement of this prospective prohibition may be seen in 1346, when Sir Godfray of Harecourt (otherwise known as 'Geoffrey d'Harcourt'), a Norman officer fighting on the English side, commanded the townspeople at the same siege of Caen not to kill citizens, 'nor to vyolate any woman'.[475] Godfray was the viscount of Saint-Sauveur, and had been appointed by King Edward III (1312–77) as one of the commanders of his campaign against France during the Hundred Years War (1337–1453).[476] Similarly, during the same siege, the English royal chronicler Froissart noted that another commander, Thomas (likely Thomas of Lancaster, the Duke of Clarence), took action to prevent violation of women by the soldiers by riding 'into the streates, and saved many lyves of ladyes, damosels, and cloysterers fro defoyling, for the soudyers were without mercy'.[477] Notably, during the later sieges of Bergnes and Damne, ladies and children were sent away and excluded from male prisoners so as to avoid violation by English soldiers.

While we are primarily considering case studies of historical practice here, it is noteworthy that — at least for this prohibition — the ways in which English commanders appeared to implement this customary prohibition seems to have

471 See Antony Anghie, 'Francisco De Vitoria and the Colonial Origins of International Law' (n 76) 321, 323, citing Alfred Rubin 'International Law in the Age of Columbus' (1992) 39(1) *Netherlands International Law Review* 5, 5–35.

472 See further Alfred P Rubin, 'The Law of Piracy: British Practice in the Nineteenth-Century' (n 77) 201, 270–1.

473 See generally Corinne Saunders, 'Sexual Violence in Wars — the Middle Ages' in Hans-Henning Kortüm (ed), *Transcultural Wars: From the Middle Ages to the 21st Century* (De Gruyter, 2006).

474 Ibid 153.

475 Ibid 154.

476 Sir John Froissart, *The Chronicles of Froissart,* tr John Bourchier and Lord Bemers (Macmillan, 1901–1903), vol i, cxxiiii, 27–33, 285.

477 Ibid 284.

matched how international legal scholars such as Hugo Grotius (1583–1645) wrote about it. This is visible through how, centuries later in his 1625 magnum opus *De Jure Belli ac Pacis* (The Rights of War and Peace), Grotius outlined several conditions where wartime sexual violence should be punished under the 'Law of Nations':

> The Ravishing of Women is sometimes permitted in War, and sometimes not. They that permit it, respect only the Inury done to the Body of an Enemy, which by the Law of Arms they think should be subject to all Acts of Hostility. But others, with more Reason, look not to that Injury alone, but also to the Act of Brutality, which behing neither necessary for the Security of those who commit it, nor proper for the Punishment of those against whom it is committed, should be as much punished in War as in Peace; and this last is the Law of Nations, if not all, yet of the most Civilized.[478]

Again, Grotius' views are particularly relevant when noting his influence on the unwritten customs of war considered by pre-Modern English commanders and their later Imperial successors.[479]

Furthermore, prohibitions against sexual violence were included by the jurist Richard Zouch's 1650 seminal treatise on International Law titled *Juris Et Judicii Fecialis, Sive, Juris Inter Gentes, Et Quaestionum De Eodem Explicatio* (An Exposition of Fecial Law And Procedure, Or Of Law Between Nations and Questions Concerning The Same). Zouch explicitly agreed with the position of earlier writers such as Grotius (1625) in concluding that the prohibition of rape *was* 'the Law of Nations, not of all nations, but of the better among them'.[480] Notably, this was in line with Grotius' earlier stance and reflected his exact wording as seen above.

---

478 Michael Schmitt, 'Assassination in the Law of War', West Point Lieber Institute (Blog Post, 15 October 2021) <https://lieber.westpoint.edu/assassination-law-of-war/>, quoting Hugo Grotius, *De Iure Belli Ac Pacis* [*On the Law of War and Peace*] (1625). See also Tuba Inal, *Looting and Rape in Wartime* (University of Pennsylvania Press, 2013) 29.

479 GR Rubin, 'Parliament, Prerogative and Military Law: Who had Legal Authority over the Army in the Later Nineteenth Century' (1997) 18(1) *Journal of Legal History* 45, 46.

480 Richard Zouche, *Juris et Judicii Fecialis, sive, Juris inter Gentes et Quaestionum de Eodem Explicatio* (1650) 180–1, <https://archive.org/stream/iurisetjudiciife12zouc/iurisetjudiciife12zouc_djvu.txt>, cited by Barbara Donagan, 'Atrocity, War Crime, and Treason in the English Civil War' (n 70) 1142, 1149. For a description of Grotius' earlier view, see Tuba Inal (n 80) 29, citing Hugo Grotius, *De Iure Belli Ac Pacis* [On the Law of War and Peace] (1625). See also Stephen C Neff, *Justice among Nations: A History of International Law* (n 308).

In with this eventual shift in the late seventeenth century towards the recognition of more universally humanitarian concepts including the safeguarding of civilians[481] — as perhaps inspired by the increasing influence of the above IHL jurists on emerging English military thought and jurisprudence[482] — we also have evidence of attempted proscriptions against sexual violence in Royalist articles of war during the English Civil War (1642–51). In the 1642 *Orders and Institutions of War* set out by the Earl of Newcastle (William Cavendish), for instance, it was emphasised that 'Whosever shall force or ravish any woman within our quarters, or any other place, shall suffer death'.[483] Similarly, in the 1643 *Laws and Ordinances of Warre* issued by the Earl of Essex (Robert Devereux), it was more expansively outlined that 'Rapes, ravishments, unnaturall abuses shall be punished with death'.[484] As summarised by Barbara Donagan, the prohibition against rape at the time was pioneering at the time for the 'formal legal and punitive machinery' involved in its formal acknowledgement in Royalist ordinances[485] — in contrast to the norms surrounding other issues such as 'surrender, plunder, and parol', which commanders only considered with regard to 'honor, morality, and not least reciprocal utility'.[486]

While commentary on the Parliamentarian approach to the emerging prohibition against sexual violence is scant in comparison, what we have does suggest some level of reciprocal recognition. Ó Siochrú has previously highlighted the notable attempts undertaken by the Parliamentarian commander Michael Jones (1606–1649) to punish soldiers under his command who had

481 Beatrice Heuser, 'Ordinances and Articles of War before the Lieber Code, 866–1863' (n 75) vol 21, 139, 139–64. See also: Christopher Duffy, *The Military Experience in the Age of Reason* (n 75) 10–13; John Collins, *Martial Law and English Laws, c.1500–c.1700* (n 64) 7–8.

482 John Collins, *Martial Law and English Laws, c.1500–c.1700* (n 64) 109, citing Francis Grose, *Military Antiquities Respecting a History of the English Army: From the Conquest to the Present Time* (n 78) vol 2, 54.

483 *Orders and Institutions of War, made and ordained by His Majesty and by him delivered to his generall His Excellence the Earle of Newcastle with the said Earles speech to the army at the delivery and publishing the said orders prefixt* (1642) 4, as cited by Barbara Donagan, 'Atrocity, War Crime, and Treason in the English Civil War' (n 453) 158, 176.

484 *Laws and ordinances of Warre, extablished for the better conduct of the army by His Excellency the Earl of Essex, lord generall of the forces raised by the authority of the Parliament for the defence of king and kingdom: and now inlarged by command of His Excellency* (1643) 11, as cited by Barbara Donagan, 'Atrocity, War Crime, and Treason in the English Civil War' in (n 453) 158, 176.

485 Barbara Donagan, 'Atrocity, War Crime, and Treason in the English Civil War' (n 70) 1142.

486 Ibid.

contravened his issued 1647 *Lawes and Ordinances of Warre, Established for the Good Conduct of the Army* by committing rape.[487]

> The vast majority of the rules dealt with discipline within the army Itself, but a number related to the civilian population. Murder, rape and theft were all punishable by death, along with unlicensed destruction of goods and property, 'be it of friend or foe'.

As England became an overseas maritime power with the dawn of the Imperial period in the sixteenth and seventeenth centuries, it became more commonplace for different Western powers to accuse their enemies of committing atrocities such as sexual violence — especially as humanist commentary became increasingly accepted by the British public.[488] A notable example of this can be seen from British commentary regarding the Bulgarian and Bosnian rebellions against the Ottoman Empire during the Great Eastern Crisis (1875–8), where the House of Commons accused and denounced the Ottoman Army for not punishing 'outrages' committed by its soldiers against Bulgarian and Bosnian women.[489]

Enforceability issues remained, however. For instance, as emphasised by Hoock, throughout the post-Cromwellian period of British expansion in North America in the eighteenth-century, 'the extent to which the proscription of rape was enforced … and prosecuted at military law, depended to a significant extent on the oversight and prosecutorial discretion exercised by local commanders'.[490] According to War Office Courts Martial Books, there were six rape trials pertaining to British army soldiers between 1776 and 1782.[491] Arthur N Gilbert notes how one of these trials led to acquittal, but does not mention

487 Micheál Ó Siochrú, *Atrocity, Codes of Conduct and the Irish in the British Civil Wars 1641–1653* (n 406) 72–3, citing Colonel Michael Jones, *Lawes and Ordinances of Warre, Established for the Good Conduct of the Army* (1647).

488 See James Heartfield, *The Aborigines' Protection Society: Humanitarian Imperialism in Australia, New Zealand, Fiji, Canada, South Africa, and the Congo, 1836–1909* (Hurst, 2011). Cf Stuart Bedford, 'Archives, Oral Traditions and Archaeology: Dissonant Narratives Concerning Punitive Expeditions on Malakula Island, Vanuatu' in Geoffrey Clark and Mirani Litster (eds), *Archaeological Perspectives on Conflict and Warfare in Australia and the Pacific* (Australian National University Press, 2022) 211, 211.

489 See United Kingdom, Parliamentary Debates, House of Commons, 7 August 1876, vol 231, col 721–46.

490 Holger Hoock, '*Jus in Bello*, Rape and the British Army in the American Revolutionary War' (2015) 14(1) *Journal of Military Ethics* 74, 78–9.

491 Arthur N Gilbert, 'British Military Justice during the American Revolution' (1979) 20(1) *The Eighteenth Century* 30–2, citing W.O. 71/54–57 and W.O. 71/82–96.

the fate of the other five trials.[492] It can be assumed that they were convicted. Gilbert does emphasise, however, that sexual offenses were rarely tried in army court-martials throughout the eighteenth century. Hoock additionally noted that 'conviction rates and punishment levels within the small number of rape cases tried at British general courts-martial were higher compared to rape cases tried in criminal courts across the eighteenth-century, but the sample of Revolutionary-era courts-martial seems too small to draw any definitive conclusions:[493]

> Officers' responses to rape and rape allegations appeared to vary, then, from collusion and tacit toleration to the imposition of discipline and, perhaps, an assertion of difference from the rank and file through courts-martial. In eighteenth-century military law generally, officers possessed considerable discretion in defining crimes; soldiers could be indicted in various ways for the same offense. Officer discretion — analogous also to the significance of prosecutorial discretion at civil law — helps explain the divergence between the formal law of rape and its application in the theater of war.[494]

Hoock has described several incidents where British soldiers were court-martial and executed for rape, including the 1779 execution of Sergeant Boswell of Lord Rawdon's regiment,[495] and the 1781 execution of two soldiers from Sir Banastre Tarleton's British Legion under General Charles Cornwallis' (1738–1805) orders.[496] Notably, however these cases all involved sexual violence towards American women.[497] More broadly, and with implications for how this emerging prohibition might have extended to non-Western peoples, Hoock has suggested that officers more typically failed to restrain their troops or silently condoned cases of sexual assault.[498] Again, this ties back to our modern understanding of the general failures of domestic enforcement at the time despite crimes against sexual violence having already been established in legislation.

---

492 Ibid.

493 Holger Hoock, '*Jus in Bello*, Rape and the British Army in the American Revolutionary War' (n 490) 74, 80.

494 Ibid.

495 Ibid 81.

496 Ibid 83.

497 Ibid 81–4.

498 Ibid 82.

The passage of the 1803 *Mutiny Act* empowered British commanders to enforce Articles of War in British Territory Overseas or wherever British soldiers served.[499] The Canadian historian Donald Graves has previously described in fine detail how British discipline in overseas territories was governed, and the extent to which this involved the operation of two interlinking but separate pieces of legislation: the *Articles of War* and the *Mutiny Act* (the latter of which was annually passed by Parliament).

> In 1813 the discipline of the British army was governed by two documents — the Articles of War and the Mutiny Act. The Articles of War were prerogative, which is to say they were drafted by royal authority (actually the Commander-in-Chief of the army, who was the Duke of York in that year), while the Mutiny Act was statutory in that it was debated and assented to by parliament. If there was a conflict between the provisions of the two documents, the Mutiny Act prevailed in England and Scotland (but not Ireland), while the Articles of War prevailed in British territory overseas. Although the Articles and the Act covered such matters as enlistment and billeting, they also had the object of maintaining discipline among both officers and enlisted men — as well as other persons (e.g. sutlers and camp followers) who were regarded as being subject to military law — and prescribed the offenses which were punishable and provided for legal procedures to try and punish offenders. Prior to 1803, the Articles and the Act only had validity within the "King's Dominions," but in that year parliament extended this power to any place where British troops served. At this point, the Articles of War were given a statutory basis in the Mutiny Act and became subordinate to it.[500]

According to Graves, British commanders were made to ensure that their assigned soldiers became familiar with the content of the *Articles of War*, to the extent that 'No magistrate would certify that a recruit was legally enlisted unless' the individual had read and understood the articles relating to desertion, mutiny and gross insubordination. Notably, these acts were punishable by death.

---

499 See GR Rubin, 'Parliament, Prerogative and Military Law: Who had Legal Authority over the Army in the Later Nineteenth Century' (1997) 18(1) *Journal of Legal History* 45, 48, where the effect of the 1803 *Mutiny Act* is discussed.

500 Donald E Graves, '"Every Horror was Committed with Impunity ... and Not a Man was Punished!" Reflections on British Military Law and the Atrocities at Hampton' (n 142). As noted by Graves, 'The relevant act was 43 Geo III, c. 20. This brief overview of the

This approach was prescribed by the regulations themselves, which explicitly required their consistent reading to soldiers in active service. At the same time, it also necessitated the reading of General Orders passed by British commanders for specific campaigns, especially those orders which concerned soldierly discipline and the associated penalties for disobedience:

> The Articles of War are to be read once in every Two Months to the Officers and Men (agreeable to His Majesty's Orders therein expressed), in presence of the Commanding Officer [of a regiment]; the Officers are to be at the head of their respective Troops or Companies: The strictest Silence is to be kept, and that respectful Attention given, which is due to the Declaration of Orders proceeding immediately from His Majesty. In like manner, whatever parts of the present or future General Orders are meant to regulate the Conduct of the Officers and Men, are to be read and carefully explained to them, at least, once in every Two Months. The obedience of this Order is to be regularly certified by the Commanding Officer.[501]

With the exception of situations involving the three offences noted above (desertion, mutiny and gross insubordination), soldiers who contravened either the *Articles of War* or the *Mutiny Acts* were punished by courts martial.[502] In correlation with the extent of offending conduct and the position of the perpetrating officer within the military hierarchy, there were 'three distinct levels of court martial available:'[503] the most inferior being the Regimental Court Martial. Involving five officers taken from the same regiment as the offending soldier, this panel could be summoned by a regimental commander who sought to punish breaches of the *Articles* or the *Mutiny Act* by servicemen from the commander's own unit. In line with the junior rank of this type of panel however, a Regimental Court Martial did not possess the mandate to

foundation of British military law is based on Charles M Clode, *The Administration of Justice under Military and Martial Law* (Kessinger, 1874)'.

501 Donald E Graves, '"Every Horror was Committed with Impunity ... and Not a Man was Punished!" Reflections on British Military Law and the Atrocities at Hampton' (n 142), quoting from *General Regulations and Orders for the Army: Adjutant General's Office, Horse-Guards, 12th August, 1811* (1811) 98–9.

502 Henry Marshall, *Military Miscellany: Comprehending a History of the Recruiting of the Army, Military Punishments* (Andesite Press, 1846) 165.

503 *Report from His Majesty's Commissioners for Inquiring into the System of Military Punishments in The Army 1836* (HMSO, 1836) 309, cited by Donald E Graves, '"Every Horror was Committed with Impunity ... and Not a Man was Punished!" Reflections on British

hand down death penalty sentences for infractions. At the same time however, the General Courts Martial Book records demonstrate that punishments at this level were still usually quite severe despite attempts throughout the eighteenth century to reform its practices.[504] According to a 1722 edition of the records book for instance, two soldiers were listed as being court martialled at the regimental level for abusing the wife of another private and assaulting a lady respectively. The first soldier was 'lead through guards with halberds and lashed', while the second was 'lashed on two successive days'.[505]

Secondly, there was the Garrison Court Martial (otherwise known as District Court Martial or General Regimental Court Martial), which for overseas cases was a tribunal of five officers summoned by the commander of a Garrison (seven officers were required for cases taking place in Britain itself).[506] As per the name, these officers could be assigned to different regiments. Similar to the Regimental Court Martial however, this higher tribunal could not try commissioned officers or hand down charges directly involving the death penalty.[507]

Finally, the highest authority was the General Court Martial, which was the sole tribunal (comprised of a judge advocate and between five and thirteen officers, contingent on the instructions of the Crown or Commander-in-Chief) with the power to inflict the death penalty and actually try senior officers.[508] In 1807, the British Parliament conferred the power to convene a General Court Martial on any officer who had command of soldiers 'beyond the seas (*or otherwise outside British territories*)'.[509]

Military Law and the Atrocities at Hampton' (n 142). See also Donald E Graves, 'British Military Discipline in the Napoleonic Period: Gleanings from the Inquiry into the System of Military Punishments in the Army, 1836' (Blog Post, January 2009), <https://www.napoleon-series.org/military-info/organization/Britain/Miscellaneous/c_militaryjusticeinquiry.html>.

504 Arthur N Gilbert, 'The Regimental Courts Martial in the Eighteenth Century British Army' (1976) 8(1) *Albion: A Quarterly Journal Concerned with British Studies* 50, 50–66, citing Letter from Hughes to Secretary at War, 3 March 1723, W.O. 71/15. See also Articles of War, 1728. W.O. 72/2.

505 Arthur N Gilbert, 'The Regimental Courts Martial in the Eighteenth Century British Army' (n 504) 50, 56.

506 Donald E Graves, '"Every Horror was Committed with Impunity … and Not a Man was Punished!" Reflections on British Military Law and the Atrocities at Hampton' (n 142). See also RW Bennett, 'Military Law in 1839' (1970) 48(196) *Journal of the Society for Army Historical Research* 225, 225–41.

507 Donald E Graves, '"Every Horror was Committed with Impunity … and Not a Man was Punished!" Reflections on British Military Law and the Atrocities at Hampton' (n 142).

508 Ibid.

509 For further information on military law and courts martial in the British army throughout the Napoleonic period, see Kevin Linch, 'Desertion from the British Army during the

As highlighted by Graves, this power matched the language of the 1813 *Articles of War* (titled the 'Rules and Articles for the Better Government of All His Majesty's Forces London') which also recognised the expanded authority of overseas commanders to summon a General Court Martial in cases involving rape:[510]

> In any Place beyond the Seas, where Our Forces now are or may be employed, where there is no Form of Our Civil Judicature in Force, the General, Governor, or other Officer commanding in Chief for the Time being, is to appoint General Courts-martial as Occasion may require, for the Trial of any such Persons under his Command, accused of wilful Murder, Theft, Robbery, Rape, Coining or Clipping the Coin of Great Britain, or any Foreign Coin current in the Garrison or Place under his Command, or of having used Violence against the Persons or Property of any of our Subjects, or of any others entitled to Our Protection: And the Persons so accused, if found guilty, shall suffer Death, or such other Punishment, according to the Nature and Degree of their respective Offenses, as by the Sentence of any such General Court-martial shall be awarded.[511]

The 1811 *Regulations for the Army* also referred to this power, and further categorised rape as a '[C]rime of such enormity' that justified the death penalty for soldiers found guilty of the charge:[512]

> Plundering and Marauding, at all times highly disgraceful to Soldiers, under the circumstance in which the Army would take the field … will become Crimes of such Enormity, as to admit of no remission of the awful Punishment [i.e. execution], which the Military Law awards against Offenses of this nature. The Provost-Marshal, in making his Rounds, will be commanded to execute it immediately, and in its greatest rigour, against all such as are detected in the fact. …

Napoleonic Wars' (2016) 49(4) *Journal of Social History* 808, 808–28; Arthur N Gilbert, 'Why Men Deserted from the Eighteenth-Century British Army' (1980) 6(4) *Armed Forces & Society* 553, 553–67.

510 Donald E Graves, '"Every Horror was Committed with Impunity … and Not a Man was Punished!" Reflections on British Military Law and the Atrocities at Hampton' (n 142).

511 *Rules and Articles for the Better Government of All His Majesty's Forces London* (1807) 81–2.

512 Ibid.

> All Officers in the Command of Guards or Detachments, are enjoined to give Assistance to the Provost-Marshal in the execution of his Duty; and any Officer or Soldier impeding him in the same, or offering him any insult, will receive the most exemplary Punishment.[513]

During the War of 1812 (1812–15) between Great Britain and the United States, there are records of proscriptions against rape were enforced by the British army in Canada. Notably however, this was a war fought between Western civilizations as opposed to one explicitly involving a non-civilised power. The Canadian military historian Donald E Graves, in his article 'Reflections on British Military Law', argues that punishment under British martial law was 'usually sure and swift' during this war:[514]

> For example, Vice-Admiral Alexander Cochrane, RN, commanding the British fleet in North America, responded to the plunder of an American civilian at Benedict, Maryland, by having the perpetrator flogged 'in the presence of the Inhabitant whose House they robbed.[515]

Graves also notes that, when a 'British soldier raped and murdered an American woman at Eastport in late 1815, he was tried by court martial, found guilty and sentenced to be hanged but committed suicide before his execution'.[516]

Conversely, through reference to anecdotal evidence, Professor Elsbeth Heamen of McGill University counter-argues that incidents of rape during a British raid on the village of Hampton, Virginia in June 1813 went clearly unpunished by Colonial Officers. Regarding the same incident however, Graves asserts that this was the primary fault of the commanding officer Colonel Thomas Sydney Beckwith — and that rape was clearly prohibited through contemporary British Imperial practice, such as the aforementioned court-martial and execution of the British soldier in 1815 for rape.[517]

---

513 Ibid.

514 Donald E Graves, '"Every Horror was Committed with Impunity … and Not a Man was Punished!" Reflections on British Military Law and the Atrocities at Hampton' (n 142).

515 Ibid, citing Memorandum from Vice-Admiral Cochrane to Captains, 25 August 1814. See also Michael J Crawford, *The Naval War of 1812: A Documentary History* (US Naval Historical Centre, 2002) vol 3, 230–1.

516 Donald E Graves, '"Every Horror was Committed with Impunity … and Not a Man was Punished!" Reflections on British Military Law and the Atrocities at Hampton' (n 142).

517 Ibid.

Most prominently, the Swiss lawyer Emmerich de Vattel's *Law of Nations* has been highlighted as the most popular codification of laws of war among British commanders by the time of the War of 1812 against the United States.[518] Published originally in 1758, five editions of de Vattel's treatise had been published in Great Britain by that point. It is noteworthy that de Vattel himself clearly contended that vulnerable civilians had to be protected from violence and 'malreat[ment]' during times of war, which again was in parallel with the jurisdiction conferred on British military tribunals to punish sexual violence:

> Women, children, feeble old men, and sick persons, come under the description of enemies ... and we have certain rights over them, inasmuch as they belong to the nation with whom we are at war, and as, between nation and nation, all rights and pretensions affect the body of society, together with all its members. ... But these are enemies who make no resistance; and consequently we have no right to maltreat their persons, or use any violence against them, much less to take away their lives ...
>
> This is so plain a maxim of justice and humanity, that at present every nation, in the least civilized, acquiesces in it. If sometimes the furious and ungovernable soldier carries his brutality so far as to violate female chastity, or to massacre women, children, and old men, the officers lament those excesses: they exert their utmost efforts to put a stop to them; and a prudent and humane general even punishes them whenever he can.[519]

As reasoned by Graves,[520] de Vattel's position pointed to a recognition of any unnecessary violence (in terms of completing the objectives of the campaign at the hand) as a *licentious* act infringing the 'law of nature' and mankind.

At the same time, a similar stance was argued by the renowned German statesman Georg Friedrich von Martens (1756–1821). Notably, his 1789

518 In Ibid, Graves notes that the 'dates of the British editions of de Vattel were 1759, 1787, 1792, 1793 and 1811 while those of the American editions were 1787, 1796 and 1805'. Similarly, Farbel also outlines that any American seeking to consult international codes the war of 1812 would probably have turned to the Swiss jurists' published works: see Robin FA Farbel, 'Laws of War in the 1812 Conflict' (1980) 14(2) *American Studies* 199, 199–218.

519 Emmerich de Vattel, *The Law of Nations, or, Principles of the Law of Nature, Applied to the Conduct and Affairs of Nations and Sovereigns*, (London, 1797) 351–2.

520 Ibid 369, cited by Donald E Graves, '"Every Horror was Committed with Impunity ... and Not a Man was Punished!" Reflections on British Military Law and the Atrocities at Hampton' (June 2009) *War of 1812 Magazine* <https://www.napoleon-series.org/military-info/Warof1812/2009/Issue11/c_hampton.html>.

Compendium of the Law of Nations: Founded on the Treaties and Customs of the Modern Nations of Europe was also admired through the British military and wider English-speaking world.[521] According to von Martens:

> From the moment we are at war, all those who belong to the hostile state become our enemies, and we have a right to act against them as such; but our right to wound and kill being founded on self-defence, or on the resistance opposed to us, we can, with justification wound or take the life of none except those who take an active part in the war.
>
> So that, 1. children, old men, women, and in general all those who cannot carry arms, or who ought not to do it, are safe under the protection of the law of nations, unless they have exercised violence against the enemy. 2. Retainers of the army, whose profession is not to kill or directly injure the enemy, such as chaplains, surgeons, and, to a certain degree, drummers, fifers, trumpeters, & cought not to be killed or wounded deliberately.[522]

Potential evidence of the enforcement of this customary prohibition may also be seen among English colonial officers during the later Anglo-Kafir Wars (1834–35) in South Africa. James Edward Alexander, who was the aide-de-camp to Benjamin d'Urban (Governor of the Cape Colony) at the time, notes how ordinances were issued for British Officers to prevent members of the indigenous Khoekhoen and other native soldiers in the Provisional Battalion from molesting or injuring Gcaleka women and children in their custody.[523] Notably, the exact timing of this conflict was concurrent with the one of the Wiradyuri Wars in modern-day New South Wales, which was part of the wider Australian Frontier Wars (1788–1934).

521 See Donald E Graves, '"Every Horror was Committed with Impunity … and Not a Man was Punished!" Reflections on British Military Law and the Atrocities at Hampton' (n 142).

522 Georg Friedrich von Martens, *A Compendium of the Law of Nations, Founded on the Treaties and Customs of the Modern Nations of Europe* tr William Cobbett (Cobbett and Morgan, 1802) 286–7.

523 James Edward Alexander, *Excursions in Western Africa and Narrative of a Campaign in Kaffirland on the Staff of the Commander-In-Chief, Vol. I and II* (Colburn, 1840) 120, cited by Denver A Webb, 'African women and the Wars of Resistance and Dispossession in the Cape Colony and Xhosaland in the Eighteenth and Nineteenth centuries' (2019) 20(3) *Journal of South African and American Studies*. See also Pamela Scully, 'Rape, Race and Colonial Culture: The Sexual Politics of Identity in the Nineteenth-Century Cape Colony, South Africa', (1995) 100(2) *American Historical Review* 335, 335–59.

Decades later, we have more comprehensive evidence in 1856 of colonial courts in British Xhosaland enforcing punishments against natives for sexual assault.[524] Elizabeth Thornberry, in particular, has provided a brief but illuminating examination on the punishment of a Xhosa man of the Gqunukhwebe Nation for sexual assault under colonial law.[525] Her study begins with a discussion of a case in 1856 at the town of Middledrift in the Eastern Cape province, where a Xhosa man was accused of rape against another tribeswoman; the case was heard by a combination of British Magistrates and Gqunukwebe Tribal Chiefs (including William Kama, the first Christian Chief):

> In 1856, the Gqunukhwebe Xhosa chief Kama and his council convened to hear a complaint by Umngeni, one of Kama's subjects. Umngeni complained that his wife had been raped, and claimed 'all the property that the offender is possessed of in compensation for the wrong done to me'. Because the offender was an employee of the colonial state, the Special Magistrate assigned to Kama was present to observe and record the proceedings. Kama confirmed to the magistrate that Umngeni's claim was indeed 'in accordance to [Xhosa] law'. However, he continued, 'in such cases … it rests with the chief whether or not the offender gives the whole or a part of the property claimed by the defendant'. In this case, after intervention from the magistrate, Kama awarded a smaller compensation payment.[526]

Thornberry compares this 1856 case to a later 1894 rape case (with similar facts), and highlights how compensation was denied for the latter in favour of corporal punishment to demonstrate how customary Xhosa methods of punishment had been replaced by that point with British punitive practices:

> Almost four decades later, in 1894, another Xhosa man was charged with a similar crime. Mkuhlwana, a resident of Ngcana's location in Nqamakwe district, was (after a trial in the colonial criminal court system) convicted of raping a married woman. Instead of paying compensation, Mkuhlwana was imprisoned for three years with hard labour, and given 20 lashes. The difference in the punishments given to these two men indicates a broad

524 See Pamela Scully, 'Rape, Race and Colonial Culture: The Sexual Politics of Identity in the Nineteenth-Century Cape Colony, South Africa' (n 253) 307.

525 See Elizabeth Thornberry, 'Defining Crime through Punishment: Sexual Assault in the Eastern Cape, c.1835–1900' (2011) 37(3) *Journal of Southern African Studies* 415, 415–30.

526 Ibid 415.

> change in the normative forms of punishment in South Africa's Eastern Cape, then part of the Colony of the Cape of Good Hope, from the late pre-colonial period through the early twentieth century. Between 1848 and 1893, the British administration of the Cape Colony extended its jurisdiction over the area between the Fish and Mtamvuna rivers. As the colony expanded, administrators sought to replace pre-colonial practices of punishment with a new punitive apparatus. In the earlier case, all parties (except perhaps the colonial magistrate) accepted the payment of cattle from the accused man to the family of his victim as an appropriate punishment. By the twentieth century, however, rape was understood — at least to the colonial state — to demand corporal punishment and incarceration. Where the pre-colonial regime was marked by an important role for family networks in mediating between individual actors and the punishments imposed, colonial officials sought to impose a model that privileged the direct relationship between the individual and the state.[527]

By1893, there was evidence of Xhosa parties both taking their cases to be decided by the Cape Colony Circuit Court and accepting British methods of punishment instead of their own historical practices:

> Between 1848 and 1893, the British administration of the Cape Colony extended its jurisdiction over the area between the Fish and Mtamvuna rivers. As the colony expanded, administrators sought to replace pre-colonial practices of punishment with a new punitive apparatus.[528]

However, the object of Thornberry's article is evidently to dispute the idea that native methods of punishment had been 'fully replaced'. Consequently, she highlights how Native customary proscriptions against rape was taken into account by British magistrates, and how:

> The fact that the Circuit Court relied almost exclusively on imprisonment and corporal punishment to punish rape conceals the degree to which non-consensual sex continued to be prosecuted and punished by a wide range of institutions, as well as the colonial state's cooperation in that process.[529]

527 Ibid 416.
528 Ibid.
529 Ibid 419, 430.

An examination of British conduct during the Karene Expedition (1898–99) waged against the Temne Tribes in Sierra Leone also points to a growing recognition among Imperial frontier commanders of a need to enforce this customary prohibition in external conflicts. While ultimately dismissing the allegations on the grounds that it was 'unsupported by evidence and incompatible with medical testimony',[530] Major RJ Norris (who commanded the expedition) personally sought to investigate claims of attempted rapes by members of the British West India Regiment of local Temne civilians[531] — to the extent of making the following assurances in official field reports:

> I however gave complainant to understand that had the charge been proved severe punishment would have been awarded, and then told her to let people in town understand that they would receive every protection.[532]

Lastly, it is also worth considering how the customary prohibition against sexual violence was treated British War Office in their pre-Hague 1899 *Manual of Military Law* issued as non-binding guidance to Imperial commanders. In particular, the chapter on 'The Customs of War' broadly outlines the need to protect vulnerable persons from unnecessary violence and maltreatment, with explicit reference to de Vattel's writings in the *The Law of Nations*: 'women, and children, wherever found, will be carefully guarded from outrage'.[533]

A holistic reading of these accounts, in line with the practice-oriented methodology, compellingly casts doubt on any notion that prohibitions on sexual violence were never implemented in colonial territories.[534] As per Tuba Inal,[535] the issues surrounding customary prohibitions against sexual violence were related to enforceability rather than the acceptance of this prohibition by international and British jurists:

530 Michelle Gordon, *Extreme Violence and the 'British Way': Colonial Warfare in Perak, Sierra Leone and Sudan* (n 97) 104, citing 'Karene Expedition: Staff Diary', WO32/7624.

531 Ibid.

532 Ibid.

533 War Office, *Manual of Military Law* (His Majesty's Stationery Office, 1899) 290, citing Emmerich de Vattel, *The Law of Nations* (1835) vol ii, 173.

534 Holger Hoock, '*Jus in Bello*, Rape and the British Army in the American Revolutionary War' (n 490) 74, 78–9.

535 Tuba Inal (n 80) 172.

> The actors necessary to help the development of a normative context in which rape is as undesirable and preventable as pillage were not effective on the international stage. The publicists who pushed for the codification of the laws of war did not include rape in the drafts they prepared, because they did not want to jeopardize their projects by putting potentially unacceptable articles in them.[536]

This is aligned with wider scholarly commentary on the treatment of sexual violence under domestic English and European legal systems generally before the twentieth century, and the low rate of convictions despite a clear acceptance of its criminality. As Dean noted in his study of pre-modern Western criminal law, 'of all the crimes perpetrated against women, rape stands out for the apparent ineffectiveness of the law'.[537] Similarly, Simpson writes with regard to English common law at the time that 'the source of many of the victims' problems was the considerable variance between what the courts were obligated to do and what they actually did'.[538] As previously noted in this chapter, these enforceability issues are interconnected with wider issues surrounding the limitations of colonial records about non-English victims of atrocities.[539]

Nonetheless, while it is clear that enforcement was always highly dependent on the will of the superior commanders on campaign, it is also apparent from the information before us that a history of customary precedence was

536 Ibid 172.

537 Trevor Dean, *Crime in Medieval Europe 1200–1550* (Routledge, 2001) 32. See also Bill McCarthy and Rosemary Gartner (eds), *The Oxford Handbook of Gender, Sex, and Crime* (Oxford University Press, 2014) 211; Marisa Silvestri and Chris Crowther-Dowey, *Gender and Crime: A Human Rights Approach* (SAGE, 2016) 61.

538 See Anthony Simpson, *Masculinity and Control: The Prosecution of Sex Offenses in Eighteenth-Century London* (New York University Press, 1984) 204). See also Bill McCarthy and Rosemary Gartner (eds), *The Oxford Handbook of Gender, Sex, and Crime* (Oxford University Press, 2014) 211.

539 See further Shohei Sato, '"Operation Legacy": Britain's Destruction and Concealment of Colonial Records Worldwide' (2017) 45(4) *Journal of Imperial and Commonwealth History* 697, 697. See also Riley Linebaugh, 'Colonial Fragility: British Embarrassment and the So-Called "Migrated Archives"'(2022) 50(4) *Journal of Imperial and Commonwealth History* 729, 734, 737; Tim Livsey, 'Open Secrets: The British "Migrated Archives", Colonial History, and Postcolonial History' (2022) 93(1) *History Workshop Journal* 95, 97, citing ML McCaul, *Destruction of Records in the Federation of Malaya* (Report, TNA DO186/17, 9 September 1957); Mandy Banton, 'Destroy? "Migrate"? Conceal? British Strategies for the Disposal of Sensitive Records of Colonial Administrations at Independence' (2012) 40(2) *Journal of Imperial and Commonwealth History* 317, 327, citing AM Mackintosh, *Disposal of Archives of Former Governor-General of the Malayan Union, 1958–59* (Report, TNA CO 1030/691, 29 December 1958).

developing by the late nineteenth-century for officers who did seek to proscript sexual violence committed by Imperial military personnel — and that there was no such blanket exclusion for sexual violence committed against alien 'Others' in pre-Hague external conflicts throughout the British Empire such as the early Australian Frontier Wars (1788–1898). Accordingly, the information so far seems to point to Imperial commanders likely taking the view that this prohibition was crystallised before the 1899 (first) *Hague Convention.*

CHAPTER 5

Prohibition on Perfidy

Perfidy relates to the idea of acting in bad faith relative to the rules of the law of armed conflict.[540] It must be recognised that this involves a broad category of wartime conduct, including issues such as breaches of oath (such as to give safe conduct); the misuse of emblems or protections; as well as the use of prohibited weapons such as poisons and assassinations. The inclusion in this category of other conduct (such as the use of torture) is arguably more contentious when we consider the extent to which States continue to avoid enforcing prohibitions against them today. On the other end of the spectrum are the acceptable, if not merely devious conduct, such as ambushes and other ruses of warfare.[541]

Despite attempts by scholars in the past few centuries to cast the history of laws of armed conflict as a recent development,[542] there is clear evidence that 'attempts to regulate war are as old as war itself'.[543] In the context of perfidious context, it is clear that attempts to prohibit its use have been undertaken since antiquity. The Hellenes (otherwise known as the ancient Greeks), for instance, viewed negotiated truces as sacrosanct and came down harshly on any polities who violated this custom.[544] Indeed, abiding by the rules of the laws of war (as they have been negotiated in each culture) is arguably one of the most basic, cardinal principles of the laws of war across time and space.[545]

---

540 Byron D Greene, 'Bridging the Gap that Exists for War Crimes of Perfidy' [2010] (August) *The Army Lawyer* 45, 49. See also Mike Madden, 'Of Wolves and Sheep: A Purposive Analysis of Perfidy Prohibitions in International Humanitarian Law' (2012) 17(3) *Journal of Conflict & Security Law* 439, 440–4.

541 For a good explanation of the difference, see Yuval Noah Harari, *Special Operations in the Age of Chivalry, 1100-1550* (Boydell & Brewer, 2007).

542 See, eg, Lassa FL Oppenheim, *Disputes, War and Neutrality* (Longmans, Green and Co, 5th ed, 1935) vol 2, 193–4.

543 Chris af Jochnick and Roger Normand, 'The Legitimation of Violence: A Critical History of the Laws of War' (1994) 35(1) *Harvard International Law Journal* 49, 55. See also Gregory P Noone, Derek M Mills, and Philip E Angeli, 'Humanitarian Restraints in Early Modern Warfare: Law of Armed Conflict from Antiquity to the Great War', in Damien Rogers (ed), *Human Rights in War* (Springer, 2022) 61, 64.

544 Cian O'Driscoll, 'Rewriting the Just War Tradition: Just War in Classical Greek Political Thought and Practice' (2015) 15 *International Studies Quarterly* 1, 5.

545 Samuel White, 'War Without Limits: How Sharp War Theory is a Historical Anomaly' (n 263).

 | DOI:10.1163/9789004515987_007

According to LC Green, these emerging prohibitions included restrictions on the use of certain 'treacherous weapons' such as poison — the latter of which the classical poet Homer famously declared to be worthy of divine wrath.[546] Past contraventions of these restrictions by belligerents, as per Bederman, were often cited as grounds for conflicts during this time period.[547]

As always however, the degree to which these prohibitions were enforced during times of war is questionable and not exactly a popular subject for detailed discourse in past commentary. As covered in Chapter 1, the worldview of the Ancient Greeks, in particular, relied upon a distinction between 'civilised' and 'barbaric' peoples that only extended these robust protections under the laws of war to societies who fell under the former category.[548] Enemies whose language, religion, and culture might denote them as being of non-Hellenic extraction would instead be considered barbaric, and would find the Ancient Greeks able and willing to abandon their customary restrictions when waging war upon them.[549] This distinction would ultimately be inherited by the Romans, whose practice of *jus gentium* unilaterally excluded non-Romans from wartime protections.[550] Commentators such as O'Driscoll have conflated this distinction with the modern-day debates over whether protections under the laws of armed conflict are capable of extended to terrorists who refuse to reciprocate them.[551]

It does not appear as if this dynamic changed much throughout the Middle Ages. It is accepted among academics, for instance, that disguises were commonly used by both Christian and Muslim armies against eachother throughout the Crusades.[552] More broadly, as emphasised by Robert Finucane,[553] any customary rules against treachery or perfidy relating to uniforms were clearly not practiced during these early transcontinental wars where both sides routinely attempted to dress in the other side's clothing 'and arms to get closer' to

546 LC Green, 'Cicero and Clausewitz or Quincy Wright: The Interplay of Law and War' (1999) 47(3–4) *Chitty's Law Journal and Family Law Review* 37, 41.

547 David Bederman, *International Law in Antiquity*, Cambridge University Press, 2001) 250.

548 Cian O'Driscoll, 'Rewriting the Just War Tradition: Just War in Classical Greek Political Thought and Practice' (2015) 15 *International Studies Quarterly* 1, 5.

549 Ibid, citing Plato, *The Republic*, tr Desmond Lee (Penguin, 1987) 196–9.

550 See, eg, ABM Mafizul Islam Patwari, Principles of International Humanitarian Law: An Oriental Perspective (Asiatic Society of Bangladesh, 1994) 19.

551 Cian O'Driscoll, 'Rewriting the Just War Tradition: Just War in Classical Greek Political Thought and Practice' (2015) 15 *International Studies Quarterly* 1, 5. See also Mark Osiel, *The End of Reciprocity: Terror, Torture, and the Law on Terror* (Cambridge University Press, 2009) 1–7.

552 Ronald C Finucane, *Soldiers of the Faith: Crusaders and Moslems at War* (n 461) 86–8.

553 Ibid.

their camps. By its nature, the use of disguises in the Crusades were therefore not perfidious; as opposed to breaches of the law of ransom,[554] or breaking parole[555] — which, while obviously not uniformly enforced during this time period, were at least discussed in contemporary commentary.[556]

As noted in the chapter on summary executions, medieval ransom law arose from a desire to maximise income on the battlefield. It follows then that the giving and actioning of an oath of ransom was particularly important. Although an oath of ransom was given on the battlefield, it was still a binding contract. Yet, for surety, captors would often require a solemn deed or charter, in writing, which promised three key undertakings: to be a good and loyal vassal; that the captive renounced any right to dispute the title to ransom; and finally invoked 'savage anathemas' if he failed his obligations.[557] A capital sum would be fixed, and the terms and place at which it was to be paid — an example being that if the ransom was not paid in five weeks, it would be doubled.[558]

Payment of a ransom could require the individual to leave his captor to go collect the ransom; thus, a knight would be *en parole*. This was legally dangerous, as 'it is arguable that a captive who is released by the enemy is not bound to return unless it is proved that he has agreed otherwise'.[559] The only legal way, absent an act that constituted *delicutm turpis quaestus*, that a captee could be released was by the individual captor; not his lord, nor his sovereign, but the captor. Thus, when Henry V made it a condition of the surrender of Meaux in 1422 that the garrison should free their prisoners, each captor who was present was required to quote his faith to each of his individual prisoners.[560] Those who were not present were required to travel to free them.[561] There would appear select occasions that when the captor himself was a captive, it could be a condition of his freedom that he would acquit his captive — 'you free my

554 Samuel White, 'The Late Middle Ages' (n 9) 101–26.

555 Ibid.

556 See, eg: AJ Forey, 'The Military Orders and the Ransoming of Captives from Islam (Twelfth to Early Fourteenth Centuries)' (1991) 33 *Studia Monastica* 259–79; Yaacov Lev, 'Prisoners of War During the Fatimid-Ayyubid Wars with the Crusaders' in Michael Gervers and James M. Powell (eds), *Tolerance and Intolerance: Social Conflict in the Age of the Crusades*, ed. (Syracuse, 2001), 11–27.

557 Maurice Keen, *The Laws of War in the Late Middle Ages* (n 8) 168.

558 Treaty Roll for 1366, PRO C76/49, m 15.

559 Baldus, *Comment in Decretal*, Lib 1, Tit 3, cap 25.

560 Thomas Rymer, *Foedera* 4:4: 65.

561 Ibid.

friend, I will free you'.[562] This legal obligation was so absolute that once a man gave his faith to his captor, not even rescue could free him.

Because the price demanded for a ransom was almost nearly always excessive, sometimes a knight could not afford to pay his ransom. In lieu, a captor could require the captive to perform services for him. This easily leads into a discussion of the prohibition of a breach of fealty. The law of ransom could, as noted previously, require an individual to provide service to their captor. This, as one academic has noted, was a dangerous custom that had dangerous results.[563]

A knight did not fight as the representative of a nation-state, but rather for his liege lord, to whom he owed an indefeasible duty of loyalty. Oaths of allegiances were consummated in two kinds of instruments: statues of orders of chivalry and congregations of knights; and contracts of service.[564] The nuances of fealty to one's lord were complicated and difficult to trace, superseding regionalism, religion and kinship. Count William of Hainault's strange predicament in 1339 was not uncommon; whilst he was content to fight Philip VI on Imperial territory, if such attacks were to occur on French territory, he would be obliged to cross the lines and defend Philip VI, as he was a vassal of the French King for his own lands held in France.[565] There could be clashes because the land a lord held feudally belonged to more than one superior; or because two lords claimed the same allegiance from him; or because there was an overlapping conflict of allegiances.[566]

Contemporary sources at the time questioned how the law of ransom interrelated and connected with the concept of fealty. In terms of strict law, a man could not have taken his brother-in-arms a prisoner.[567] Some argued that the law of ransom, as the *lex specialis,* could theoretically override fealty.[568] Others yet argued that the fealty could not ever be overridden, and that a request within the law of ransom for a captive to breach fealty would necessarily negate any ransom owed by virtue of *delicutm turpis quaestus*. As noted above, there was always a lot of room for doubt about the priority of obligations, and one example will substitute for all in attempting to navigate this esoteric maze

562 See *First English Life of King Henry V*, (ed Charles Kingsford, 1911) 171.
563 Maurice Keen, *The Laws of War in the Late Middle Ages* (n 8) 161.
564 Ibid.
565 Clifford J Rogers, *War: Cruel and Sharp: English Strategy under Edward III, 1327–1360* (Boydell Press, 2000) 165.
566 Maurice Keen, *The Laws of War in the Late Middle Ages* (n 8) 87.
567 Bartholomew of Saliceto, *Super VIII, Cod,* Tit 51, 1.2.
568 Maurice Keen, *The Laws of War in the Late Middle Ages* (n 8) 163.

of uncertainties. When Guillaume de Bruyn was charged in 1389 with treason — because he as a French subject had ridden with the King's enemy Geoffroy Tête-Noire — he replied that he had made merely made an oath to serve, provoked by his inability to pay his own ransom after being captured.[569] He was hanged for his offences. Often, the correct answer to feudal complexities was simply who was the victor. Breach of oath was one of the critical crimes on the medieval battlefield, and ensuring that 'the great principle' of the laws of war continued to be followed was particularly important.

While the landmark international ecumenical councils established by the early Catholic Church, such as the Second Council of the Lateran organised by Pope Innocent II in 1139, had attempted to 'enforce weapons symmetry' by prohibiting the use of poisons and crossbows against fellow Christians,[570] they had also clearly outlined their legal use against heretics and 'infidels'.[571]

By the late sixteenth-century however, the first instances of direct commentary regarding perfidy began to appear among the pioneer European international law scholars. Thomas C Wingfield suggests that Balthazar Ayala, an influential Dutch military lawyer during the Eighty Years' War (1566–1648) fought between England and the Netherlands against the Spanish, was potentially the first to propose that there was a prevailing obligation to not commit treachery.[572] In doing so, Ayala had 'looked beyond the existence of an actual contract or agreement between the two parties'.[573] Instead, he proposed that impermissible 'treachery could arise [even] in the absence of a specific understanding between the aggressor and the defender'.[574] As further emphasised by Michael Schmitt, Ayala's commentary distinguished permissible *trickery* and impermissible *frauds and snares*, which he argued as analogous to the modern-day conception of ruses and perfidy.[575]

569 Ibid.

570 Rain Livoja, 'Chivalry Without a Horse: Military Honour and the Modern Law of Armed Conflict (2012) 15 *Estonian Journal of Military Studies* 75, 85–6. See generally Robert L O'Connell, *Of Arms and Men: A History of War, Weapons, and Aggression* (Oxford University Press, 1989).

571 ABM Mafizul Islam Patwari, *Principles of International Humanitarian Law: An Oriental Perspective* (n 550) 22.

572 Thomas C Wingfield, 'Chivalry in the Use of Force' (2001) 32(2) *University of Toledo Law Review* 111, 131–3.

573 Ibid 131.

574 Ibid, citing Balthazar Ayala, *Three Books on The Law of War and The Duties Connected with War and Military Discipline,* tr John P Bate (Carnegie Institution, 1912) 84.

575 Wingfield (n 572) 131, citing Michael N Schmitt, 'State-Sponsored Assassination in International and Domestic Law' (1992) 17(2) *Yale Journal of International Law* 609, 614. See also Ayala (n 574) 84.

As further emphasised by Michael Schmitt, '[t]he key for Ayala was a distinction between permissible *trickery*, similar to our understanding ruses of war, and impermissible *frauds and snares*, which we would equate to perfidy. The distinction between the two [were] to be made in the mind of the reasonable defender'.[576]

This prospective prohibition was later taken up and discussed by the Italian-English canon law jurist Gentili, who defined illegal perfidy in 1598 as constituting impermissible treacherous behaviour.[577] Gentili went on to cite the use of poison as a specific example of conduct which fell within this unlawful category.[578] According to Kyle Walker, the justification for these restrictions appears to have been 'rooted in whether they met the standard considered appropriate to a sovereign'.[579]

Particularly relevant to the development of English legal norms due to his role as an influential professor at Oxford,[580] Gentili also went on to classify the assassination of foreign leaders as illegal and treacherous.[581] In doing so, he declined to agree with the alternative view of the Tudor Lord Chancellor Sir Thomas More, who instead advanced that assassination was permissible to avoid the consequences of direct warfare.[582] As per Walker, Gentili's counter-argument was that the 'successor to the slain would be frenzied by the illegitimate means of killing thereby perpetuating the conflict'.[583]

As interpreted by Wingfield, who again seems to be heavily influenced by Michael Schmitt's writings on the topic,[584] Gentili's expansion of the notion of perfidy included not merely those who committed illegal treachery, but also sought to punish those who motivated or paid for violations of bonds of

576 Ibid, citing Michael N Schmitt, 'State-Sponsored Assassination in International and Domestic Law' (n 575) 614. See also Ayala (n 574) 84.

577 See generally Gentili (n 399).

578 See Kyle Walker (n 259) 127, 140, citing Gentili (n 399) 156.

579 Kyle Walker (n 259) 140.

580 Andres Wagner, 'Alberico Gentili: Sovereignty, Natural Law, and the System of Roman Civil Law' (Kyle Walker (n 259)) 104–6.

581 Kyle Walker (n 259) 138, citing Gentili (n 399) 169. See also: Shannon Brincat, 'The Legal Philosophy of Internationally Assisted Tyrannicide' (2009) 34(1) *Australian Journal of Legal Philosophy* 151, 161; Michael N Schmitt, 'State-Sponsored Assassination in International and Domestic Law' (n 575) 614.

582 Shannon Brincat, 'The Legal Philosophy of Internationally Assisted Tyrannicide' (n 581) 160, citing Sir Thomas Moore, *Utopia* (1516) ch 8. See also Kyle Walker (n 259) 167.

583 Kyle Walker (n 259) 138, citing Gentili (n 399) 167.

584 Wingfield (n 572) 132, citing Michael N Schmitt, 'State-Sponsored Assassination in International and Domestic Law' (n 575) 615.

loyalty and fealty.[585] Therefore, 'under Gentili's model, it would be permissible for a warrior to stealthily make his way into an enemy's camp to kill him as he sleeps, but not to hire one of the enemy's own soldiers to perform the same act'.[586] Similar to Ayala's earlier view, it has been suggested that Gentili also did not require a prohibition on perfidy to be included in any binding agreements between combatants for the custom to be applicable.[587]

With regards to his categorisation of poison as forbidden, Walker points to two reasons for why Gentili considered its usage as inappropriate for conventional wars. Firstly, he describes how it contravenes Gentili's conception of contemporary warfare as 'a contest of arms'[588] and, secondly, because of poison's furtive nature.[589] In particular, Gentili considered '[s]uch conduct [as] worthy of brigands and not of princes'.[590] To illustrate this point, comparisons were made between the use of poison with 'incantations and magic', which were similarly described as unlawful for its clandestine and ungodly character.[591]

As per Rain Livoja, it is also worthy to notes that 'the special contempt for poisoning was not limited to the battlefield' but also extended to mid-16th century domestic English criminal law.[592] Parallel to other crimes such as high treason and heresy, which also resulted in execution through methods of torture for those found guilty, poisoners at this time were 'boiled to death'.[593]

Noting the wide extension of Gentili's concept of treachery however, it is unlikely that his contemporaries agreed with him on the exact scope of the prohibition. In particular, other scholars such as the eminent sixteenth-century Spanish canon law jurist Francisco de Vitoria constrained the extent of the custom to merely the killing of commanders or sovereigns and other high-ranking civilians. Well known for being a legal advisor to leaders from all across Western Europe, Vitoria wrote in his commentaries that the poisoning of essential

585 Wingfield (n 572) 132, citing Gentili (n 399) 168.

586 Ibid.

587 Michael N Schmitt, 'State-Sponsored Assassination in International and Domestic Law' (n 575) 614–15.

588 Kyle Walker (n 259) 140, citing Gentili (n 399) 155.

589 Kyle Walker (n 259) 140, citing Gentili (n 399) 156. See also Leslie C Green, *The Contemporary Law of Armed Conflict* (Manchester University Press, 3rd ed, 2018) 142.

590 Kyle Walker (n 259) 155–6.

591 Ibid 160–1.

592 Rain Livoja, 'Chivalry Without a Horse: Military Honour and the Modern Law of Armed Conflict (2012) 15 *Estonian Journal of Military Studies* 75, 85, citing Sir James Fitzjames Stephen, 1883. *A History of the Criminal Law of England* (Macmillan, 1883) vol 1, 476. See also Sir James Fitzjames Stephen, 1883. *A History of the Criminal Law of England* (Macmillan, 1883) vol 3, 44–5.

593 Ibid, citing.

public resources such as 'water supplies' was justifiable on the basis of military necessity:

> [S]ince the enemy rely upon the resources of its people to sustain an unjust war ... their strength is therefore weakened if their subjects are plundered.[594]

Grotius, who belonged to the generation just after Gentili and de Vitoria, also clearly accepted and applied this notion of illegal treachery albeit without noting whether he specifically agreed with Gentili's wider scope.[595] In 1625, Grotius contended that

> a distinction must be made between assassins who violate an express or tacit obligation of good faith, as subjects resorting to violence against a king, vassals against a lord, soldiers against him whom they serve, those also who have been received as suppliants or strangers or deserters, against those who have received them; and such as are held by no bond of good faith.[596]

An element of pragmatism (rather than purely humanitarian concerns) in Grotius' approach may also be seen through his statement in his magnus opus *De Jure Belli ac Pacis Libri Tres* that a prohibition against the use of poison 'originated with kings, whose lives are better defended by arms than those of other men, but are less safe from poison'.[597]

When we look towards English conduct during their seventeenth century colonisation of the Americas, we can observe a mixed reception to this emerging prohibition, notably at a time when the preclusive principle of excluding non-Western peoples from international legal norms was also becoming influential. Particular regard should be given to the assassination of the imprisoned Powhatan Confederacy leader Opechancanough in 1646 by English settlers of

594 Francisco de Vitoria, *Political Writings* (n 300) 317.

595 Bert Brandenburg, 'The Legality of Assassination as an Aspect of Foreign Policy' (1987) 27(3) *Virginia Journal of International Law* 655, 657–8.

596 Leon Friedman (ed), *The Law of War, A Documentary History* (Random House, 1972) vol 1, 38–9, quoting Hugo Grotius, *The Law of War and Peace* (1625); See also Michael N Schmitt, 'State-Sponsored Assassination in International and Domestic Law' (n 575) 615.

597 Rain Livoja, 'Chivalry Without a Horse: Military Honour and the Modern Law of Armed Conflict (n 570) 75, 85, citing Gentili, Alberico, *De Jure Belli Libri Tres* [Three Books on the Law of War] (Clarendon Press, 1925) vol 3, 652.

the Jamestown colony in Virginia, an incident which led to the end of the Third Anglo-Powhatan War (1644–46).[598] Not only was the killer unpunished for this; remarkably, this was after a previous failed attempt had been made to poison Opechancanough during a peace meeting to end the Second Anglo-Powhatan War (1622–6).

As narrated by Kupperman, 'the English brought with them a large barrel of white wine containing poison' which had been prepared by John Pott (a physician at the time, and later the 5th Crown Governor of Virginia from 1629–30).[599] Supposedly, after the English first drank a separate barrel of wine themselves as a ruse, '[a]round two hundred Indians were poisoned, and the colonists fired upon those who survived the poisoning'.[600]

Back in England the poisoning incident was denounced by the Earl Warwick, notable for being one of the leading investors in North American ventures, who wrote to the Viscount Conway (principal Secretary of State from 1623–28) to have Dr Pott temporarily dismissed from the Virginian Governor's Council for being a 'poysoner of the savages'.[601] However, as per Horton, the investigation was inconclusive and Pott was ultimately restored to his position in 1626 — two decades before the eventual assassination of Opechancanough.[602]

More than a hundred years later, de Vattel went on to directly consider the prohibition on perfidy in 1758. It should be highlighted that the English translation of his work was published in 1760, and as emphasised by Graves, de Vattel's interpretations on natural law were stunningly popular in the English-speaking world. This to the extent that they were even cited by British frontier commanders in later colonial wars such as the War of 1812 (1812–15) in North America.[603] Most notably, and largely in parallel with the prior writings of Ayala, Gentili and Grotius,[604] de Vattel identified the treacherous breaking of

598 Lars C Adams, '"The Battle of Weyanoke Creek": A Story of the Third Anglo-Powhatan War in Early Carolina' (2013) 6 *Native South* 170, 182.

599 Karen Ordahl Kupperman, *The Jamestown Project* (Harvard University Press, 2007) 316.

600 Ibid.

601 Letter from Robert Rich (Earl of Warwick) to Edward Conway (Secretary of State), 9 August 1624, quoted in *Calendar of State Papers* (HMSO, 1830) vol 1, 69. See also.

602 Charles E Horton and Charles E Horton Jr, 'Dr. John Pott: America's First Physician-Governor and Revolutionary' (1983) 59(7) *Bulletin of the New York Academy of Medicine* 678, 679.

603 See generally Donald E Graves, '"Every Horror was Committed with Impunity ... and Not a Man was Punished!" Reflections on British Military Law and the Atrocities at Hampton' (n 142).

604 Bert Brandenburg, 'The Legality of Assassination as an Aspect of Foreign Policy' (n 595) 657–9.

a bond of fealty or other forms of sacred trust as the *shameful* element that separates unlawful assassination and perfidy from lawful killing during wars:

> But in order to reason clearly on this question we must first of all avoid confusing assassination with surprises, which are, doubtless, perfectly lawful in warfare. When a resolute soldier steals into the enemy's camp at night and makes his way to the general's tent and stabs him, he does nothing contrary to the natural laws of war, nothing, indeed, but what is commendable in a just and necessary war.
>
> Hence I mean by assassination a murder committed by means of treachery, whether the deed be done by persons who are subjects of him who is assassinated, or of his sovereign, and who are therefore traitors, or whether it be done by any other agent who makes his way in as a suppliant or refugee, or as a turncoat, or even as an alien; and I assert that the deed is a shameful and revolting one, both on the part of him who executes and of him who commands it.[605]

It is also worth considering British practice surrounding the allegedly deliberate use of disease in colonial wars against Native American peoples, as an instance of biological warfare by trickery. Scholars such as Elizabeth A Fenn and Erica Charters have particularly considered the conduct of Lord Amherst (Commander-in-Chief of the British Army in North America from 1758–63) at the siege of Fort Pitt in 1763 during the Pontiac's War that erupted that year against a confederation of Native American communities. As per an instructing letter from Lord Amherst to his subordinate Colonel Henry Bouquet,[606] the British Army was recorded to have distributed smallpox-infested blankets to Ohio Country First Nations emissaries sent by the besieging army:

> To Sundries got to Replace in kind those which were taken from people in the Hospital to Convey the Smallpox to the Indians Viz:
> 2 Blankets ....@ 20/ £2" 0" 0

605 Ibid.

606 See Letter from Lord Jeffery Amherst (Commander-in-Chief of the British Army in North America from 1758–63) to Colonel Henry Bouquet, 7 July 1763, as cited in Elizabeth A Fenn, 'Biological Warfare in Eighteenth-Century North America: Beyond Jeffrey Amherst' (2000) 68(4) *Journal of American History* 1552, 1555–6. See also Philip Ranlet, 'The British, the Indians, and Smallpox: What Actually Happened at Fort Pitt in 1763?', (2000) 67(3) *Pennsylvania History* 427, 427–41.

Silk Handkerchef........ 10/
& 1 linnen do:..........3/60" 0" 13" 6[607]

As Charters explains, British commanders such as Lord Amherst and Colonel Bouquet clearly did not view their conduct as falling within the category of illegal treachery. Instead, it has been argued that they were justified as reprisals on the basis that 'the conventions of regular warfare had been contravened by Amerindian [Native American] attacks on civilians or non-combatants' during the Siege at Fort Pitt. The report of Major Henry Gladwin, for instance, which appeared in correspondence between Amherst and Bouquet directly before the incident, reported that the besieging forces had 'murdered some of our people' despite claiming a 'friendly visit'.[608] Taken together, this seems to suggest that the commanders had regard to the general contravention against perfidious wartime conduct (or at least the moral dimension of it) but also applied a wide scope to an exception for reprisal based on military necessity.

As the influence of the preclusive position receded during the nineteenth century and later High Imperial period, international lawyers hoping to codify restrictions on wartime conduct increasingly considered whether there was a customary prohibition against perfidy. Perhaps the most compelling evidence we have on the nascent nature of this custom throughout the late nineteenth-century was its inclusion in the 1863 American *Lieber Code*, which was in turn expressly referenced in the pre-*Hague* 1899 *Manual of Military Law* published by the British War Office and has also been said to largely align with customs and laws of warfare at this time.[609] While the *Code* did not exactly offer a clear definition for what constituted illegal treachery or perfidy, several of its articles mention obligations for parties to desist from committing perfidious behaviour against enemy combatants during warfare. Article 16 in particular,

607 See Fenn (n 606), quoting the invoice from Levy, Trent and Company: Account against the Crown, 13 August 1736 as it appears in Sylvester K Stevens and Donald H Kent, *Papers of Henry Bouquet* (Pennsylvania Historical Commission, Series 21634, 1940).

608 See Letter from Lord Jeffery Amherst (Commander-in-Chief of the British Army in North America from 1758–63) to Colonel Henry Bouquet, 23 June 1763, as discussed in Erica Charters, 'Military Medicine and the Ethics of War: British Colonial Warfare during the Seven Years War (1756–63)' (2010) 27(2) *Criminal Behaviour and Mental Health* 274, 290. See also Peter Silver, *Our Savage Neighbors: How Indian War Transformed Early America* (WW Norton, 2008).

609 See Lia Brazil, 'British War Office Manuals and International Law, 1899–1907' in Edward Cavanagh, *Empire and Legal Thought: Ideas and Institutions from Antiquity to Modernity*

distinguishes between permissible ruses and prohibited perfidy by stating that 'Military necessity … admits of deception, but disclaims acts of perfidy'.

More broadly, art 148 admonished the use of assassination in warfare among '[c]ivilized nations':

> [t]he sternest retaliation should follow the murder committed in consequence of such proclamation, made by whatever authority. Civilized nations look with horror upon offers of rewards for the assassination of enemies as relapses into barbarism.[610]

At the same time, art 101 of the *Code* also more specifically noted the hostile position of the 'common law of warfare' against unhonourable conduct and the liability of instigators to having capital punishment enforced against them and their soldiers:

> While deception in war is admitted as a just and necessary means of hostility, and is consistent with honourable warfare, the common law of war allows even capital punishment for clandestine or treacherous attempts to injure an enemy, because they are so dangerous, and it is difficult to guard against them.[611]

However, Sean Watts notes both the limitations and nuances of this article when taking into account the lack of guidance offered on what specifically constitutes 'clandestine or treacherous attempts'.[612] Evidently, the operation of arts 16 and 101 was likely not calculated to forbid all aspects of concealed operations. Rather, it potentially gave a significant discretion to commanders, in line with the wartime purpose of the *Code*. At the same time, the fact that art 101 explicitly covers 'attempts to injure an enemy' as opposed to merely killings suggests a potentially broader scope than even the earlier position offered by Gentili. Regardless of these uncertainties however, its codification of the custom still attests to the growing acceptance of the custom at the time among Western nations.

(Brill, 2020) 548, 563, citing *Manual of Military Law* (n 533) 285. See also Schindler and Toman (n 533) 3–23.

610 *Lieber Code* art 148.

611 *Lieber Code* art 101.

612 Sean Watts, 'Law-of-War Perfidy' (2014) 219(1) *Military Law Review* 106, 126.

It may also be useful to refer to the American General and international lawyer Henry Halleck's (1815–72) contemporaneous writings on perfidy. Particularly notable given his post-war status as an authoritative source on international law, he was known for extensively considering treatises from other jurisdictions when planning his own wartime operations.

> Whenever we have expressly or tacitly engaged to speak the truth to an enemy, it would be perfidy in use to deceive his confidence in our sincerity. But if the occasion imposes upon us no moral obligation to disclose to him the truth, we are perfectly justifiable in leading him into error, either by words or actions ... it is the breach of good faith, express[ed] or implied, which constitutes the perfidy, and gives to such acts the character of lies.[613]

More than a decade after the *Lieber Code*, the 1874 *Brussels Declaration* organised by Tsar Alexander II of Russia prohibited under its art 13(b) the 'murder by treachery of individuals belonging to the hostile nation or army'.[614] Although ultimately not ratified by other leading European powers,[615] including Britain, its conclusions would be carried over into the more comprehensive 1880 *Oxford Manual of the Laws and Customs of War* ('*Oxford Manual*').[616]

While also of a non-binding nature, the draft commentaries supplied by the *Oxford Manual* would later become a persuasive influence on the 1899 and 1907 *Hague Conventions*.[617] A general principle against perfidious wartime conduct is set out in art 4 of the *Oxford Manual*, which notes that '[t]he laws of war do not recognize in belligerents an unlimited liberty as to the means of

613 Henry Wager Halleck, *Halleck's International Law, or, Rules Regulating the Intercourse of States in Peace and War* (Kegan Paul, Trench, Trübner, 1893) 562.

614 See *Project of an International Declaration Concerning the Laws and Customs of War*, opened for signature 27 July 1874, (1907) 1(2) *American Journal of International* Law 96 (entered into force 27 August 1874). See also: Schindler and Toman (n 533) 24; Greene, 'Bridging the Gap that Exists for War Crimes of Perfidy' (n 540) 46.

615 Tuba Inal (n 80) 169.

616 Institute of International Law, *The Laws of War on Land* (1880). See Emily Crawford, *Non-Binding Norms in International Humanitarian Law: Efficacy, Legitimacy, and Legality* (Oxford University Press, 2021) 40–9. See also Schindler and Toman (n 533) 29–40.

617 See Michael H Hoffman, 'Can Military Manuals Improve the Law of War: The San Remo Manual on the Law of Non-International Armed Conflict Considered in Relation to Historical and Contemporary Trends' (2007) 37 *Israel Yearbook on Human Rights* 241, 244, citing Schindler and Toman (n 533).

injuring the enemy. They are to abstain especially from all needless severity, as well as from all perfidious, unjust, or tyrannical acts'.[618]

Most relevantly, art 8 then outlines that 'the struggle must be honourable' and accordingly prohibits the following:

a) To make use of poison, in any form whatever;
b) To make treacherous attempts upon the life of an enemy; as, for example, by keeping assassins in pay or by feigning to surrender;
c) To attack an enemy while concealing the distinctive signs of an armed force;
d) To make improper use of the national flag, military insignia or uniform of the enemy, of the flag of truce and of the protective signs prescribed by the Geneva Convention.[619]

More authoritatively, in the pre-*Hague* 1899 *Manual of Military Law* published by the British War Office and provided to Imperial commanders, the non-binding chapter on 'The Customs of War' noted both assassination and poison as 'forbidden' modes of warfare where they are intended to cause 'unnecessary pain or injury'. Notably, the chapter cited Vattel and Halleck in doing so:

> The poisoning of water or food is a mode of warfare absolutely forbidden, but the turning off the water supply or stopping convoys of food to the enemy is one of the usual methods of reducing him to submission. The use of poisoned weapons and of weapons calculated to produce unnecessary pain or injury is prohibited, on the ground that, as the object of war isc onfined to disabling the enemy, the infliction of any injury beyond that which is required to produce disability is needless cruelty.
>
> Assassination is against the customs of war. Assasination is the murder by treachery of individuals of the hostile forces. The essence of the crime is treachery, as a surprise is always allowable, and a small force may penetrate into the enemy's camp, dispatch the sentinels, and take the general prisoner or kill him without infringing any of the customs of war, or subjecting themselves if taken to be treated otherwise than as prisoners of war. It is the duty of the enemy to be prepared against a military surprise, but not to guard himself against the treacherous attacks of individuals introduced in disguise into his camp.[620]

618 Institute of International Law, *The Laws of War on Land* (1880), as reproduced in Rain Livoja, (n 570) 75, 83–4.

619 Ibid 84.

620 *Manual of Military Law* (n 533) 286–7, citing de Vattel, *The Law of Nations* (n 143) 183–9 and Henry Wager Halleck, *Halleck's International Law* (1878) vol ii, 22–4.

Again however, while the aforementioned evidence seems to overwhelmingly point to the prominent featuring of this customary prohibition in late nineteenth-century inter-European conflicts,[621] the uncertainty lies in whether it was actually extended to Imperial wars against non-Western peoples. The primary obstacle here are the racialised and exclusionary writings of British commanders such as Callwell, who has been popularly regarded as 'occupying an interesting position in the history of savage warfare in that he reflected contemporary military practice and experience as much as he shaped it'.[622] As emphasised earlier, Callwell had alleged that uncivilised non-Western peoples lacked targetable formal military institutions, and that accordingly civilised armies were 'forced to resort to ... village burning and [other] operations ... which the laws of warfare do not sanction'.[623] The test of military necessity appeared to be Callwell's justification for permitting European armies to stray from traditional norms of warfare when taking part in small frontier conflicts. He argued that 'refractory subjects of the ruling power must all be chastised and subdued,' as 'part and parcel of the system of overawing and terrifying the enemy, which is the great object always to be kept in view'.[624] As part of his recommendations, Callwell primarily cited the late nineteenth century Plains campaigns conducted against Native American tribes by the US army, 'which included the indiscriminate massacring of men, women and children at places like Sand Creek (1864), Washita (1868), and later Wounded Knee (1890)'.[625]

Gordon also notes how British Imperial conduct in the Perak War (1875–6), especially following an initial Malay victory,[626] eventually shifted to 'methods of burning and blockading'[627] — which draws similarities to the

621 Rain Livoja (n 570) 75, 84.

622 Kim A Wagner (n 153) 223.

623 Daniel Whittingham, *Charles E Callwell and the British Way in Warfare* (n 246) 30, citing Charles Edward Callwell, *Small Wars: Their Principles and Practice* (n 177).

624 Charles Edward Callwell, *Small Wars: Their Principles and Practice* (n 177) 41, 80.

625 Kim A Wagner (n 153) 222.

626 Michelle Gordon, *Extreme Violence and the 'British Way': Colonial Warfare in Perak, Sierra Leone and Sudan* (n 97) 48, citing JFA McNair, *Perak and the Malays* (Tinsley Brothers, 1878) 377. See also: CD Cowan, *Nineteenth Century Malaya: The Origins of British Political Control* (Oxford University Press, 1961) 234; 'The Perak Expedition', *The Straits Times* (Singapore, 20 November 1875) 2 <https://eresources.nlb.gov.sg/newspapers/digitised/article/straitstimes18751120-1.2.12>; 'Untitled', *The Straits Times* (Singapore, 27 November 1875) 3 <https://eresources.nlb.gov.sg/newspapers/digitised/article/straitstimes18751127-1.2.21>.

627 Michelle Gordon, *Extreme Violence and the 'British Way': Colonial Warfare in Perak, Sierra Leone and Sudan* (n 97) 61.

previously-described burning practices that Imperial commanders otherwise employed against other non-Western peoples such as the Pashtun tribes at Malakand (1897–8).[628]

However, there were also those who adopted a more expansive view of applying a customary prohibition against perfidy towards non-Western peoples, especially in the case of reprisals against unnecessary Western conduct. Likely reflecting the well-accepted nature of this custom in the public consciousness by this point (as this took place the year before the 1899 first *Hague Convention* was signed), Ernest N Bennett argued that Dervish reprisals against the British in 1898 were legally justified given the unnecessary wartime conduct practised by the British Army during the Anglo-Egyptian conquest of Sudan (1896–9)[629] —a conflict infamous for the use of Dum-Dum bullets by the British despite the efforts of other powers to ban them.[630] In particular, this affair related to accounts of British soldiers killing and neglecting wounded Dervish soldiers who could have been saved. According to Bennett (later elected to Parliament in 1906):[631]

> the actual instances in which our men have been injured by wounded Dervishes are, after all, extremely few in number, and in any case it does not seem fair, because of occasional acts of treachery on the part of individuals, to decree the slaughter of the wounded indiscriminately.[632]

As emphasised by Michelle Gordon,[633] Bennett also notably argued that the past behaviour of British troops in the Sudan was partially accountable for the violent actions of the wounded: 'The wounded Dervish has become dangerous because he fully expects to be killed'.[634] She further points out the clear lack of military necessity associated with the killing and neglecting of the enemy

628 See Winston Churchill, *The Story of the Malakand Field Force: An Episode of Frontier War* (n 252) 272–4. See generally: Helen Bradford, 'Gentlemen and Boers: Afrikaner Nationalism, Gender and Colonial Warfare in the South African War' (n 252) 39; Frank Emery, *Marching Over Africa: Letters from Victorian Soldier* (n 252) 26; Lewis Gann and Peter Duignan, *The Rulers of British Africa, 1870–1914* (n 252) 143–4.

629 Michelle Gordon, 'British Colonial Violence in Perak, Sierra Leone and the Sudan' (n 97) 137, citing Ernest N Bennett, 'After Omdurman' (1899) 75(1) *Contemporary Review* 18, 25.

630 See, eg, Bennett (n 629) 18–35. See also Kim A Wagner (n 153) 227.

631 Matthew Johnson, *Militarism and the British Left, 1902–1914* (Palgrave Macmillan, 2013) 60.

632 Bennett (n 629) 21.

633 Ibid, cited by Michelle Gordon, 'British Colonial Violence in Perak, Sierra Leone and the Sudan' (PhD Thesis, University of London, 2017) 152.

634 Bennett (n 629) 25.

combatants. Of particular relevance here is the contemporary account of the British General Neville Lyttelton, who admitted that 'some of the men thoroughly enjoyed this sort of work:'[635]

> I rode over the battlefield, a grisly sight. I saw two wounded Arabs who had been shot through both thighs and unable to walk. They were propelling themselves along the ground in a sitting position with short sticks and left a conspicuous track in the sand. A day or two later after I came across the two just arriving in our lines, I should say nearly 3 miles from where I had first seen them.[636]

The British government's response to the German Army's killings of the Herero and Nama Peoples also directly engages with this custom. Of particular relevance here was an incident where 'Two of the Herero chiefs ... came to [the] German headquarters [at Ombakaha] for a parley' and were instead 'shot as rebels'. Tragically, the 'murder of the chief of the Budelswartz Hottentots at the end of 1903' has been highlighted as the cause for further uprisings by the Herero and consequently, the 'notorious' violence committed by German soldiers under the command of General Lothar von Trotha (which modern commentators have noted as one of the deadliest colonial-era mass killings).[637]

Notably, the 1918 'Blue Book' published by the British Government as its official commentary on the massacres outlines the exact promise that had been broken. According to the Herero headman Gerard Kamaheke, one of the few survivors of the massacre:

> the German commander had invited [the chieftains] all to come in and make peace; that our lives would all be spared; that we would be allowed to retain our cattle and other possession ... on arrival at Ombakaha ... the Germans opened fire ... and bayoneting the wounded.[638]

635 Edward M Spiers, 'Campaigning under Kitchener' in Edward M Spiers (ed), *Sudan: The Reconquest Reappraised* (Routledge, 1998) 73; See also Michelle Gordon, 'British Colonial Violence in Perak, Sierra Leone and the Sudan' (n 97) 152.

636 Neville Lyttelton, *Eighty Years: Soldiering, Politics, Games* (Hodder & Stoughton, 1927) 195.

637 Gray (n 451) 33.

638 Jeremy Silvester and Jan-Bart Gewald, *Words Cannot Be Found: German Colonial Rule in Namibia* (Brill, 2003), 46.

This government report would go on to describe the massacre as a 'treacherous and most disgraceful piece of business'.[639] As highlighted by Albert Gray, in his capacity as Legal Counsel to the British Colonial Office, the conduct by the German army 'murder[ing] … Herero leaders who came under promises of safe-conduct' was evidence that the former had 'shrank from no acts of treachery or breaches of the laws of war'.[640]

Ultimately, with the current information provided, an application of the practice-oriented approach might suggest that a customary prohibition against perfidious conduct among British commanders was developing by the late nineteenth-century in British Imperial wars against other Western nations (as seen through the 1880 *Oxford Manual*). It is likely too that a prohibition on perfidy was crystalising in frontier conflicts of the Empire, in general principles around keeping oaths, avoiding treacherous behaviour (such as stabbing in the back, etc) in conflicts against non-Western peoples before the first Hague Convention.

639 Ibid.

640 Gray (n 451) 25, 33. See also Frédéric Mégret (n 91) 265, 280.

CHAPTER 6

Prohibition on Slavery

> How then can the House refuse its belief to the multiplied testimonies, before the Privy Council, of the savage treatment of the negroes in the middle passage? Nay, indeed, what need is there of any evidence? The number of deaths speaks for itself, and makes all such inquiry superfluous. As soon as ever I had arrived thus far in my investigation of the slave trade, I confess to you, sir, so enormous, so dreadful, so irremediable did its wickedness appear, that my own mind was completely made up for the abolition. A trade founded in iniquity, and carried on as this was, must be abolished, let the policy be what it might, let the consequences be what they would, I from this time determined that I would never rest till I had effected its abolition.[641]

It would be remiss for an assessment of the laws of war of the late British Empire to ignore an assessment of its approach to slavery, which is particularly curious given its role as a celebrated instrument for the abolition of an institution so crucial to its initial success.

The shift in pre-modern English wartime ordinances towards notions of humanitarian concepts, caused by the influence of jurists such as the Oxford-based Alberico Gentili and Richard Zouche[642] on the emerging military traditions and the training of officers,[643] included a gradual rejection of the enslavement of fellow Christians. Maurice Keen notes the early influence of Thomas Aquinas on this, whose view in the thirteenth century of slavery as an 'unnatural' is particularly meaningful given its longstanding acceptance under Roman law.[644]

641 See William Wilberforth's famous abolition speech of 1789, as extracted in Brycchan Carey, 'William Wilberforce's Sentimental Rhetoric: Parliamentary Reportage and the Abolition Speech of 1789' (2003) 14 *The Age of Johnson: A Scholarly Annual* 298–9.

642 Andres Wagner (n 79) 92, 104–6.

643 John Collins (n 64) 109, citing Francis Grose (n 78) 54.

644 Maurice Keen, *The Laws of War in the Late Middle Ages* (n 8) 12, citing *Digest*, XVI Tit 3, 1. 31.

 | DOI:10.1163/9789004515987_008

The legal status of a medieval prisoner — especially one who was a knight — was complex. Following Roman law, a person taken in a just war became a slave; yet, the rule of *postliminium* — as this Roman law concept was called — did not apply between Christians.[645] Accordingly, the relationship between the captor and the captive was one of *contract*.

This contractual relationship was not unilateral, instead but required certain conduct on behalf of both the captor and the captive. Because a ransom was a valuable asset, a captor was anxious to establish his right incontrovertibly and absolutely, for a ransom could be shared by a co-captor, or a brother-in-arms.[646] It was thereby no surprise to see, in the closing moments of the Battle of Poitiers in 1356, 'the French scattered, and the English running and making prisoners'.[647] From surviving accounts, it truly sounds like a game of tag in the schoolyard.

Yet, it took more than a simple tap to take charge of a captive. To prevent confusion, it was an established custom that to claim a ransom, the captive must offer his right gauntlet; the ransom and contractual obligations were then accepted by the captor by placing his right hand into the captive's gauntlet.[648] The contractual obligation included safe escort to a protected place behind the lines, either personally or in the carriage of an individual who could do so, before returning to the battlefield to take another captive.

Throughout the Age of Commerce, however,[649] an expansion of the slave trade was itself a goal of the early Imperial wars waged in the Americas and Africa. The profitability of this enterprise resulted in the swathe of charters granted to trade companies by the Crown to grow the African Slave Trade in 1618, 1631, and 1662.[650] This was clearly accepted in international law at the time, which explicitly differentiated between the treatment of Christians and non-Christians in warfare.[651]

The sixteenth-century Spanish canon law jurist Francisco de Vitoria (1483–1546) — well known for being a legal advisor to leaders from all across Western

645 Giovanni da Legnano (John of Legnano), *Tractatus De Bello, De Represalis et De Duello*, tr. JL Brierly (Oxford University Press, 1917) ch 9.

646 Maurice Keen, 'Brotherhood-In-Arms' (n 368) 1, 1–17.

647 Chandos Herald, *Le Prince Noir* (Roxburghe Club, HO Coxe ed, 1842), 108.

648 Richard II, *Durham Ordinances*; see further *Black Book of the Admiralty*, vol I, at page 4457.

649 Nordin Hussin, *Trade and Society in the Straits of Melaka: Dutch Melaka and English Penang, 1780–1830* (National University of Singapore Press, 2007) 338.

650 William Black, *The History of Slavery and the Slave Trade* (Franklin, 1858) 107.

651 See Antony Anghie, 'Francisco De Vitoria and the Colonial Origins of International Law' (n 76) 321, 323, citing Alfred Rubin, 'International Law in the Age of Columbus' (n 76) 5, 5–35.

Europe — had for instance argued that the traditional prohibition against the enslavement of women and children only applied to wars between Christians, and accordingly did not govern the conduct of Europeans in the New World:

> And so when a war is at that pass that the indiscriminate spoliation of all enemy-subjects alike and the seizure of all their goods are justifiable, then it is also justifiable to carry all enemy-subjects off into captivity, whether they be guilty or guiltless. And in as much as war with pagans is of this type, seeing that it is perpetual and that they can never make amends for the wrongs and damages they have wrought, it is indubitably lawful to carry off both the children and women of the Saracens into captivity and slavery.[652]

In setting this set out, Vitoria's approach appears parallel to the approach taken in the Papal Bull of 1452 by Pope Nicholas V. As translated by Diana Hayes, Nicholas V had used the occasion of the Bull to permit King Afonso V of Portugal to reduce any non-believer to 'perpetual slavery':

> [F]ull and free permission to invade, search out, capture, and subjugate the Saracens and pagans and any other unbelievers and enemies of Christ wherever they may be, as well as their kingdoms, duchies, counties, principalities, and other property ... and to reduce their persons into perpetual slavery.[653]

By the 1670s however, the acceptance of slavery in the British Empire became less assured following the passage of the *Habeas Corpus Act* (1979) and the increased protections that it afforded to victims of slavery who lived within English borders. As per Helen Nutting, the *Habeas Corpus Act*, while initially intended as a legal device to bring detained prisoners into court, had instead transformed into a judicial remedy against the illegal arrest, detainment or evacuation to another territory of people already inhabiting or residing in England.[654] In 1706, this uncertainty became even more prevalent after the

652 Antony Anghie, 'Francisco De Vitoria and the Colonial Origins of International Law' (n 76) 321, 330, citing Francisco de Vitoria, *De Indis et de Ivre Belli Relectiones* (n 178) 181.

653 Nicholas V, 'Dum Diversas' (1452), as discussed in Diana Hayes, 'Reflections on Slavery', in Charles Curran (ed), Change in Official Catholic Moral Teachings (Paulist Press, 2003) 67; See also Samuel White, 'The Late Middle Ages' (n 2) 144–5.

654 Helen A Nutting, 'The Most Wholesome Law — The Habeas Corpus Act of 1679' (1960) 65(3) *American Historical Review* 529, 529.

decision of Lord Chief Justice Holt in the seminal case of *Smith v Gould* to dismiss the ability of slave owners to utilise remedies related to property rights.[655] As noted by Holly Brewer, the decision in *Smith v Gould* is particularly striking for the chilling effect it had on slavery in British colonies in the Americas:

> [S]lave ownership in the colonies and in England itself [became] less secure [given that] Judges in colonial courts were constantly citing and quoting from published common law decisions, and colonial legislatures framed their laws around the common law. To do otherwise was to risk their very charters. Massachusetts and other colonies had passed laws that violated the common law, and their charters had been confiscated in the 1680s, just as Chief Justice Rainsford (among others) had recommended in 1677. The idea that in the colonies there was a different law, as determined by the king, was generally rejected by the Holt rulings and by broader policies under William III and Anne.[656]

Finally in 1772 the judgment of the King's Bench in *Somerset v Stewart* sounded the death knell for slavery within the British Isles — and the start of the reconfiguration of this gradually-developed domestic position against slavery into a prohibition that applied to Imperial warfare overseas:

> The state of slavery is of such a nature that it is incapable of being introduced on any reasons, moral or political, but only by positive law, which preserves its force long after the reasons, occasions, and time itself from whence it was created, is erased from memory. It is so odious, that nothing can be suffered to support it, but positive law. Whatever inconveniences, therefore, may follow from the decision, I cannot say this case is allowed or approved by the law of England; and therefore the black must be discharged.[657]

In contrast to the days of early European colonialism,[658] the Empire of the High Imperial period (from 1850 onwards)[659] publicly pursued anti-slavery

655 *Smith v Gould* 2 Salk 666 (1706).

656 Holly Brewer, 'Creating a Common Law of Slavery for England and its New World Empire' (2021) 39(4) *Law and History Review* 824, 824.

657 *Somerset v Stewart* (1772) 98 ER 499 (Lord Mansfield).

658 William Black, *The History of Slavery and the Slave Trade* (Franklin, 1858) 107.

659 See Anthony Reid, 'A New Phase of Commercial Expansion in Southeast Asia, 1760–1850' (n 424) 57, 57–82.

policies that extended to its conduct in overseas campaigns.[660] Public outrage following the 1781 Zong Massacre — where British sailors had thrown overboard 130 enslaved Africans to avoid rationing drinking water[661] — had resulted in a torrent of attempted abolitionist bills in Parliament, consequently leading to both Houses' passage of the 1807 *Slave Trade Act* after years of arduous campaigning by various anti-slavery groups.[662] The Act, while explicitly legalising (and thus legitimising) past slave trading,[663] also criminalised the future 'Purchase, Sale, Barter, or Transfer' of slaves to territories under British possession and empowered Royal Navy servicemen to seize ships suspected of engaging in the trade.[664] Following this, British diplomats began pivoting to a platform of convincing other Western and American countries to formally end slave-trading practices in the Atlantic Ocean[665] — in the High Imperial period this humanitarian mission shifted to Asia and Africa.

This initial focus is evident when assessing the bilateral and multilateral treaties signed between Great Britain and the other Great Powers throughout the nineteenth century. In 1814, for instance, the *Treaty of Paris* signed between Britain and France included a clause that sought to abolish the slave trade within France itself:

> His Most Christian Majesty, concurring without reserve in the sentiments of His Britannic Majesty, with respect to a description of Traffic repugnant to the principles of natural justice and of the enlightened age in which we live, engages to unite all his efforts to those of His Britannic Majesty, at the approaching Congress, to induce all the Powers of Christendom to decree the abolition of the Slave Trade, so that the said Trade shall cease universally as it shall cease definitely, under any circumstances, on the part of the French Government, in the course of five years; and that, during the said period, no Slave Merchant shall import or sell Slaves, except in the colonies of the State of which he is a subject.[666]

---

660 See, eg, Michelle Gordon, *Extreme Violence and the 'British Way': Colonial Warfare in Perak, Sierra Leone and Sudan* (n 97) 20.

661 *Gregson v Gilbert* (1783) 3 Doug KB 232.

662 See *Slave Trade Act 1807* (UK), <http://www.esp.org/foundations/freedom/holdings/slave-trade-act-1807.pdf>.

663 Ibid s VI.

664 Ibid s I, XIV.

665 See Jean Allain, *Slavery in International Law: Of Human Exploitation and Trafficking* (Brill, 2013) 72–4. See also Laura Benton, Abolition and Imperial Law, 1790–1820 (2011) 3(39) *Journal of Imperial and Commonwealth History* 355, 355–74.

666 See *Treaty of Paris 1814*, Additional Article I.

Although preliminary attempts to assimilate slavery into pre-existing universal prohibitions against piracy (which would allow Royal Navy ships to search international vessels for slaves even during peacetime) fizzled out in the face of widespread international defiance, the other Great Powers did ultimately agree to more indirectly phrased treaties.

First in 1815, and then later again in 1822,[667] the extraterritorial effect of the 1807 proscription on slavery was more clearly materialised through the *Declaration at the Congress of Vienna*, where state actors from Austria, France, Great Britain, Prussia and Russia agreed to '[put] a stop to' the slave trade:

> the commerce, known by the name of the "Slave Trade" (Traite des Negres d'Afrique) has been considered, by just and enlightened men in all ages, as repugnant to the principles of humanity and universal morality; ... at length the public voice, in all civilized countries, calls aloud for its prompt suppression ... [and] several European Governments have virtually come to the resolution of putting a stop to it.[668]

That 1815 pan-European treaty was soon followed by a bilateral treaty signed between Britain and the Kingdom of the Netherlands on 4 May 1818. As set out in Article I of that treaty, its purpose was almost solely to prohibit slave trade participation by the subjects of both countries:

> The Laws of the United Kingdom of Great Britain and Ireland rendering it already highly penal for the Subjects of His Britannic Majesty to carry on, or to be in any way engaged in Trade in Slaves, His Majesty the King of the Netherlands, referring to the Eighth Article of the Convention entered into with His Britannic Majesty on the Thirteenth August One thousand eight hundred and fourteen, engages in pursuance thereof, and within Eight Months from the Ratification of these Presents, or sooner if possible, to prohibit all his Subjects in the most effectual Manner and especially by penal Law the most formal, to take any Part whatever in the Trade of Slaves; and in the Event of the Measures already taken by the British Government, and to be taken by that of the Netherlands, being

667 Renee Colette Redman, 'The League of Nations and the Right to be Free from Enslavement: The First Human Right to Be Recognized as Customary International Law — Freedom: Beyond the United States' (1994) 70(2) *Chicago-Kent Law Review* 769.

668 *Declaration of the Congress Treaty of Vienna*, 8 February 1815, as cited by Ibid.

> found ineffectual or insufficient, the High Contracting Parties mutually engage to adopt such further Measures, whether by legal Provision or otherwise, as may from time to time appear to be best calculated in the most effectual Manner to prevent all their respective Subjects from taking any Share whatever in this nefarious Traffic.[669]

In doing so, the treaty also contained provisions empowering the British Royal Navy with the right of visit and search in relation to Dutch ships (and vice-versa). A mixed Court of Justice was set up in order to specifically try sailors and commanders found to be in breach of these clauses:

> The Mixed Courts of Justice to be established by the Treaty of this Date, upon the Coast of Africa and in a Colonial Possession of His Majesty the King of the Netherlands, are appointed to decide upon the Legality of the Detention of such Vessels as the Cruizers of both Nations shall detain in pursuance of this same Treaty.
>
> The above mentioned Courts shall judge definitively and without Appeal, according to the present Treaty.
>
> The Proceeding shall take place as summarily as possible; the Courts are required to decide, as far as they shall find it practicable, within the Space of Twenty Days, to be dated from that on which every detained Vessel shall have been brought into the Port where they shall reside; — First, upon the Legality of the Capture; — Secondly, in the Cases in which the captured Vessel shall have been liberated, as to the Indemnification which the said Vessel is to receive.
>
> And it is hereby provided, that in all Cases the final Sentence shall not be delayed, on account of the Absence of Witnesses or for Want of other Proofs, beyond the Period of Two Months, except upon the Application of any of the Parties interested, when, upon their giving satisfactory Security to charge themselves with the Expence and Risks of the Delay, the Courts may at their Discretion grant an additional Delay, not exceeding Four Months.[670]

669 *Treaty between His Britannic Majesty and His Majesty the King of the Netherlands, for Preventing their Subjects from engaging in any Traffic in Slaves*, 4 May 1818.

670 Ibid.

As argued by Bernard H Nelson, the enforcement of these provisions, however, proved to be a difficult task for Great Britain.[671] Despite the success of Lord Castlereagh's foreign ministry in pressuring foreign nations to sign such treaties, British commissioners consistently noted flagrant breaches committed by Dutch and French subjects.[672]

More worryingly for Great Britain, its diplomats and commissioners also started receiving pushback over its attempts to adopt mutual rights of visits and search into international treaties — as a way to bolster enforcement efforts. As aptly summarised by Jean Allain, this manifested into an eighty-year struggle where Imperial policymakers agitated for the expansion of the right to visit through the use of its dominant navy.[673]

The issue came to a head in *Buron v Denman*.[674] Commander Joseph Denman (as the eventual Rear Admiral then was) engaged in a policy of punishment operations against slave ships along the West African coast, blockading river entry points and destroying slave holding pens. An action was brought against Denman by the Spanish merchants who had owned the slave ships destroyed. Denman was acquitted by the relevant English court, who found that there was no case to answer for the legality of the action could not be questioned as it was an Act of State. Importantly, although the actions taken were not done under a valid act of war, nor under any rule of international law at the time, the punishment operations were retrospectively supported by the British government.[675] The Crown was thus able to 'by virtue of its prerogative over foreign affairs ... subject only to the risk of provoking war' have a free hand 'in its dealings with aliens outside the jurisdiction of the English courts'.[676]

But is it limited purely to actions against a foreign national? A majority of the case law would appear to fall under the Diceyian approach to Acts of State — that is, the lawful authority only extends to actions taken against those not subject to the relevant Crown. *Buron v Denman* makes clear that the act must be done to an alien:

> Courts of law are established for the express purpose of limiting public authority in its conduct towards individuals. If one British subject puts

671 Bernard H Nelson, 'The Slave Trade as a Factor in British Foreign Policy 1815–1862' (1942) 27(2) *Journal of Negro History* 192, 200.

672 Ibid.

673 Jean Allain, 'The Nineteenth Century Law of the Sea and the British Abolition of the Slave Trade' (2008) 78(1) *British Yearbook of International Law* 342, 342.

674 (1848) 2 Ex 167.

675 Holdsworth, Act of State, 1321.

676 Ibid.

> another to death, or destroys his property by the express command of the King, that command is no protection to the person who executes it unless it is in itself lawful, and it is the duty of the proper courts of justice to determine whether it is lawful or not.[677]

In this respect, the Act of State doctrine covered the field of anti-slavery operations, due to its clear prohibition under British law.

Distinction between Slavery and Indentured or Forced Labour

A distinction must be made between the British conceptions of chattel slavery and 'mere' indentured labour. It is clear that, while successive challenges to the formal regimes of colonial slavery throughout the late eighteenth century led to its eventual collapse, the latter remained explicitly lawful. In Australia alone, systems of Aboriginal forced labour were actively encouraged by state colonial governments despite its similar 'standards of brutality' to the slave system abhorred by the British public.[678]

The Role of Abolitionist Policies to Justify Imperial Expansion

Michelle Gordon expertly summarises the particular way that Imperial frontier commanders or 'men on the spot' wielded abolitionism as a tool in wars of conquest throughout the late nineteenth century:

> As the men on the spot sought to increase British influence on a local level, issues that caused tensions between the colonial administrations and indigenous leaders include the abolition of slavery and the implementation of tax systems. British approaches to these issues demonstrate a failure to understand (or even consider) local customs and traditions and the disastrous effects that the implementation of these policies could have. Furthermore, Britain used the issue of slavery to 'prove' preconceived notions of the 'natives' and their alleged 'propensity' towards 'barbarism'. The approach and attitudes of colonial administrators on the

677 (1848) 2 Ex 167, 169.

678 Frank Stevens, 'Aboriginal Labour' (1971) 41(1) *Australian Quarterly* 70–8.

> ground were informed by the advocacy of the imperial project as a 'civilising mission' and the belief that colonialism was a 'moral duty'.[679]

This is connected to the wider issue of the significant discretion afforded to the actors of Imperial authority, including governors, commanders and administrative officers who advanced their own interests, and that oftentimes this led to varied applications of wartime prohibitions — especially as overseas campaigns were waged increasingly away from the Colonial and Foreign Offices in the Imperial metropole.[680] The logistical challenges that this created[681] resulted in significant discretion being afforded to colonial commanders[682] — as seen in how 'men on the spot' such as Lord Lytton in Afghanistan (1878) and Sir Henry Bartle Frere in Zululand (1879) initiated colonial wars without Parliamentary sanction.[683] Keith Surridge summarises this aptly, while describing late nineteenth-century British expeditions in the African Gold Coast:

> For example, [Governor] Wolsley was given full responsibility in the Gold Coast/Ashanti in 1874, owing to the lack of Imperial government locally and the need for comprehensive powers to ensure that the demands of the campaign were met. In northern Nigeria Brigadier-General Sir Frederick Lugard was made High Commissioner in 1899 and subsequently used his position and authority to launch an attack against the Sokoto Caliphate, which by 1903 was absorbed into the British Empire.[684]

In line with this, Victor Kiernan also notes how violations against the British ban on slave-trading were publicly referenced by colonial officers to justify the 1873–4 expeditions undertaken against the Ashanti people of modern-day

679 Michelle Gordon, 'British Colonial Violence in Perak, Sierra Leone and the Sudan' (PhD Thesis, University of London, 2017) 20.

680 See generally Roger Long, *The Man on the Spot: Essays on British Empire History* (Greenwood Press, 1995).

681 Emrys Chew, 'The Naning War, 1831–1832: Colonial Authority and Malay Resistance in the Early Period of British Expansion' (1998) 32(2) *Modern Asian Studies* 351, 381.

682 Frédéric Mégret (n 91) 265, 281–2.

683 See Damian O'Connor (n 89) 5, 14.

684 Keith Surridge, 'The Politics of War: Lord Kitchener and the Settlement of the South African War, 1901–1902' in Greg Cuthbertson, Albert Grundlingh and Mary-Lynn Suttie (eds), *Writing a Wider War: Rethinking Gender, Race, and Identity in the South African War, 1899–1902* (Ohio University Press, 2002) 213, 215. See also, T Lloyd, 'Africa and Hobson's Imperialism' (1972) 55(1) *Past and Present* 130, 130–53.

Ghana and subsequently the Perak-Malays in 1875.[685] Despite criticisms of how this 'civilising mission' merely disguised more economic considerations,[686] it is arguable that this custom was routinely enforced by British administrators throughout the imperial frontiers ever since the 1807 *Slave Trade Act*.[687]

In addition to the abolition laws issued after the conquests of Ghana and Perak,[688] it may be pertinent here to refer to Sir Andries Stockenström (Lieutenant-Governor of British Kaffraria from 1836 to 1838), who drafted proclamations in 1817 to punish colonial settlers who had enslaved members of the local San peoples.[689] As highlighted by Nigel Penn,[690] local enforcement of this ruling was so prioritised that it eventually culminated in the 1822 Commission of Enquiry,[691] where frontier farms were inspected to ensure compliance with Stockenström's ordinances. Given the persuasiveness of relevant State practice here, this prohibition would likely be enforceable under the practice-oriented framework.

At the same time however, it is also worth considering the differing opinions of the colonial men on the spot in Malaya. In 1866, Sir Orfeur Cavenagh (the last Straits Governor appointed by the Indian Office) had written to the Governor-General in Bengal regarding the existence of chattel slavery in Perak and Selangor when compared to its supposed eradication in the Settlements.[692] More than a decade earlier however, the British Resident-Councillor in Melaka had explicitly noted the continued existence of slavery on British territories (even after the Naning War):

> Slavery ... exists to a great extent on the western boundaries of Malacca, vizt. Rembau and Sungei Ujong, and extends even to Perak. It is a fact well-known that several boats, annually, in the S.W. monsoon, about the months of July and August, import into the above-named places several

685 Victor Kiernan, *The Lords of Human Kind: Black Man, Yellow Man, and White Man in the Age of Empire* (Cresset, 1988) 83; See also William McIntyre, 'The Ashanti Expedition of 1873–4' (1962) 5(1) *Historical Journal* 19, 19–22.

686 Walter Knaggs, 'A Visit to Perak' (1875) 1(1) *Journal of Eastern Asia* 36–7.

687 *Slave Trade Act 1807* (UK).

688 William McIntyre, 'The Ashanti Expedition of 1873–4' (1962) 5(1) *Historical Journal* 19, 19.

689 Nigel Penn, 'The British and the "Bushmen": The Massacre of the Cape San, 1795 to 1828' (2013) 15(2) *Journal of Genocide Research*, 18—200.

690 Ibid 183–95.

691 Ibid.

692 Letter from Sir Orfeur Cavenagh (Governor of Straits Settlements) to Sir John Lawrence (Viceroy and Governor-General of India), 6 April 1866, no 65/406, FO 37/450, cited by Nicholas Tarling, 'British Policy in the Malay Peninsula and Archipelago, 1824–71' (1957) 30(3) *Journal of the Malaysian Branch of the Royal Asiatic Society* 176 n 837.

> hundreds of slaves of both sexes from Batu Bahru on the Sumatran coast.[693]

Overarchingly, when adopting a practice-oriented approach to appraising a pre-*Hague* customary prohibition against slavery in the late nineteenth century British Empire, it appears that this custom was certainly enforceable in Imperial wars. Although the exact nature and success of its enforcement appears to have been ad-hoc or problematic in parts of the Empire, these seem to have been a departure from what was expected of Imperial commanders by both their peers and superiors (including in Parliament).[694]

693 Letter from William Thomas Lewis (Resident Councillor of Malacca) to Secretary to Major General William John Butterworth (Governor of the Straits Settlements), 27 November 1854, 164938 at 63, as quoted in Nicholas Tarling, 'British Policy in the Malay Peninsula and Archipelago, 1824–71' (1957) 30(3) *Journal of the Malaysian Branch of the Royal Asiatic Society* 176 n 837.

694 See generally Damian O'Connor (n 89) (2009) 6(1) *Journal of Australian Naval History* 5, 14.

CHAPTER 7

Prohibition on Unnecessary Looting of Cultural Heritage

> You must understand what the Parthenon Marbles mean to us. They are our pride. They are our sacrifices. They are the supreme symbol of nobility. They are a tribute to democratic philosophy. They are our aspiration and our name. They are the essence of Greekness.[695]
>
> My Lords, may I ask my noble friend to tread very warily when it comes to returning booty which we have collected in this country, because the process might turn into rather a strip-tease?[696]

Given its heavy emphasis in international disputes, as seen in the current attempts by India to recover the Koh-i-Noor diamond seized by the British after the 1849 Second Anglo-Sikh War,[697] there has been a recent focus by scholars from the Third World Approaches to International Law ('TWAIL') school on the viability of establishing colonial-era prohibitions against the 'wartime looting of cultural property'.[698] When taken together with rising public outcries for

695 Nadia Banteka, 'The Parthenon Marbles Revisited: A New Strategy for Greece' (2016) 37(4) *University of Pennsylvania Journal of International Law* 1231, 1249–50, citing Melina Mercouri, 'Greece's Claim to the Elgin Marbles' (Speech, Oxford Union, June 1986).

696 See United Kingdom, *Parliamentary Debates*, House of Lords, 10 December 1974, vol 355, col 534–5 (Jennie Lee, Baroness Lee of Asheridge).

697 Tanner Wadsworth, 'The Advantages of Giving Up: Greece and the Futile Quest to Force the Parthenon Marbles Home by Judgment' (2023) 1(29) *Columbia Journal of European Law* 129, 129.

698 Yue Zhang, 'The Right to Restitution of Cultural Property Removed as Spoils of War during Nineteenth-Century International Warfare' (n 309). It must be noted that it remains uncertain regarding what types of human artifacts would have been classified as 'cultural property' by pre-*Hague* Imperial commanders. While modern commentators today may have regard to the categories outlined in the 1995 *UNIDROIT Convention on Stolen or Illegally Exported Cultural Objects*, international jurists historically appeared to have outlined their own lists of what types of property should be protected — grounded on Eurocentric ideas of art to the exclusion of colonial takings: see Fiona Macmillan,

 DOI:10.1163/9789004515987_009

apologies from Western States, the dismantling of statues honouring Imperial heroes, and the repatriation of cultural artefacts to their original countries,[699] this is clearly a space that needs further assessment.

An application of the practice-oriented methodology will be particularly meaningful here to address the perceived flaws of traditional TWAIL commentary in this area. In particular, the international lawyer Dr Doreen Lustig has noted that a recurring criticism of postcolonial scholars from the TWAIL school has been a perceived failure on their part to sufficiently 'capture the porous and contested aspects' of international legal history.[700] As previously argued, any assessment of the applicability of Imperial laws of war in colonial conflicts must factor in the concept of the 'Othering' of non-Western peoples under international law in order to avoid the 'unrealistic' contextualising of early IHL developments.[701] This notion, and its impact on how a prohibition against unnecessary looting must be considered, has been summarised generally in a very apt fashion by Tanisha M. Fazal and Brooke C. Greene:

> Because indigenous peoples fought war differently from Europeans, often employing what we consider today to be guerrilla tactics, they could thus not be expected to reciprocate compliance with norms of warfare with which they were wholly unfamiliar. … As a result, Europeans did not view themselves as bound to restrictions vis-à-vis the 'savage'.[702]

Moving on, the starting point here must be the current view on the existence of this potential prohibition. Yue Zhang has persuasively argued that a rule against the 'unnecessary' plunder of substantial cultural property was developed as a custom of war in the eighteenth century and was 'well-established'

Cultural Property and Community Rights to Cultural Heritage in Ting Xu and Jean Allain (eds), *Property and Human Rights in a Global Context* (Hart Publishing, 2015) 41, 41–2.

Given its persuasive role as largely aligning with European custom at the time, however, this chapter will place particular weight on the categories of cultural property identified in art 35 of the *Lieber Code*: 'Classical works of art, libraries, scientific collections, or precious instruments.'

699 See, eg, Tristram Hunt, 'Should Museums Return their Colonial Artefacts?', *The Guardian*, (online, 29 June 2019) <https://www.theguardian.com/culture/2019/jun/29/should-museums-return-their-colonial-artefacts>.

700 Doreen Lustig, 'Governance Histories of International Law' (n 230) 859, 859–882.

701 See, eg, Ingo Venzke, 'The Path Not Taken: On Legal Change and its Context' (n 229) 309.

702 Tanisha M Fazal and Brooke C Greene, 'A Particular Difference: European Identity and Civilian Targeting' (n 192) 829, 835, citing Geoffrey Parker, 'Early Modern Europe' in Michael Howard, George J Andreopoulos and Mark R Shulman, *Laws of War: Constraints on Warfighting in the Western World* (Yale University Press, 1994) 40, 57.

even before its inclusion in post-*Hague Conventions* treaties.[703] Of particular interest is Zhang's focus on the international reaction to France's looting of artefacts from Greece and Egypt. Zhang emphasises how, during the 1815 Treaty of Paris negotiations, the Duke of Wellington 'argued that stolen artistic treasures should be returned ... because Napoleon's looting was contrary to the law[s] of war.[704]' Taking into account the wide-acceptance by other European countries of the British position,[705] and the enforced restoration of artefacts that occurred afterwards, Zhang reasons that this event confirmed the existence of a proscription against the unnecessary looting of cultural property.[706] In order to reliably (or as reliably as reasonably possible) assess this according to the practice-oriented methodology, these instances highlighted by Zhang must be situated and then considered within the wider context of pre-*Hague Convention* international legal developments within the British Empire.

Early Developments of a Prohibition against Looting of Cultural Property

Despite current controversies surrounding the exact scope of a 'duty' to return looted cultural heritage to their countries of origin, it is clear that the idea of such an obligation is not new. Rather, advocates of a general prohibition on looting cultural property have been verbalising their views since before the dawn of the Roman Empire — the issue is that actual enforcement of this duty by military commander has been sporadic and inconsistent with the consensus achieved among international lawyers and scholars.

For a summary of very early scholarship in this space, the French diplomat Louis-Jacques Rollet-Andriane's 1979 commentary remains an illustrative introduction.[707] In particular, Rollet-Andriane points to the writings of

703 Yue Zhang, 'The Right to Restitution of Cultural Property Removed as Spoils of War during Nineteenth-Century International Warfare' (n 309) 22–4.

704 Ibid 33, quoting Letter of the Duke of Wellington to Viscount Castlereagh, 23 September 1815.

705 Wayne Sandholtz, 'Plunder, Restitution, and International Law' (2010) 17 *International Journal of Cultural Property* 152.

706 Yue Zhang, 'Customary International Law and the Rule Against Taking Cultural Property as Spoils of War' (n 309) 940.

707 See Louis-Jacques Rollet-Andriane, 'Precedents' (1979) 31(1) *Museum International* 4–7. See also Geoffrey Lewis, 'The Return of Cultural Property' (1981) 129 [June] *Journal of the Royal Society of the Arts* 435.

the classical Greek historian Polybius (active during the 2nd century BC, and also noteworthy for his exploits as a statesman in the Achaean League), who wrote in support of a prohibition against the appropriation of foreign cultural heritage:

> The city should not owe its beauty to adornments brought in from elsewhere, but to the valour of its inhabitants. … I trust that future conquerors will learn from these reflexions not to plunder the cities they bring into subjection and not to take advantage of the distress of other peoples to adorn their homelands.[708]

Rollet-Andriane also took care to highlight the later commentary produced by the late Roman Republican statesman and lawyer Cicero, who verbally commended the conduct of Scipio Aemilianus (otherwise known as Scipio Africanus the Younger) during the Third Punic War (149–146 BC).[709] Infamously, having conquered Carthage in the conflict, Scipio had proceeded to repatriate to Sicily artefacts which Carthaginian commanders had themselves looted from the various city-states there — rather than opting to bring the objects to Rome itself.[710]

Despite this aforementioned evidence of early wartime protections for cultural heritage during the classical Greek and Roman periods,[711] an examination of later state practice during the Anglo-Spanish War (1585–1604) casts significance doubt on the existence of a recognisable prohibition among English commanders towards the end of the sixteenth Century. The storming of the prominent Spanish city of Cádiz by English and Dutch forces under the command of Robert Devereux (1576–1601), the 2nd Earl of Essex, highlights this. Devereux, well-documented for strictly enforcing other developing customary practices such as the prohibition against sexual violence,[712] expressly permitted the soldiers under his authority to sack Catholic churches in the

---

708 Louis-Jacques Rollet-Andriane, 'Precedents' (n 707) 4, quoting volume 2 of S Seferiades, 'La Question du Rapatriement des Marbres d'Elgin Considérée plus Spécialementau Point de Vue du Droit des Gens' (1932) *Revue du Droit International*.

709 Louis-Jacques Rollet-Andriane, 'Precedents' (n 707) 4.

710 Ibid, citing Marcus Tullius Cicero, *C Verrem Oratio*, lib XXXIII.

711 See book 3, ch 12 in Hugo Grotius, *The Rights of War and Peace*, tr AC Campbell (M Walter Dunne, 1905): 'On Moderation in Despoiling an Enemy's Country'.

712 Beatrice Heuser notes how Devereux, as the Commander-in-Chief of Queen Elizabeth I's army during the Anglo-Spanish War (1585–1604) had 'applied the laws of war which Matthew Sutcliffe had compiled in his official publication on war': Beatrice Heuser, 'Ordinances and Articles of War before the Lieber Code, 866–1863' (n 75) 155.

city[713] — in doing so, turning a blind eye to the unfortunate devastation of the famous paintings and statues of Christian saints.[714]

While provisions related to general obligations to return looted artefacts did begin to emerge in the early seventeenth century, these appeared to be sporadically enforced and not yet supported by the views of contemporary English and international jurists. As noted by Rollet-Andriane, the 1662 Treaty of Whitehall is perhaps the most notable instance of this, where the Dutch Republic agreed to return works of art which had been taken from the personal collection of King James I of England (1603–1625).[715]

The writings of the great pre-Modern pioneer scholar of international law, Hugo Grotius (1583–1645), arguably represent a turning point towards a growing recognition of the need to protect the 'elegant works and monuments of art'. Grotius' position was evidently informed by the contemporaneous shift towards humanitarian concepts such as limiting wartime conduct to only what was necessary, which so characterised his wider generation of fellow international lawyers[716] — but it also stands out for his use of careful references to the aforementioned views of classical writers such as Cicero and Polybius. As helpfully translated by AC Campbell, Grotius cited these celebrated ancient writers when specifically contending that cultural property should be excluded from destruction in wartime:

> III.XII.V. There are some things of such a nature, as to contribute, no way, to the support and prolongation of war: things which reason itself requires to be spared even during the heat and continuance of war. Polybius calls it brutal rage and madness to destroy things, the destruction of which does not in the least tend to impair an enemy's strength, nor to increase that of the destroyer: Such are Porticos, Temples, statues, and all other elegant works and monuments of art. Cicero commends Marcellus for sparing the public and private edifices of Syracuse, as if he had come with his army to protect them, rather than to take the place by storm.
>
> III.XII.VI. As this rule of moderation is observed towards other ornamental works of art, for the reasons before stated, there is still greater

713 Ibid 156.

714 Ibid.

715 Louis-Jacques Rollet-Andriane, 'Precedents' (n 707) 6.

716 John Collins, *Martial Law and English Laws, c1500–c1700* (n 64) 109, citing Francis Grose, *Military Antiquities Respecting a History of the English Army: From the Conquest to the Present Time* (n 78) vol 2, 54.

> reason, why it should be obeyed in respect to things devoted to the purposes of religion. For although such things, or edifices, being the property of the state may, according to the law of nations, be with impunity demolished, yet as they contribute nothing to aggravate the calamities, or retard the successes of war, it is a mark of reverence to divine things to spare them, and all that is connected therewith: and more especially should this rule be adhered to among nations, worshipping the same God according to the same fundamental laws, although differing from each other by slight shades of variation in their rights and opinions. Thucydides says that it was a law among the Greeks of his time, in all their invasions of each other's territories, to forbear touching the edifices of religion: and Livy likewise observes that, upon the destruction of Alba by the Romans, the temples of the Gods were spared.[717]

More than a century later, the international jurist Emmerich de Vattel took a similar approach in his 1758 seminal essay 'Le Droit des Gens' or the *Law of Nations*. In particular, he deplored the 'wilful destruction of public monuments, temples, tombs, statues, paintings, etc', which was 'absolutely condemned, even by the voluntary law of nations, as never being conducive to the rightful object of war'.[718] De Vattel's emphasis on the need to consider wartime objectives, however, is striking here and points to an extension of Grotius's previous regard to a perceived nexus between the destruction of cultural property and the 'the support and prolongation of war'. As highlighted by Roger O'Keefe, '[De] Vattel made clear, however, that if it were "necessary to destroy buildings of this sort to pursue military operations or to erect siegeworks," a belligerent "no doubt ha[d] the right to do so"'. While not himself representative of the views of British commanders in this space, it is noteworthy that de Vattel's interpretations on natural law were stunningly popular in the English-speaking world — to the extent that they were even directly cited by British frontier commanders in later colonial wars such as the War of 1812 (1812–15) in North America.[719]

---

717 Hugo Grotius, *The Law of War and Peace* (1625) 273, as cited by Evelien Campfens, 'The Bangwa Queen: Artifact or Heritage?' (2019) 26 *International Journal of Cultural Property* 75, 86.

718 Emer de Vattel, *Le Droit des Gens, ou Principes de la Loi Naturelle, appliqués à la Conduite et aux Affaires des Nations et des Souverains* (*text of 1758*) (Carnegie Institution, 1916), book III, 143–4 [173], cited by Roger O'Keefe, 'Protection of Cultural Property Under International Criminal Law' (2010) 11(2) *Melbourne Journal of International Law* 339.

719 See generally Donald E Graves, '"Every Horror was Committed with Impunity … and Not a Man was Punished!" Reflections on British Military Law and the Atrocities at Hampton' (n 142).

While a specific enforceable provision regarding long-term legal obligations to return cultural property or refrain from unnecessary looting was not included in the treaties that followed the Napoleonic Wars (1803–1815), the widespread practice of pillage among commanders of the French Imperial War resulted in considerable outcry from victimised nations 'who had suffered extensive plundering from their churches, museums'.[720] Later writers would contrast the scale of the pillaging of cultural property with instances of earlier State practice amongst European nations, in order to showcase its jarring effect:

> During their wars, Louis XIII and Louis XIV, while they annexed provinces, scrupulously refrained from despoiling the vanquished of the monuments which were the mementoes of their nation's past, which embodied their scientific, literary or artistic achievements.[721]

State Actors representing European Great Powers such as the United Kingdom appeared to share this outrage against French wartime conduct during the Napoleonic Wars (1803–1815), as reflected in the writings of the Duke of Wellington who 'argued [in 1815] that stolen artistic treasures should be returned … because Napoleon's looting was contrary to the law[s] of war.[722]' According to Tuba Inal, this emerging consensus 'paved the way for the emergence of a prevalent norm that considered pillage an uncivilized practice'.[723] As a result of this outrage, the Great Powers then compelled France at the Congress of Vienna (1815) to repatriate the majority of its looted treasures — itself a remarkable act as perhaps the first instance of mass restitution of objects of cultural heritage (on a far grander scale than what Scipio had undertaken in Sicily around two millennia prior).[724] Even more strikingly, Rollet-Andriane has also noted how some of the returned cultural objects were not merely transferred to the last previous owner prior to seizure by the French Army.[725] Notably, manuscripts which had been appropriated from the Papal

---

720 Geoffrey Lewis, 'The Return of Cultural Property' (1981) 129 [June] *Journal of the Royal Society of the Arts* 435, 435.

721 Louis-Jacques Rollet-Andriane, 'Precedents' (n 707) 6.

722 Yue Zhang, 'The Right to Restitution of Cultural Property Removed as Spoils of War during Nineteenth-Century International Warfare' (n 709) 33, quoting Letter of the Duke of Wellington to Viscount Castlereagh, 23 September 1815.

723 Tuba Inal, 'Looting and Rape in Wartime' (n 80) 169.

724 See Louis-Jacques Rollet-Andriane, 'Precedents' (n 707) 6, citing Henry Wheaton, *Elements of International Law* (FA Brockhaus, 1852) vol 1, 15. See also Geoffrey Lewis (n 707) 435.

725 Louis-Jacques Rollet-Andriane, 'Precedents' (n 707) 6.

Libraries in Rome and transferred to the Bibliotheque Nationale in Paris, were instead restored back to the University of Heidelberg archives[726] — which had itself been looted by Holy Roman-Papal armies under the command of Duke Maximilian I of Bavaria during the Thirty Years' War (1618–48).[727]

The cultural heritage lawyer Evelien Campfens has also supported that position that the 1815 Congress of Vienna was a 'turning point' for the nascent crystallisation of a prohibition against unnecessary looting of cultural property.[728] Most strikingly, Campfens has noted Castlereagh and the British's delegation at Vienna's view on how restitution of the artefacts looted by France was the right and proper measure in order to 'effectuate what justice and policy require'.[729]

Taking place towards the end of the Napoleonic Wars (1803–1815), the 1813 *Marquis de Sommerueles* case may be the first instance where this nascent prohibition made its way into British domestic commentary. Involving a dispute over paintings purchased by the Pennsylvania Academy of the Fine Arts in Philadelphia, which had then been seized by a British ship from an Italian vessel during the War of 1812, the case ultimately came before Justice Alexander Croke of the Nova Scotia Court of Vice-Admiralty.[730] Justice Dr Croke ordered the restitution of the paintings to the Pennsylvania Academy of the Fine Arts on the basis of a perceived duty among 'all civilized nations' to safeguard the 'arts and sciences':

> The same law of nations, which prescribes that all property belonging to the enemy shall be liable to confiscation, has likewise its modifications and relaxations of that rule. The arts and sciences are admitted amongst all civilized nations, as forming an exception to the severe rights of warfare, and as entitled to favour and protection. They are considered not as the peculium of this or that nation, but as the property of mankind at large, and as belonging to the common interests of the whole species.[731]

---

726 Ibid, citing Johann Kaspar Bluntschli, *Le Droit International Codifié* (1870) art 650.

727 See generally Fred Lerner, *The Story of Libraries: From the Invention of Writing to the Computer Age* (Continuum Publishing, 1999) 107–8.

728 Evelien Campfens, 'The Bangwa Queen: Artifact or Heritage?' (n 717) 75, 87.

729 Ibid, citing 'Note Delivered by Viscount Castlereagh to the Allied Ministers, and Placed upon their Protocol, Respecting the Restitution of the Works of Art', Paris, 11 September 1815.

730 Vice-Admiralty Court of Halifax, Nova Scotia Stewart's Vice-Admiralty Reports 482 (1813), as reproduced in John Henry Merryman, Note on The Marquis Someruele (1996) 5 *International Journal of Cultural Property* 321–9.

731 Evelien Campfens, 'Whose Cultural Objects? Introducing Heritage Title for Cross-Border Cultural Property Claims (2020) 67 *Netherlands International Law Review* 257, 263.

As per John Henry Merryman, who also notes how the reasoning in *Marquis de Sommerueles* 'provides a rare and eloquent judicial statement of cultural property internationalism', Dr Croke's language is 'striking' in its similarity to a book written by the French archaeologist Quatremère de Quincy in 1796 — the purpose of which was to condemn the looting undertaken by Napoleon's commanders:

> [T]he arts and sciences belong to all of Europe and are no longer the exclusive property of any nation. ... [I]t is as a member of that general republic of arts and sciences, and not as an inhabitant of this or that nation, that I will discuss the interest that all parties have in the conservation of all. What is that interest? It is that of civilization, of perfection of the means of welfare and pleasure, of the advancement and progress of education and thought, of amelioration of the human condition. Everything that could contribute to this end belongs to all peoples; no one has the right to dispose arbitrarily of it.[732]

Accordingly, there is some clear evidence that pieces of art (statues and works of art) were beginning to be protected under crystallising laws of war. As noted by Campfens, it is clear that a customary prohibition was already recognised by the time of the 1899 Hague Convention — with art 56 of the *Hague Regulations* providing that:

> The property of municipalities, that of institutions dedicated to religion, charity and education, the arts and sciences, even when State property, shall be treated as private property. All seizure of, destruction or willful damage done to institutions of this character, historic monuments, works of art and science, is forbidden, and should be made the subject of legal proceedings.[733]

While the 'exact moment' when the prohibition achieved customary status is uncertain,[734] pre-*Hague* American commentary in this space seems to further support the application of this prohibition in conflicts between Western nations. The early nineteenth century jurist Henry Wheaton (famous for his

732 John Henry Merryman, 'Cultural Property Internationalism' (2005) 12 *International Journal of Cultural Property* 11, 15, citing Quatremère de Quincy, *Lettres au général Miranda sur le déplacement des monuments de l'art de l'Italie,* (1796) 141–6.

733 Evelien Campfens, 'The Bangwa Queen: Artifact or Heritage?' (n 717) 75, 90.

734 Ibid.

treatise *Elements of International Law*), for instance, noted that that purely civil monuments were 'exempted' from wartime conduct based on principles of military necessity:

> By the ancient law of nations, even what were called *res sacrae* were not exempt from capture and confiscation ... But by the modern usage of nations, which has now acquired the force of law, temples of religion, public edifices devoted to civil purposes only, monuments of art, and repositories of science, are exempted from the general operations of war.[735]

Henry Halleck, who later served as General-in-Chief of the Armies of the United States from 1862 to 1864, also supported the application of a proscription against unnecessary plunder of cultural property — although he also adopted a narrow view of its character, in effect arguing that 'movable' property could be taken provided that the former owner accepted this 'by means of treaty stipulations':

> No belligerent would be justifiable in destroying temples, tombs, statutes [sic], paintings, or other works of art (except so far as their destruction may be the accidental or necessary result of military operations.) But, may he not seize and appropriate to his own use such works of genius and taste as belong to the hostile state, and are of a moveable character? This was done by the French armies in the wars of conquest which followed the revolution of 1789. ... The acquisitions of the Parisian galleries and museums from the conquest of Italy, were generally obtained by means of treaty stipulations, or forced contributions levied by Napoleon on the Italian princes.[736]

Finally, the most relevant example of the nascent nature of this custom throughout the late nineteenth-century is likely its inclusion in the 1863 American *Lieber Code* — arts 34 to 36 of which provide the following commentary:[737]

---

735 Henry Wheaton, *Elements of International Law* (1836) s 347, as quoted in John Henry Merryman, 'Cultural Property Internationalism' (n 732) 11, 17.

736 Henry Wager Halleck, *Halleck's International Law, or, Rules Regulating the Intercourse of States in Peace and War* (Kegan Paul, Trench, Trübner, 1893) vol 1, ch XIX, ss 10–11, as cited in John Henry Merryman, 'Cultural Property Internationalism' (n 732) 11, 17.

737 Dietrich Schindler and Jiří Toman (eds), *The Laws of Armed Conflicts: A Collection of Conventions, Resolutions, and Other Documents* (n 441) 3–23.

34. As a general rule, the property belonging to churches, to hospitals, or other establishments of an exclusively charitable character, to establishments of education, or foundations for the promotion of knowledge, whether public schools, universities, academies of learning or observatories, museums of the fine arts, or of a scientific character — such property is not to be considered public property in the sense of paragraph 31 [authorizing seizure of enemy public property]; but it may be taxed or used when the public service may require it.
35. Classical works of art, libraries, scientific collections, or precious instruments, such as astronomical telescopes, as well as hospitals, must be secured against all avoidable injury, even when they are contained in fortified places whilst besieged or bombarded.
36. If such works of art, libraries, collections, or instruments belonging to a hostile nation or government, can be removed without injury, the ruler of the conquering state or nation may order them to be seized and removed for the benefit of the said nation. The ultimate ownership is to be settled by the ensuing treaty of peace.[738]

However, the particular scope of the prohibition also remains difficult to establish. Zhang contends that the protection of cultural property was applicable to non-European nations under natural law. While this would be supported under the naturalist framework advanced by Bluntschli, this prospective custom is clearly rebutted by evidence of wider State practice. Even in the case of the 1815 Treaty of Paris, Zhang mistakenly does not refer to how Egyptian artefacts seized by the French were not returned. Accordingly, while the looting of cultural property is relevant to raise given the growing academic focus on the subject, its contemporary enforceability to non-Western peoples is doubtful under both the preclusive and social contract perspectives. With the current information before us, it seems instead that a prohibition against the unnecessary looting of cultural property was enforceable only in external Imperial wars against other Western nations. Its application against non-Western peoples was nascent and developing, however it still could not yet be seen in actual Imperial practices on the frontier.

738 Francis Lieber et al, *General Orders No 100: Adjutant-General's Office, Instructions for the Government of Armies of the United States in the Field* (D Van Nostrand, 1863) arts 34–6.

CHAPTER 8

Prohibition on Brigandry

> The pirate destroys all government and all order, by breaking all those ties and bonds that unite people in a civil society under any government.[739]

...

> 'To those who knew the Straits of Malacca in 1872–73, or who choose to look up the old files of the local journals, it will probably seem a notable achievement that no piracy has ever taken place in these waters since the British Government abandoned the policy of inaction for the policy of protection.[740]

...

> Justice being taken away, then, what are kingdoms but great robberies? For what are robberies themselves, but little kingdoms?[741]

∴

This chapter will consider whether a prohibition against brigandry and piracy was enforced by Imperial British commanders prior to the 1899 (first) *Hague Convention*, noting that this relates to the prosecution of violent acts committed by unlawful non-State actors usually for personal gain. Accordingly, this

739 Eric Wilson, *Savage Republic: De Indis of Hugo Grotius, Republicanism and Dutch Hegemony Within the Early Modern World-System (c. 1600–1619)* (Brill, 2008) 427 quoting Daniel Defoe, *A General History of the Robberies and Murders of the Most Notorious Pyrates* (1724).

740 Frank Athelstane Swettenham, *About Perak* (Singapore Straits Times Press, 1893) 5. See generally Eric Wilson, 'Magnum Latrocinium and Private Avengers: Carl Schmitt and Hugo Grotius' (2011) 26 *Leidschrift* 75, 75–97.

741 See Augustine, *On the City of God Against the Pagans* (426), as quoted in Marcus Dodds (ed), *The Works of Aurelius Augustine, Bishop of Hippo: The City of God* (T&T Clarke, 1917) at 140.

 | DOI:10.1163/9789004515987_010

space will be treated separately in this text from the prohibition against private warfare, which instead involves organized cross-border armed conflicts conducted by private entities without State authorisation, usually with wider objectives than mere theft or robbery.[742]

Drawing upon the writings of pioneering jurists including Francis Lieber, modern IHL commentators such as Richard Shelly Hartigan have briefly considered the treatment of brigands and pirates under twentieth century international laws of war.[743] However, in contrast to the other categories of customary prohibitions described in this work, which have previously received more in-depth treatment, there is clearly a need for a comprehensive exploration of whether a pre-*Hague* contemporary prohibition on brigandry existed during the late nineteenth-century British Empire.[744]

As emphasised by Alfred P Rubin, whose commentaries on piracy under global international law remains the foundational text in this space,[745] any assessment must first distinguish between the various ways that 'brigandry', 'piracy' and other terms ascribed to 'enemies of all mankind' have been used in different legal contexts,[746] The meaning of this term has transformed constantly across legal history, confusingly compounded even further through the inconsistent discourse adopted by late nineteenth-century international lawyers.[747] As summarised by Rubin:

> All of these uses ... have been argued from time to time to rest on classical writings and precedents. In the days leading up to the Westphalian settlement of Europe in 1648, citations to Greek and Latin sources were a major element of legal argumentation. Those renaissance legal arguments and the municipal law of the European sea powers, particularly England, purported to rest on Roman law and usage.[748]

742 See pt II ch IX.

743 Richard Shelly Hartigan, *Lieber's Code and the Law of War* (Precedent, 1983) 95.

744 While this chapter will refer to the global and Imperial British treatment of pirates and brigands interchangeably, it must be noted that its focus will primarily be on the exploration of a legal customary prohibition against brigands as perceived by commanders in the late nineteenth century British Empire.

745 WE Butler, 'Alfred P. Rubin (1931–2014)' (2016) 1(1) *Jus Gentium: Journal of International Legal History* 317.

746 Alfred P Rubin, 'The Law of Piracy' (1987) 2(15) *Denver Journal of International Law and Piracy* 173, 173.

747 Inge Van Hulle, *Britain and International Law in West Africa: The Practice of Empire* (n 285) 23.

748 Alfred P Rubin, 'The Law of Piracy' (n 746) 174.

Accordingly, this chapter will focus specifically on instances where British or Imperial commanders prosecuted against individuals or groups who conducted brigandry or piratical practices, based on a perception that these acts had been illegal under custom or law. A useful example of Imperial anti-piracy policies is seen through a letter written in 1811 by Sir Stamford Raffles (British Governor-General of the Dutch East Indies, 1811–1816) to his superior, the Earl of Minto (Governor-General of India, 1807–1813):

> The increase of piracy must necessarily be contemplated, as well as the adoption of vigorous measures on our part for the protection of our Malay and Javanese subjects, and the security of the commerce of the Eastern Seas ... the greatest necessity will be to oblige every Rajah to refuse to every description of pirates and Lanuns any sort of assistance or protection in his own territories.[749]

In this instance, it is notable that Raffles was clearly avoiding any use of the legal category of piracy, which might have created an obligation on either himself or his fellow Imperial officers to expunge the pirates from British or international territories. Rather, instead of relying upon any customary prohibition against brigandry, the Governor-General (later famous for developing Singapore into an Imperial colony) was merely using the sociological definition and seeking support for treaties with local Rajahs that would shift this obligation on to them. With this scope now in mind, it would be helpful to shift to identifying how brigandry was treated in pre-Modern international law.

It must be noted that one of the primary differences between the prohibition against brigandry, when compared against the proscription against private warfare, is that the former seems to stem from Roman law instead of Anglo-Saxon military tradition. In particular, Roman writers referred to the phenomenon of *latrocinium* as a catch-all category for individuals (*latro*) or groups (*latrones*) who participated in brigandry or violence outside of the normal usages of warfare.[750] As aptly defined by the second century Roman jurist Ulpian (170–228AD), whose commentary was in turn later relied upon by Grotius:[751]

749 Sophia Raffles, Memoir of the Life and Public Services of Sir Thomas Stamford Raffles (J Murray, 1830) 48, as discussed by Alfred P Rubin, 'The Law of Piracy' '(n 746) 175. It must also be noted that the use of the word 'Lanun' here is a reference to the Sama-Bajau peoples of maritime Southeast Asia, whose military exploits were the stuff of legend and fear during this time period: see LA Mills, *British Malaya, 1824–67* (Constable & Company, 1925) 196, 202.

750 Brent D Shaw, 'Bandits in the Roman Empire' (1984) 105 *Past and Present* 3, 6–7.

751 Alberico Gentili, *De Jure Belli Libri Tres* (n 398) 12.

> Enemies are these against whom the Roman people have publicly declared war, or who themselves have declared war against the Roman people; others are called robbers or brigands. Therefore, anyone who is captured by robbers, does not become their slave, nor has any need of the right of *postliminium*.[752]

Postliminium, a recurrent concept, refers to the right of the rule by which persons or things captured in war resume their original status when restored to the jurisdiction of their own country. As highlighted by Brent D Shaw, it was common for the charters of municipalities (*municipium*) throughout the Roman world to explicitly task local officials with the duty of punishing brigands 'for the sake of common peace' or public vengeance.[753] Curiously, sometimes this went further, with even private individuals being permitted to use force against brigands, to the extent that private actors could be exempted from being penalised under orthodox laws against homicide.[754] Among classical historians, a prominent instance of Roman Imperial support for brigandry suppression efforts was the 190AD letter sent by Commodus (177–192) to the municipality of Bubon in ancient Lycia (in modern day Turkey),[755] where the infamous Emperor praised the residents of the city for imprisoning and killing local bandits.[756]

This early othering of brigands and bandits would make its way to the traditional *jus armorum* or domestic chivalric customs later applied by West European courts and military tribunals in the early medieval period.[757] Despite this, brigandry and piracy was rife in England throughout this period, particularly during times of war when the Crown's ability to prosecute brigands and outlaws was weakened. As noted by Peter Crook:

---

752 *Corpus Juris Civilis*, XLIX, 15.24, as cited by Alfred P Rubin, 'The Law of Piracy' (1987) 2(15) *Denver Journal of International Law and Piracy* 186.

753 Brent D Shaw, 'Bandits in the Roman Empire' (n 750) 19.

754 Ibid.

755 See, eg: Wynne Williams, 'Individuality in the Imperial Constitutions: Hadrian and the Antonines' (1976) 66 *Journal of Roman Studies* 67, 82; RJA Talbert, Commodus as Diplomat in an Extract from the Acta Senatus (1988) 71 *Zeitschrift für Papyrologie und Epigraphik* 137, 142.

756 See Brent D Shaw, 'Bandits in the Roman Empire' (n 750) 19, citing Friedel Schindler, *Die Inschriften von Bubon (Nordlykien)* (Böhlau, 1972) 11–23.

757 Samuel White, 'The Late Middle Ages' (n 2) 101, 102. See also John Collins, *Martial Law and English Laws, c1500–c1700* (n 64) 22–3.

> The problem seems to have been particularly acute in the first half of the fourteenth century, when outlaws were reportedly terrorising the countryside, notably Derbyshire and Leicestershire, and were employed by respectable landholders and churchmen to carry out their more sordid business. The members of such gangs fled their natural habitats on being declared criminals and banded together because survival outside the law was better assured in groups than alone.[758]

The shift during Henry II's reign (1133–89) towards the use of contract soldiers instead of merely feudal levies, following the ravaging of the country as a result of the Anarchy (1138–53), had already initiated a military revolution that would strengthen sovereign authority.[759] As was the case with other categories of customary laws of war however, the Hundred Years War (1337–1453) fought intermittently between France and Plantagenet England — and the centralisation of royal authority over the legitimate use of violence that followed — seems to have been a watershed moment for the eventual codification of proscriptions against brigandry. As per BJH Rowe, official records from the fifteenth century English-Burgundian administration in northern France points to an overwhelming number of executions of local brigands or *brigans de boys*.[760] Notably, this definition was applied to all outlaws regardless of nationality or

---

758 Peter Crooks, 'Factions, Feuds and Noble Power in the Lordship of Ireland, c. 1356–1496' (2007) 35(140) *Irish Historical Studies* 425, 436–7. See also Barbara A Hanawalt, 'Fur-Collar Crime: The Pattern of Crime among the Fourteenth-Century English Nobility' in Barbara A Hanawalt, *Of Good and Ill Repute': Gender and Social Control in Medieval England* (Oxford University Press, 1998) 53, 53–69.

759 See Michael Prestwich, 'Money and Mercenaries in English Medieval Armies' in Alfred Haverkamp and Hanna Vollrath (eds), *England and Germany in the High Middle Ages* (Oxford University Press, 1996) 129, 129–150. See also JO Prestwich, 'War and Finance in the Anglo-Norman State' (1955) 5(4) *Transactions of the Royal Historical Society* 19, 19–43.

760 BJH Rowe, 'John Duke of Bedford and the Norman "Brigands"' (1932) 47(188) *English Historical Review* 583, 583, 585. For more information on the Anglo-Burgundian alliance towards the end of the Hundred Years War (1337–1453), see Clifford J Rogers, 'The Anglo-Burgundian Alliance and Grand Strategy in the Hundred Years War' in Peter R Mansoor and Williamson Murray (eds), *Grand Strategy and Military Alliances* (Cambridge University Press, 2016) 216, 216–53. It is important, however, to reflect on the uncertainties and immeasurable bias in the records kept during this time period. For instance, the medieval French historian and Normandy-based bishop Thomas Basin (1412–1491) wrote that upwards of ten thousand brigands were executed by Anglo-Burgundian commanders: Thomas Basin, *Hist. de Charles VII* (Soc. de 1'Hist. de France, 1855) vol 1, ii, 6, 60. As argued by Rowe, although the 'executions certainly reached a terrible figure', Basin's estimates were certainly exaggerated: BJH Rowe, 'John Duke of Bedford and the Norman "Brigands"' (n 760) 600, citing Charles de Beaurepaire, *Le Patriotisme en Normandie Pendant L'occupation Anglaise* (H Delesques, 1904).

partisanship, and was focused on those who generally 'preyed upon [English] subjects' rather than soldiers who had mutinied and turned to pillaging:[761]

> An Englishman who held the woods and preyed upon the people was dubbed 'brigand' and executed 'for his ill deeds', and his captor was paid the regulation 6 *livres tournois* without any comment as to the type of brigand he had caught ... on another occasion eight Englishmen were executed at Rouen as brigands.[762]

Curiously it must be noted that this same period is also associated with an expansion of the use of mercenaries by the English Crown in its wars. John of Gaunt's (1340–99) English contingent which fought victoriously with John I of Portugal (1357–1433, King from 1385–1433) against the Castilians at Aljubarrota during the Portuguese War of Succession (1383–5), for instance, contained many mercenary archers amongst its ranks.[763] As highlighted by Prestwich, by this point the costs of military campaigns and mustering men at arms was rising drastically to the point where it was 'increasingly difficult for magnates to supply the very large numbers of men traditionally due when the king summoned the feudal host'.[764]

The development of more effective State enforcement regimes against piracy and brigandry began with the upending of the old English feudal order brought about during the Tudor period (1485–1603), and the political consolidation processes implemented by Henry VII (1457–1509). In 1536, The government of his son Henry VIII (1491–1547) hastened this further by explicitly

761 BJH Rowe, 'John Duke of Bedford and the Norman "Brigands"' (n 760) 596.

762 Ibid. 590, citing Arch. Dép. Seine-Inferieure. Compte de la Vicomte de Rouen. St. Michel 1431, fos. 83v and 11. It must be noted that *livres tournois* was a type of currency used in France during this period: see generally Sussman N Debasements, 'Royal Revenues, and Inflation in France During the Hundred Years' War, 1415–1422' (1993) 53(1) *The Journal of Economic History* 44, 44–70; Mark Greengrass, 'Money, Majesty and Virtue: the Rhetoric of Monetary Reform in Later Sixteenth-Century France' (2007) 21(2) *French History* 165, 165–186.

763 See Malyn Newitt, 'The Portugese Nobility and the Rise and Decline of Portugese Military Power 1400–1650' in DJB Trim, *The Chivalric Ethos and the Development of Military Professionalism* (Brill, 2003)89, 95. See also Matthew Bennett, 'Why Chivalry? Military "Professionalism" the Twelfth Century: The Origins and Expressions of a Socio-Military Ethos' in DJB Trim, *The Chivalric Ethos and the Development of Military Professionalism* (Brill, 2003) 41, 41–64; Tiago Viúla de Faria, 'Tracing the "Chemyn de Portyngale": English Service and Servicemen in Fourteenth Century Portugal' (2011) 37(3) *Journal of Medieval History* 257, 257–268.

764 Michael Prestwich, 'Money and Mercenaries in English Medieval Armies' (n 759) 129, 132.

penalising acts of piracy through legislation. As noted by Heebøll-Holm, this statute was novel at the time for how it made criminalising pirates and brigands more readily enforceable by grouping them with 'the vilest of malefactors' including traitors:

> Where traytors, pirates, thieves, robbers, murderers and confederates upon the sea, many times escaped unpunished, because the trial of their offences hath heretofore been ordered, judged and determined before the admiral, or his lieutenant or commissary, after the course of the civil laws, ... suffer such pains of death, losses of lands, goods and chattels, as if they had been attainted and convicted of any treasons, felonies, robberies, or other the said offences done upon the lands.[765]

Towards the late sixteenth and seventeenth centuries, proscriptions against brigandry began to more commonly appear in the writings of the pioneering international law scholars, whose views would in turn influence nascent formal military traditions and the training of officers. First, the Italian-born lawyer Alberico Gentili (who was Regius Professor of Civil Law at Oxford from 1587–1608) argued in his *Three Books on the Law of War* that brigands and pirates violated the laws of nations, as taken from natural law and the advancement of civilisation:[766]

> Neither brigands nor pirates are entitled to the privileges of international law ... since they themselves have utterly spurned all intercourse with their fellowmen and, so far as in them lies, endeavor to drag back the world to the savagery of primitive times. In that age, as you know, men passed their lives in the manner of wild beasts, and each one carried off what fortune offered to him as prey, trained to use his strength in accordance with his own impulses and to live for himself alone.[767]

---

765 See Thomas K Heebøll-Holm, 'Towards a Criminalisation of Piracy in Late Medieval England' in Louis Sicking and Alain Wijffels, *Conflict Management in the Mediterranean and the Atlantic, 1000–1800* (Brill, 2020) 165, 165–6, citing D Pickering, *The Statutes at Large, From the First Year of King Richard II to the Thirty-first Year of King Henry VIII* (J Bentham, 1763) vol 4, 441–3.

766 Alberico Gentili, *De Jure Belli Libri Tres* (n 398) vol 2, 122–7, as discussed by Brian Lockey, 'Conquest and English Legal Identity in Renaissance Ireland' (2004) 65(4) *Journal of the History of Ideas* 543, 547.

767 Alberico Gentili, *De Jure Belli Libri Tres* (n 398) 79, as discussed by Christopher N Warren, 'Hobbes's Thucydides and the Colonial Law of Nations' (2009) 24(2) *The Seventeenth Century* 260, 260–86.

As summarised by Daragh Grant, Gentili's Christian-informed world view would therefore deposit 'faithless' persons including brigands and atheists into a wider category of 'common foes of all mankind'.[768] Accordingly, as per Bassiouni, brigands were seen by Gentili as incapable of reciprocating civilised practices and therefore deserving of universal punishment by all States under *jus gentium*.[769]

The jurist Richard Zouche (1590–1661), who was Regius Professor of Civil Law at Oxford during the English Civil War (1642–51) and post-Cromwellian period, would later similarly opine that brigands and other enemies of mankind were clearly excluded from the category of 'lawful enemies ... to whom are due all the rights of war'.[770] In doing so, both of these early jurists advocated for a customary prohibition against brigandry, to be enforced by English and international commanders as based on the principles of natural law — on the understanding that brigands and pirates were posing threats to the laws of civilised nations. As suggested by Megan Wachspress, this clearly appears to be an adaptation of the equally broad Roman concept of the *latro*,[771] albeit without the transfer of rights and privileges attached with State-sanctioned violence to private individuals.

A brief consideration of contemporary pre-Modern writers suggests that the recognition of a customary prohibition against piracy was becoming crystallised by the sixteenth and seventeenth centuries. The Dutch international lawyer Hugo Grotius (1583–1645) pointed out that 'if any one violates a sworn or unsworn pledge given to a brigand he will not on that account be liable to punishment among other nations. For because of the hatred of brigands the nations have decided to overlook illegal acts committed against them'.[772]

Regard may also be given to the Elizabethan-era courtier and historian Sir William Segar (1554–1633), whose military commentaries drew upon the

768 Daragh Grant, 'Francisco de Vitoria and Alberico Gentili on the Juridical Status of Native American Polities' *Renaissance Quarterly* (2019) 72.3 (2019): 910–52.

769 M Cherif Bassiouni, 'Universal Jurisdiction for International Crimes: Historical Perspectives and Contemporary Practice' (2001) 42 *Virginia Journal of International Law* 81, 109.

770 Richard Zouche, *Juris et Judicii Fecialis, sive, Juris inter Gentes et Quaestionum de Eodem Explicatio* (1650) vol 2, 37–8, cited by Barbara Donagan, 'Atrocity, War Crime, and Treason in the English Civil War' (n 70) 1141.

771 Megan Wachspress, 'Pirates, Highwaymen, and the Origins of the Criminal in Seventeenth-Century English Thought' (2014) 26(2) *Yale Journal of Law and the Humanities* 301, 308.

772 Hugo Grotius, *De Iure Belli Ac Pacis* [*On the Law of War and Peace*] (1625) tr (Carnegie Institution of Washington, 1925) 796.

dishonour associated with brigands and other 'enemie of base reputation' to highlight that only conflicts between honourable foes were deserving of wartime obligations — in doing so, he curiously used the example of Roman triumphs and how they could only be awarded to generals who met the criteria for honourable victories:

> Posthumius being Consul, in his seruice of the warre proceeded coldly and sparing of blood.
>
> Also in one other expedition before, he fought most infortunately, with losse of many men, and by fleeing saued his owne person.
>
> Other causes do seeme of this Triumph Ouante: as if the warre was not iustly pronounced, or the enemie of base reputation, as a Pirate, a bondman, or a coward.[773]

Likewise, the sixteenth-century French philosopher and jurist Jean Bodin, whose writings were later considered influential among Oxford-based politico-legal scholars such as John Locke,[774] also advocated for brigands to be excluded from protections otherwise afforded to prisoners of war:

> The law has always distinguished robbers and pirates from those who are recognized to be enemies legitimately at war, in that they are members of some commonwealth founded upon that principle of justice that brigands and pirates seek to subvert. For this reason brigands cannot claim that the conventions of war, recognized by all peoples, should be observed in their case, nor are they entitled to those guarantees that the victors normally accord to the vanquished.[775]

By the eighteenth century, following the Acts of Union in 1706 and 1707, the Crown was starting to take more active steps to punish acts of piracy and brigandry. In doing so, English State actors even drew upon customary international law to justify domestic laws in this space. In 1739, the Earl of Illay

773 Sir William Segar, Honor, Military, and Ciuill contained in Foure Bookes (1633) ch 21, as discussed by Megan Wachspress, 'Pirates, Highwaymen, and the Origins of the Criminal in Seventeenth-Century English Thought' (n 771) 308–9.

774 Edward Andrew, 'Jean Bodin on Sovereignty' (2011) 2(2) *Republics of Letters* 70, 76.

775 MJ Tooley, *Six Books of the Commonwealth* (Alden Press, 1967) book 1 at ch 1, as discussed by Megan Wachspress, 'Pirates, Highwaymen, and the Origins of the Criminal in Seventeenth-Century English Thought' (n 771) 308.

(1682 –1761), in his capacity of the Lord Justice-General of Scotland, noted the following regarding customary international law influences on British anti-piracy laws such as the *Smugglers Act* (1736):

> The liberty of searching the ships of foreigners upon the high seas, on suspicion of piracy, is a liberty that is established and regulated by the law of nations alone; but the liberty which every nation enjoys, of searching, on suspicion of unlawful trade, the ships of foreigners that approach near to their coast without any necessity, is a liberty that is not only established by the law of nations, but is generally regulated by the particular laws or customs of each respective society.[776]

In a further reflection of the curious relationship between the two issues, these developments ran parallel to the continued exploitation of privateers and mercenaries by the British Crown to achieve its national interests. Most famously this was seen during the British colonisation of the Americas during its Age of Commerce (1450–1680) where private citizens were licensed by the Crown to commit acts of piracy against foreign nations without breaching this contravention.[777] Strikingly though, it was during the beginning of the later High Imperial period (from 1850 onwards)[778] that Imperial campaigns began utilising paid mercenary soldiers on a significantly higher scale. As noted by Kiernan, '[e]mpires brought with them a need for specialised troops in permanent readiness for colonial duty. Of all these the most remarkable was the East India Company's army' and its reliance on Gurkha mercenaries from neighbouring Nepal.[779] Again, the usage of these mercenaries and their conduct in external conflicts such as the Naning War (1831–2) and Perak War (1875–6) was viewed by Imperial commanders as outside the scope of this customary

776 United Kingdom, *Parliamentary Debates*, House of Lords, 22 February 1739, vol 10, col 1232 (Earl of Illay).

777 Andrew Read, 'Pirates and Privateers in Elizabethan England' in Samuel White (ed), *The Laws of Yesterday's Wars* (n 9) 171, 171–86. See also Peter Lehr, *Pirates: A New History, from Vikings to Somali Raiders* (Yale University Press, 2019) 86.

778 See Anthony Reid, 'A New Phase of Commercial Expansion in Southeast Asia, 1760–1850' (n 424) 57, 57–82.

779 VG Kiernan, *Colonial Empires and Armies 1815–1960* (Sutton Publishing, 1998) 23. See also: Katerina Galai, 'Companies of Past and Present: Lessons from the East Indian Company on the Use and Regulation of Private Forces Today' (2016) 4(1) *Legal Issues Journal* 1, 3; Christopher Spearin, *Private Military and Security Companies and States: Force Divided* (Palgrave McMillan, 2017) 63.

prohibition[780] — although issues pertaining to state responsibility were swept aside following the establishment of the British Raj in 1858 and the expansion of crown colonies around that period.

The writings of these aforementioned scholars such as Segar, Gentili and Bodin,[781] in conjunction with evidence of medieval proscriptions against brigandry under *jus gentium*, evidently affected the treatment of these class of persons during the High Imperial period (from 1850 onwards).[782] As defined by Francis Lieber, whose famous 1863 American *Lieber Code* for instance was said to largely align with European and Imperial customs and laws of warfare at the time,[783] 'the word Brigand ... soon came to be applied to armed strollers, a class of men which swarmed in all countries in the middle ages'.[784] In this same text, which was later published by the US War Department, Lieber further noted that 'Wherever the freebooter is taken, at sea or on land, death is inflicted upon him now as in former times, for freebooters are nothing less than armed robbers of the most dangerous and criminal type'.[785]

Indeed, the need to prosecute international acts of piracy and brigandry became a common *casus belli* utilised by overseas State agents such as Governors, Superintendents and Residents in the High Imperial period to wage wars against external foes on all the frontier of the Empire.[786] British control

780 See C Northcote Parkinson, *British Intervention in Malaya 1867–1877* (n 90) 255. For more commentary on these two Malayan wars, see: Sir Frank Swettenham, *Footprints in Malaya* (Hutchinson & Co, 1942) 64; Sir J George Scott, 'Needs Explaining' (July–December 1907) *Blackwood's Magazine* 483, 484–5; Sir P Benson Maxwell, *Our Malay Conquests* (PS King, 1878) 61; Mervyn Llewelyn Wynne, *Triad and Tabut: A Survey of the Origin and Diffusion of Chinese and Mohamedan Secret Societies in the Malay Peninsula A.D. 1800–1935 1935* (US Government Printing Office, 1941) 329.

781 The aforementioned influence of Segar is in contrast to Lord Mansfield's statement in *Triquet v Bath* (1764) 3 Burr 1478 that there was a lacking of early English authoritative writers about the customs of the Law of Nations: see further KR Simmonds, 'Some English Precursors of Hugo Grotius ' (1957) 43 *Transactions for the Year* 143, 143.

782 See Anthony Reid, 'A New Phase of Commercial Expansion in Southeast Asia, 1760–1850' (n 424) 57, 57–82.

783 Dietrich Schindler and Jiří Toman (eds), *The Laws of Armed Conflicts: A Collection of Conventions, Resolutions, and Other Documents* (n 441) 3–23.

784 See Francis Lieber, *Guerrilla Parties Considered with Reference to the Laws and Usages of War* (D Van Nostrand, 1862) 10, which was developed by Lieber and General Henry Halleck and then circulated by the US War Department. See also Willard B Cowles, 'Universality of Jurisdiction over War Crimes' (1945) 33(2) California Law Review 177, 183, citing Francis Lieber (ed), *The Miscellaneous Writings of Francis Lieber* (JB Lippincott & Co, 1881).

785 Francis Lieber, *Guerrilla Parties Considered with Reference to the Laws and Usages of War* (n 784) 10.

786 See Damian O'Connor, 'Defending Australia: Imperial Expansion and Local Defence' (n 89) 5, 14. See also John Collins, *Martial Law and English Laws, c.1500–c.1700* (n 64) 282–3.

over the island of Borneo in modern-day Brunei, Malaysia and Indonesia, for instance, was summarised by the Royal Navy officer Sir John Dalrymple-Hay in 1849 as being due to the 'prompt measures undertaken by Sir Thomas Cochrane, Sir James Brooke and Captains [Henry] Keppel and [William] Farquhar [to extirpate] the pirates along its north-west shore'.[787] When the context of the othering of non-Western peoples is considered, however, then it is clear that Imperial commanders applied a much wider definition of what constituted brigandry and piracy when the conduct was undertaken by non-Western combatants. Farish A Noor describes this expertly in his description of how Imperial commanders applied the prohibition against brigandry in Borneo during the 1830s to 1840s:

> Though the 'campaign against piracy' that they fought was a bloody affair — and, at times, Keppel and Marryat did frankly admit that the precise definition of 'piracy' eluded them — they were nonetheless certain that they were on the right side and that piracy was the problem of the Other.
>
> The advocates of imperial expansion may have fumbled with their ad hoc definition of what piracy was, but they were clear in their consensus that the Dayaks and all things Dayak were warlike and hostile.[788]

Broadly, it is apparent that Imperial military commanders before the 1899 (first) *Hague Convention* would have firmly viewed this customary prohibition as being applicable to external military conflicts including those with non-Western peoples. Instead, the primary obstacle in this space relate to the 'ad hoc' nature of what could have constituted piracy or brigandry and the tendency of Imperial commanders to more readily extend and enforce this custom to non-Western enemies — in contrast to its own licensed privateers or hired mercenaries, who would historically be seen as outside the scope of the prohibition.

787 Sir John Charles Dalrymple Hay, *The Suppression of Piracy in the China Sea, 1849* (Edward Stanford, 1889) 7.

788 Farish A Noor, 'Hostis Humanis Generis: The Invention of the "Warlike Dayak Race" during the "War on Piracy" in Borneo, 1830–1848' in Farish A Noor and Peter Carey (eds), *Racial Difference and the Colonial Wars of 19th Century Southeast Asia* (Amsterdam University Press, 2021) 73, 97.

CHAPTER 9

Prohibition against the Forced Dispersal or Deportation of Civilians

> Look at me —I've lost my home, the two of you, my country,
> they've stripped me of all they could take,
> yet my talent remains my joy, my constant companion:
> over *this*, Caesar could have no rights. What if
> some savage's sword should cut short my existence?
> When I'm gone, my fame will endure,
> and while from her seven hills Mars' Rome in triumph
> still surveys a conquered world, *I shall be read.*[789]

∵

Modern-day international humanitarian law forbids the deportation, dispersal or forcible transfers of civilians for reasons related to conflicts.[790] As highlighted in 2003 by the Trial Chamber of the International Criminal Tribunal for the Former Yugoslavia (ICTY) in *Prosecutor v Milomir Stakić*:

> the prohibition against deportation serves to provide civilians with a legal safeguard against forcible removals in time of armed conflict and the uprooting and destruction of communities by an aggressor or occupant of the territory in which they reside.[791]

---

789 Ovid, *Tristria.* tr George Luck (Winter Publishing House, 1967) vol 3, 7, 45–52. See generally Juliane Prade's excellent discussion of Ovid's poetry after his deportation from Rome by Augustus: 'Ovid in the "Wilderness": Exile and Autonomy' in Agnieszka Gutthy (ed), *Exile and the Narrative/Poetic Imagination* (Cambridge Scholars Publishing, 2010) 7, 15–6.

790 It must be noted that the act of displacing civilians during wartime has been referred to under various different names throughout history, including but not limited to: deportation, dispersal, forcible transfer, population transfers, mass expulsion, demographic manipulation, forced relocation and ethnic cleansing. See generally Jean Marie Henckaerts, *Mass Expulsion in Modern International Law and Practice* (Martinus Nijhoff, 1995); Joseph Schechla, 'A Righteous Inconsistency: Applying International Norms to Population Transfer in Bosnia and Palestine' (1998) 7(12) *Critique: Critical Middle Eastern Studies* 77, 77–105. Interestingly, Schechla also notes how the general term 'removal' was associated with 'transfer policies affecting indigenous populations in North America' during the administration of President Andrew Jackson (1829–37): at 78.

791 *Prosecutor v Milomir Stakić*, IT-97-24-T, para 681 (ICTY, Trial Chamber ii, Judgment, 31 July 2003). See also Etienne Henry, 'Deportation and Forcible Transfer of Civilian Populations

 | DOI:10.1163/9789004515987_011

The first multilateral treaty to set out this prohibition was the Fourth Geneva Convention of 1949. Article 49 of the Fourth Geneva Convention specifically asserts that '[i]ndividual or mass forcible transfers, as well as deportations of protected persons from occupied territory to the territory of the Occupying Power or to that of any other country, occupied or not, are prohibited, regardless of their motive'. It is clear that the Fourth Geneva Convention was adopted in response to the atrocities of the two World Wars,[792] including the mass deportations of civilians by the Nazi regime.[793]

Notably, a prohibition of deportations or the forcible transfer of civilians was not explicitly set out in the prior 1907 *Hague Regulations*.[794] The International Committee of the Red Cross' (ICRC) Commentary to GC IV explains that this was likely on the basis that 'the practice of deporting persons was regarded at the beginning of this century as having fallen in abeyance'.[795] Accordingly, Pictet implies that the authors of the *Hague Regulations* saw no urgent need to address deportations,[796] noting that its drafting process occurred years before the World Wars — the events of which 'made it necessary to make more detailed provisions on this point'.[797] As pointed out by de Zayas, '[a]nalogously, it would have seemed unnecessary to the delegates convened at The Hague in 1907 to draft special articles to prohibit cannibalism or human sacrifices'.[798]

---

in Fourth Geneva Convention and Beyond' in Md Jahid Hossain Bhuiyan and Borhan Uddin Khan (eds), *Revisiting the Geneva Conventions: 1949–2019* (Brill, 2020) 75, 77.

792 See Jean S Pictet (ed), *The Geneva Conventions of 12 August 1949 Commentary — IV Geneva Convention Relative to the Protection of Civilian Persons in Time of War* (International Committee of the Red Cross, 1958) 3.

793 See Alfred M de Zayas, 'International Law and Mass Population Transfers' (1975) 16(2) *Harvard International Law Journal* 207, 213.

794 See Regulations annexed to Convention No. IV of The Hague respecting the Laws and Customs of War on Land, Oct. 18, 1907, 36 Stat. 2277, T.S. No. 539, cited by Joseph Baker and Henry Crocker (eds), *Laws of Land Warfare: Concerning the Rights and Duties Of Belligerents As Existing On August 1, 1914* (US Government Publishing Office, 1919). See generally Adam Roberts & Richard Guelff, *Documents on The Laws of War* (eds) (Oxford University Press, 1989) 48.

795 See, eg, Jean S Pictet (ed) T*he Geneva Conventions of 12 August 1949 Commentary — IV Geneva Convention Relative to the Protection of Civilian Persons in Time of Wa*r (n 792) 4–5, 278, 279. See also Jean-Marie Henckaerts, *Deportation And Transfer Of Civilians In Time Of War* (1993) 26(3) *Vanderbilt Law Review* 469, 480. See generally Theodor Meron, *War Crimes Law Comes of Age* (n 84) 143.

796 Jean S Pictet (ed) T*he Geneva Conventions of 12 August 1949 Commentary — IV Geneva Convention Relative to the Protection of Civilian Persons in Time of Wa*r (n 792) 279.

797 Ibid.

798 Alfred M de Zayas, 'International Law and Mass Population Transfers' (n 793) 207, 211.

At the same time, however, modern commentators such as Etienne Henry have contended that, prior to the adoption of GC IV in 1949, it was generally ambiguous whether deportations and the forcible transfer of civilians in times of armed conflict were prohibited by customary international law.[799] This view can be supported by literature published in that period by the ICRC, which noted in the preamble to its 'Draft Convention for the Protection of Civilian Persons in Time of War' that:

> In present circumstances, however, it would be difficult to claim that this principle should be applicable at all times and in all places, even within the territory of a State. Nevertheless, if Governments agreed to subscribe to this ruling, the ICRC would welcome their action.[800]

In the face of this ambiguity, it is worth exploring the extent to which a pre-*Hague* customary prohibition against the dispersal or deportation of civilian populations was applicable on British or Imperial commanders. As argued by Frédéric Mégret, forcible transfers of population appear to have been common practice by other Imperial powers who conducted colonial wars[801] — with the cruel deportations of Herero peoples from German South West Africa, as ordered by General Lothar von Trotha during the Herero Wars (1904–1908) being a prominent example of this:

> I, the great general of the German troops, send this letter to the Herero people … All Hereros must leave this land … Any Herero found within the German borders with or without a gun, with or without cattle, will be shot. I shall no longer receive any women or children. I will drive them back to their people or I will shoot them. This is my decision for the Herero people.[802]

---

799 Etienne Henry, 'Deportation and Forcible Transfer of Civilian Populations in Fourth Geneva Convention and Beyond' in Md. Jahid Hossain Bhuiyan and Borhan Uddin Khan (eds), *Revisiting the Geneva Conventions: 1949–2019* (n 791) 75, 77 citing Alfred M de Zayas, 'International Law and Mass Population Transfers' (n 793) 207, 207.

800 See the 'Draft Convention for the Protection of Civilian Persons in Time of War' in *Revised and New Draft Conventions for the Protection of War Victims: Remarks and Proposals Submitted by the International Committee of the Red Cross*, (International Committee of the Red Cross, 1949) 66.

801 Frédéric Mégret, 'From "Savages" to "Unlawful Combatants": A Postcolonial Look at International Humanitarian Law's "Other"' (n 91) 265, 281.

802 Order of 2 October 1904, as quoted in Jon M Bridgman, *The Revolt of the Hereros* (Berkeley, 1981) 129. See also Frédéric Mégret, 'From "Savages" to "Unlawful Combatants": A Postcolonial Look at International Humanitarian Law's "Other"' (n 91) 265, 281.

Evidence pointing towards the prohibition of forced civilian dispersal during and subsequent to conflicts has a long-standing and storied history, dating back to the time of Alexander the Great. Prior to this, it must be highlighted that the relocation of conquered civilians was undoubtedly a common practice in the ancient world.[803] Pharaonic Egyptians, for example, depended significantly on the exploitation labour extracted from subject populations for State construction projects including mining and the building of the Great Pyramids.[804] Greg Woolf particularly emphasises how the so-called workers' town at Giza for those labouring on the construction of the pyramids was likely filled through forced population transfers.[805] These labour deportation practices was especially apparent in the fifteenth century BC, as seen in the transfer of thousands of Ancient Syrians, Canaanites and Nubians to Egypt by Amenhotep III, Thutmose III and Hatshepsut respectively — following the conquest of their homelands by these monarchs.[806]

The Babylonian Empire was also especially well-recorded for their dispersal practices, notably in contradiction of an early prohibition set out in the Code of Hammurabi (1755–1750 BC) prohibiting forced deportation (albeit specifically for 'minor offence[s]').[807] The Babylonian Chronicles, as set out in ancient cuneiform text during the reign of Nabû-nāṣir (747 to 734 BC) specifically mentions how the old King Nebuchadnezzar II had deported the residents of Jerusalem and Tyre following his occupation of those cities. Accounts of Nabonidus (556 to 539 BC), the last monarch of the Second Babylonian Empire (otherwise known as the Neo-Babylonians), similarly point to forced relocation being a primary focus of his imperial policies.[808]

It must be emphasised that the ancient concept of what constituted 'civilians' and their associated rights was markedly different from the modern-day

803 Greg Woolf, 'Moving Peoples in the Early Roman Empire' in Elio Lo Cascio and Rens Tacomaby (eds), *The Impact of Mobility and Migration in the Early Roman Empire* (Brill, 2017) 6–7. See generally Bustenay Oded, *Mass Deportations and Deportees in the Neo-Assyrian Empire* (Reichert, 1979).

804 Greg Woolf, 'Moving Peoples in the Early Roman Empire' (n 803) 4.

805 Ibid.

806 See, eg, Giovanni B Lanfranchi, Simonetta Ponchia and Robert Rollinger (eds), *Making Peace in the Ancient World* (Zaphon, 2022) vol 5, 85. See also Jeremy I Levitt, 'The African Origins of International Law: Myth or Reality' (2015) 19 *University of California Journal of International Law and Foreign Affairs* 113, 151.

807 See Martha Tobi Roth, *Law collections from Mesopotamia and Asia Minor* (Scholars Press, 1999) 106.

808 See Trevor Bryce and Jessie Birkett-Rees, *Atlas of the Ancient Near East: From Prehistoric Times to the Roman Imperial Period* (Routledge, 2016) 235–37.

view, in that civilians were considered by custom to be the property of conquering States or polities. This is evidently reflected through the commentary of the fifth century BC Athenian general and military historian Thucydides, for instance, who noted the view held by his countrymen that '[a]nything done under the pressure of war and danger ... might reasonably claim indulgence'.[809]

At the same time however, aside from the *Code of Hammurabi*, there are numerous instances of ancient rulers or statesman issuing decrees or edicts prohibiting the deportation or forcible transfer of civilians — clearly insufficient, particularly in the face of the previously described customary practices to establish a distinct universal prohibition, but arguably enough to suggest that the ban on forced dispersal did not spring, as Athena did, from the minds of the drafters of the Fourth *Geneva Convention*. In his 338 BC conquest of the kingdom of Lydia in Anatalia, for example, Alexander the Great expressly prohibited the deportation of its citizens from their homeland[810] — particularly striking when contrasted with the infamous relocation of various other populations throughout the new Hellenic empire that he forged.[811]

In contrast to the development of other customary prohibitions, which received some level of acknowledgement or treatment under *jus armorum* or the domestic chivalric customs restated and applied by Medieval European courts and military tribunals,[812] forced dispersal appears to have been actively accepted throughout most of the Middle Ages. This is especially so when considering its close connection to the separate regimes surrounding siege warfare[813] — where generally it was understood that commanders had full

809 See R Crawley *The Peloponnesian War* (Random House, 1951) 261, which is a translation of Thucydides' original *The Peloponnesian War* from 400BC. New York: Random House. See also Gregory A Raymond, *International Norms and the Resort to War* (Palgrave Macmillan, 2021) 90. See generally David Cohen, 'War, Moderation, and Revenge in Thucydides' (2006) 5(4) *Journal of Military Ethics* 270, 270–289 where Cohen discusses the Mytilenean Debate that took place among Athenian generals and statesmen during the Peloponnesian War, regarding how their State should engage in reprisals against civilians from the city-State of Mytilene, a key Spartan ally.

810 See, eg, Anne Fitzpatrick-McKinley, *Empire, Power and Indigenous Elites: A Case Study of the Nehemiah Memoir* (Brill, 2015) 81–95.

811 See generally: Robert Garland, *Wandering Greeks: The Ancient Greek Diaspora from the Age of Homer to the Death of Alexander the Great* (Princeton University Press, 2014); Peter Marshall Fraser, *Cities of Alexander the Great* (Clarendon Press, 1996).

812 Samuel White, 'The Late Middle Ages in Northern Europe' in Samuel White (ed), *The Laws of Yesterday's Wars* (n 9) 101, 102. See also John Collins, *Martial Law and English Laws, c1500–c1700* (n 64) 22–3.

813 See Jan Willem Honig's commentary on siege conventions during the 1415 Agincourt Campaign during the Hundred Years' War (1337–1453): Jan Willem Honig, 'Reappraising

discretion to treat the inhabitants of captured settlements (who had refused to surrender or submit) however they wished, including to deport or execute them.[814]

This is seen through the conduct of King Henry V (1413–1422) after the siege of Harfleur in 1415 (during the Hundred Years' War (1337–1453)). As summarised by Theodor Meron, '[o]f considerable legal importance is the fact that, in the negotiations preceding its surrender, the leaders of Harfleur had offered "to deliver the towne into the kings hands, their lives and goods saved"'.[815] After accepting the offer of surrender, however, Henry V then forcefully expelled the local population and provided their former dwellings to English settlers.[816] As recorded by the sixteenth century English chronicler (and later Member of Parliament for Bridgnorth from 1542–1547) Edward Hall:

> a greate part of the women and children [were] … expelled out of their habitations … parents with their children, yoong maids and old folke went out of the towne gates with heavie harts.[817]

Curiously, contemporary French chroniclers such as Michel Pintoin (otherwise referred to as the Monk or Religieux of Saint-Denis) did not condemn

---

Late Medieval Strategy: The Example of the 1415 Agincourt Campaign' (2012) 19(2) *War in History* 123, 123–151.

814 See, for instance, the letter written by the Duke of Wellington to the British East India Company as part of his capacity as Master-General of the Ordnance, where he noted that 'it has always been understood that the defenders of a fortress stormed have no claim to quarter': Geoffrey Parker, 'The Etiquette of Atrocity: The Laws of War in Early Modern Europe', (n 72) 155, citing Letter from Arthur Wellesely (Master-General of the Ordnance) to George Canning (President of the Board of Control of the British East India Company), 1820.

815 Theodor Meron, 'Shakespeare's Henry the Fifth and the Law of War' (n 400) 1, 22.

816 Ibid., citing See Richard Grafton's 1809 collection of Edward Hall's chronicle regarding the Hundred Years War at 63: Edward Hall and Richard Grafton, *Hall's Chronicle: Containing the History of England, During the Reign of Henry the Fourth, and the Succeeding Monarchs, to the End of the Reign of Henry the Eighth, in which are Particularly Described the Manners and Customs of Those Periods* (J Johnson, 1809) 63.

817 Edward Hall and Richard Grafton, *Hall's Chronicle: Containing the History of England, During the Reign of Henry the Fourth, and the Succeeding Monarchs, to the End of the Reign of Henry the Eighth, in which are Particularly Described the Manners and Customs of Those Periods* (J Johnson, 1809) 63. See also R Holinshed, Holinshed's Chronicles tr R Wallace and A Hansen (Clarendeon Press, 2nd ed, 1923) 58, where Holinshed notes how King Henry V treated the residents of Caen similarly.

the incident but instead focused on how King Henry had been lenient for not executing the residents of Harfleur.[818]

In line with the evolving nature of warfare throughout the pre-Modern period and its ceaseless stream of continental conflicts,[819] adjacent to the rise of nation-States and centralised militaries,[820] Western countries would later codify early military regulations into written articles intended for specific campaigns.[821] Despite the increasing emphasis on the protection of State sovereignty and interests in nineteenth century international law, this was clearly coupled with the measured development of humanitarian constraints and norms regarding wartime conduct such as the enslavement or execution of non-combatants.[822] An appraisal of the 'the first modern codification of the laws of war' points to this progress extending also to resurfaced norms regarding forced dispersal.[823]

Article 23 of the 1863 American *Lieber Code*, which Dietrich Schindler and Jiří Toman have noted as largely aligning with European customs and laws of warfare at this time,[824] provides that:

> Private citizens are no longer ... carried off to distant parts, and the inoffensive individual is as little disturbed in his private relations as the commander of the hostile troops can afford to grant in the overruling demands of a vigorous war.[825]

818 Theodor Meron, 'Shakespeare's Henry the Fifth and the Law of War' (n 400) 1, 23, discussing *Chronique du Religieux de Saint-Deny* (Collection de Documents Inedits sur l'Histoire de France, lere serie, 1844) 545. See also J Wylie, *The Reign of Henry the Fifth* (1914) 59.

819 See, eg, Warren Chin, 'Technology, War and the State: Past, Present and Future' (n 66) 765, 765–83. David Eltis, *The Military Revolution in Sixteenth Century Europe* (n 66) 6–42.

820 See, eg: Kenneth F McKenzie Jr, 'Elegant Irrelevance: Fourth Generation Warfare' (n 67) 51, 51–60; William S Lind et al, 'The Changing Face of War: Into the Fourth Generation' (n 67) 1, 2–11; Martin Van Creveld, *The Transformation of War* (n 67).

821 Timothy McCormack and Gerry Simpson, *The Law of War Crimes: National and International Approaches* (n 68) 41.

822 See Rotem Giladi, 'A Different Sense of Humanity: Occupation in Francis Lieber's Code' (2012) 94(885) *International Review of the Red Cross* 81, 81. See also Part II, Chapters 1 and 4 of this book.

823 Rotem Giladi, 'A Different Sense of Humanity: Occupation in Francis Lieber's Code' (n 822) 81, 82.

824 Dietrich Schindler and Jiří Toman (eds), *The Laws of Armed Conflicts: A Collection of Conventions, Resolutions, and Other Documents* (n 441) 3–23. See also: Karma Nabulsi, *Traditions of War: Occupation Resistance, and the Law* (Oxford University Press, 1999); Eyal Benvenisti, *The International Law of Occupation* (Princeton University Press, 1993).

825 Jean Marie Henckaerts, *Mass Expulsion in Modern International Law and Practice* (n 790) 143.

Notably, it is this provision that IHL commentators have historically looked toward as the progenitor of the modern-day law of war, with Meron noting that article 23 'anticipat[ed] the prohibition on deportations in the Fourth Geneva Convention'.[826] Of particular interest is the apparent emphasis on force and coercion in the language of article 23,[827] which has led to some commentators arguing that the Lieber Code did not intend to prohibit voluntary population transfers. Also pertinent here is the inconsistency between the absolute prohibition established in article 23, with the exception seen in article 26 which suggests that populations may be 'expel[led]' if they fail to submit to victorious commanders:

> Commanding generals may cause the magistrates and civil officers of the hostile country to take the oath of temporary allegiance or an oath of fidelity to their own victorious government or rulers, and they may expel everyone who declines to do so. But whether they do so or not, the people and their civil officers owe strict obedience to them as long as they hold sway over the district or country, at the peril of their lives.[828]

According to Rotem Giladi, this was again a reflection of the focus of international law at the time on the protection of State interests: '[e]ven if absolute prohibitions can be identified in the Code, and if lawfulness is cumulative to necessity, nothing in the Code suggests that this is grounded in humanity or human dignity in the sense used today'.[829] Accordingly, although the existence of an absolute proscription against deportation in article 23 suggests that a prohibition against wartime civilian dispersal existed by 1863, it is evident that this was not unqualified — and instead subject to tests of military necessity and the war aims of belligerents.

Nowhere is that more apparent than in the instructions issued by Major-General William T Sherman (Commander of the Army of the Tennessee from

826 See also Joseph Schechla, 'A Righteous Inconsistency: Applying International Norms to Population Transfer in Bosnia and Palestine' (n 790) 77, 77–105.

827 See Jack Goldsmith, United States Department of Justice, 'Voluntary Departure from Occupied Territory' (16 July 2004) <https://www.justice.gov/sites/default/files/olc/legacy/2009/12/30/aclu-ii-071604.pdf>.

828 Francis Lieber et al, *General Orders No 100: Adjutant-General's Office, Instructions for the Government of Armies of the United States in the Field* (D Van Nostrand, 1863) art 26, quoted by Rotem Giladi, 'A Different Sense of Humanity: Occupation in Francis Lieber's Code' (n 822) 81, 111.

829 Rotem Giladi, 'A Different Sense of Humanity: Occupation in Francis Lieber's Code' (n 822) 81, 111.

1863–4 and later Commanding General of the US Army from 1869–83) to a subordinate commander during the latter stages of the American Civil War (1861–5). While drawing upon the Lieber Code for general advice on how to treat hostile local residents, Sherman also explicitly cited English conduct during the Williamite War in Ireland (1689–91):

> I will only instance one when in the reign of William and Mary the English Army occupied Ireland then in a state of revolt. The inhabitants were actually driven into foreign lands and were dispossessed of their property and a new population introduced. To this day a large part of the North of Ireland is held by the descendants of the Scotch emigrants sent thereby by William's order & an Act of Parliament.[830]

Ultimately, General Sherman's instructions to Major Sawyer indicated the reality on the ground that American state practice had not yet reflected widespread acceptance of an absolute prohibition against deportation among its commanders:

> I would advise the commanding officers at Huntsville, and such other towns as are occupied by our troops, to assemble the inhabitants and explain, self-evident propositions, and tell them that …
>
> The Government of the United States has in North Alabama any and all rights which they choose to enforce in war— to take their lives, their homes, their lands, their everything— because they cannot deny that war does exist there, and war is simply power unrestrained by constitution or compact. If they want eternal war, well and good; we accept the issue, and will dispossess them and put our friends in their places.[831]

Accordingly, with the current information available, a practice-oriented approach to a prohibition against forced dispersal suggests that it was developing as an acknowledged pre-*Hague* custom the time of the late nineteenth-century in Imperial wars (as per its inclusion in art 23 of the influential Lieber

830 Letter from Sherman to Major Sawyer (Assistant Adjutant General), 31 January 1864. See also Ronald E Colvin, 'The Just Objects of War: Conduct of Union troops toward Noncombatants and Private Property in Alabama, 1862–1865' (MA Thesis, College of William & Mary) 27–8.

831 Letter from Sherman to Major Sawyer (Assistant Adjutant General), 31 January 1864. See also Ronald E Colvin, 'The Just Objects of War: Conduct of Union troops toward Noncombatants and Private Property in Alabama, 1862–1865' (n 830) 28.

Code), but that it was not universally enforceable and certainly did not extend to conflicts against non-Western peoples. Rather, than a specific customary prohibition that Imperial commanders might have been expected by their peers or superiors to implement, it was instead seemingly open to the wide discretion provided to these men on the spot.[832]

832 See, eg, Frédéric Mégret, 'From "Savages" to "Unlawful Combatants": A Postcolonial Look at International Humanitarian Law's "Other"' (n 91) 281–2.

CHAPTER 10

Prohibition on Private Warfare

> Two households, both alike in dignity, In fair Verona, where we lay our scene, From ancient grudge break to new mutiny, Where civil blood makes civil hands unclean. …[833]
>
> Great empires rarely enjoy peace. If there is no foreign foe to engage them, their sword is turned upon themselves; and like healthy bodies free from external menace, they collapse from their own excess of strength.[834]

In this chapter, 'private warfare' will be used to refer to conflicts between private individuals or organisations, in contrast to 'public warfare' between governments or nation-states.[835] As always, given their influence on the development of the late eighteenth-century Imperial warfare that we are seeking to understand, we must first consider evidence of initial English wartime practices throughout the medieval and pre-modern periods.[836]

At a time when the notion of a centralised, cohesive authority was only starting to re-establish itself both in England and across Europe, Kaminsky notes how medieval aristocrats commonly waged war against one another through blood-feuds or 'private wars, guerres privies [and] *Privatkriege*'.[837] These countless petty wars would go on to form the majority of the 'large-scale, organised violence' that we associated with the Middle Ages, in contrast to the

833 William Shakespeare, *Romeo and Juliet*, Prologue.

834 Sir Thomas Craig, *De Unione Regnorum Britanniae Tractatus* (1605) 470–1, as reproduced in See Roger Manning, 'Explanations and Justifications of War in the British Kingdoms in the Seventeenth Century' (2020) 41(1) *Quidditas* 134, 134.

835 The phrase 'privatised warfare' on the other hand, refers more generally to the use of mercenaries in wartime.

836 See introduction.

837 See Howard Kaminsky, 'The Noble Feud in the Later Middle Ages' [2002] (177) *Past & Present* 55, 55. See also Edward Jenks, *A Short History of English Law: From the Earliest Times to the End of the Year* (Methuen & Co, 1912) 8.

 | DOI:10.1163/9789004515987_012

royal wars waged by sovereigns against each other.[838] More broadly, it could be summarised as such: that that 'enmity was an institution, at least in the sense that lordship or vassalage were; that is, it was a generally recognized relationship hedged by ritual, expectation and sanction'.[839] While vassals were usually bound by oaths of loyalty to not wage war or harm against their superiors, in exchange for special privileges such as land or title, this did not extend to other vassals under the same system. In fact, history shows us that their right to wage war on eachother was one closely guarded by the nobility, as indicated by the numerous violent uprisings that would erupt when sovereigns attempted to restrain aristocratic feuds between their vassal magnates.[840]

It must be emphasised that private warfare during this period was governed by the same traditional *jus armorum* as applied to public wars.[841] Banners were raised during by military commanders' private wars, just as they would have when serving the English Kings against the French. These customs also included nascent prohibitions on violence against children and priests, which have been explored in more detail in other chapters.[842]

In the English context the historical treatment of blood-feuds and its norms is useful to consider, particularly as it developed independently of the Roman right of vengeance or *latrocinium*.[843] Halsall provides the following useful definition of its place in English society prior to the Norman Conquest in 1066:

> when one social group, usually a family or kindred but occasionally an institution such as a monastery, is wronged, it makes a great display of its anger, of the fact that it has been wronged and of the fact that it has

838 Justine Firnhaber-Baker, 'Techniques of Seigneurial War in the Fourteenth Century' (n 385) 90.

839 Robert Bartlett, *'Mortal Enmities': The Legal Aspect of Hostility in the Middle Ages* (University of Wales Press, 1998) 1–3. See also Howard Kaminsky, 'The Noble Feud in the Later Middle Ages' (n 387) 55, 59.

840 The Knights' War (1522–3) that erupted in central Germany is an apt example of this type of conflict occurring in medieval Europe, where assemblies of Franconian knights revolted against the attempts of their liege Prince-Bishops to enhance their feudal authority: see, eg, Benjamin Arnold, 'German Bishops and Their Military Retinues in the Medieval Empire' (1989) 7(2) *German History* 161, 182–3. See also HS Brather, 'Administrative Reforms in Electoral Saxony at the end of the Fifteenth Century' in Gerald Strauss, *Pre-Reformation Germany* (Macmillan, 1972) 225–62.

841 David A Schlueter, 'The Court-Martial: A Historical Survey' (n 65) 129, 131–2. See also Samuel White, 'The Late Middle Ages in Northern Europe' (n 9) 103, 106.

842 See, eg, pt II ch I.

843 See Brent D Shaw, 'Bandits in the Roman Empire' (n 750) 3, 6–7. See also pt II ch VI.

> the right to extract vengeance upon the wrongdoers. Pressure is thereby brought upon the original attackers to make reparation, either informally or through the local officers of the law, or sometimes through the mediation of the church. Where compensation is not paid, the aggrieved party sometimes carries out a retaliatory attack. If the correct procedures have been followed, a successful vengeance killing is held to be quite legal, and terminates the dispute.[844]

Indeed, legal scholars writing about Anglo-Saxon England have looked pointedly towards its custom of enforcing the remittance of the *wergild* or blood payments to the kin of murder victims.[845] Most strikingly, non-payment would be punished by Anglo-Saxon law then legitimising the use of force from the wrong parties against the perpetrator.[846] As contended by Hyams, this system of privileging vengeance killings was made necessary by the entrenched feud culture that 'pre-Alfredian kings shared with their nobility'[847] as notably illustrated by the series of twelve sanctified Anglo-Saxon murdered royals through the seventh to the ninth centuries including Saint Cynehelm of Mercia (786–821).[848] The eventual ascension of Alfred the Great of Wessex (849–899) to the kingship of a united England, and its associated intensification of royal authority, is said to have yielded a wave of new *leges* or early uniform law codes intended to curtail undesirable customs such as blood-feuds between Anglo-Saxon *ealdormen* and their retainers.[849] For instance, as translated by Frederick Levi Attenborough, Alfred declared the following as part of his collection of laws intended to solidify royal authority:

844 See Guy Halsall, 'Reflections on Early Medieval Violence: The Example of the "Blood Feud"' (1970) 2(1) *Memoria y Civilización* 7, 10.

845 See, eg, WD Aston, 'Problems of Roman Criminal Law' (1914) 13(2) *Journal of the Society of Comparative Legislation* 213, 216.

846 William Ian Miller, 'Choosing the Avenger: Some Aspects of the Bloodfeud in Medieval Iceland and England' (1982) 1(2) *Law and History Review* 159, 161. See also JM Wallace-Hadrill, 'The Bloodfeud of the Franks' in JM Wallace-Hadrill, *The Long-Haired Kings and Other Studies in Frankish History* (Routledge, 1962) 121, 129.

847 Paul Hyams, *Rancor and Reconciliation in Medieval England* (Cornell University Press, 2003) 77. See also the discussion of bloodfeuds in Laura Wangerin, 'Royal Feuds and the Politics of Sanctity in Anglo-Saxon England and Ottonian Saxony' (2014) 18(January-June) *Mirabilia Journal of Antiquity, Middle and Modern Ages* 78, 84; Marc Bloch, *Feudal Society* (University of Chicago Press, 1964) 128.

848 Laura Wangerin, 'Royal Feuds and the Politics of Sanctity in Anglo-Saxon England and Ottonian Saxony' (n 847) 78, 82.

849 See Frederick Levi Attenborough, *The Laws of the Earliest English Kings* (Cambridge University Press, 1922) 85, where Attenborough describes the laws of King Alfred. See also

> § 5. We further declare that a man may fight on behalf of his lord, if his lord is attacked, without becoming liable to vendetta. Under similar conditions a lord may fight on behalf of his man.
>
> § 6. In the same way a man may fight on behalf of one who is related to him by blood, if he is attacked unjustly, except it be against his lord. This we do not permit.[850]

According to Stephen White, a directly proportional relationship may be established between frequent feuding and regions lacking centralised higher authorities capable of effectively arbitrating disputes between violent parties.[851] Therefore, from this early example of King Alfred's attempts to constrain blood-feuds and other forms of private, non-sovereign warfare, we can start observing the nascent development of a wider prohibition on such conduct. Generally, the traditional view amongst scholars of English and Imperial history has been that England treated noble feuds differently given the 'process of political consolidation and the corresponding monopoli[s]ation of power' by the twelfth and thirteen century Angevin Kings and their successors, which succeeded in curtailing aristocratic feuds when compared to their contental peers such as the French and Germans.[852] White, for instance, points to the inability of weakened French rulers after the first millennium to prevent armed conflicts among their nominal subjects, in clear contrast to the province of Normandy whose dukes had achieved a monopoly over the legitimate use of violence and armed force by the time of William the Conqueror (1028–87).[853] Strikingly, historians such as Hyams and Garnett have further argued that aristocratic violence in medieval England was largely channelled through centripetal conflicts over kingship between the claims of members of the royal

---

William Ian Miller, 'Choosing the Avenger: Some Aspects of the Bloodfeud in Medieval Iceland and England' (n 846)159, 170–2; Laura Wangerin, 'Royal Feuds and the Politics of Sanctity in Anglo-Saxon England and Ottonian Saxony' (n 847) 78, 92.

850 Frederick Levi Attenborough, *The Laws of the Earliest English Kings* (n 849) 85.

851 Stephen D White, 'Feuding and Peace — Making in the Touraine Around the Year 1100' (1986) 42(1) *Traditio* 195, 200. See also Guy Halsall, 'Reflections on Early Medieval Violence: The Example of the "Blood Feud"' (n 844) 7, 15; Jacob Black-Michaud, *Feuding Societies* (Basil Blackwell, 1975) ch 4.

852 See Howard Kaminsky, 'The Noble Feud in the Later Middle Ages' (n 837) 55, 57. Whereas, Kauerper writes about how English noble feuds were common: 3 Richard W. Kaeuper, Chivalry and Violence in Medieval Europe (Oxford University Press, 1999) 110.

853 Stephen D White, 'Feuding and Peace — Making in the Touraine Around the Year 1100' (n 851) 195, 200. See also Mark Hagger, *Norman Rule in Normandy*, 911–1144 (Boydel Press, 2020) 105.

family themselves,[854] which assisted in maintaining the general coherence of the English State.

Nonetheless, an examination of English State conduct still points to a tradition of private warfare persisting until at least after the War of the Roses (1455–87) and the upending of the old feudal order brought about during the Tudor period (1485–1603). In particular, when considering post-Conquest England, much has been similarly made about the feud sub-culture which gripped lands between its northern border and Scotland during the times when neither entity could meaningfully establish their jurisdiction and instead had to rely on local armed bands for coercive force.[855] As per Summerson, '[t]he nature of the war fought on the border was such that the king could only protect his subjects there by employing the services of just those magnates whose power he needed to restrain, but whose local predominance he was, for all that, obliged to maintain and all too often to increase'.[856]

The usual aristocratic perpetrators of these Anglo-Scottish private wars are well-known to historians both past and modern. For example, a 1378 English statute during the reign of Richard II (1367–1400, King of England from 1377–99) complains about the conduct of warring nobles acting as if 'it were a land of war'.[857] While the powerful Douglas and Dunbar families commonly warred against each other in Scotland, alike to the passionate Neville-Percy feud in northern England,[858] the Percies and Douglases also engaged in cross-border

854 See, eg, Paul R Hyams, *Rancor and Reconciliation in Medieval England* (n 847) 71–154. See also George Garnett, 'Ducal Succession in Early Normandy' in George Garnett and John Garnett, *Law and Government in Medieval England and Normandy: Essays in Honour of James Holt* (Cambridge University Press, 1994) 80–110.

855 See, eg, Guy Halsall, 'Reflections on Early Medieval Violence: The Example of the "Blood Feud"' (n 844) 7, 16. In the words of Cynthia Neville, the borderlands were governed by 'a system of law that distinguished the March lands of both realms, and acknowledged their quasi-independence from the normal machinery of the common law': see further Cynthia J Neville, *Violence, Custom and Law: The Border Lands in the Later Middle Ages* (Edinburgh University Press, 1998) 100; Jean-Philippe Genet, 'Scotland in the Later Middle Ages: A Province or a Foreign Kingdom for the English?' in Hannah Skoda, Patrick Lantschner, and RLJ Shaw (eds), *Contact and Exchange in Later Medieval Europe: Essays in Honour of Malcolm Vale* (Boydell Press, 2001) 127, 132.

856 See Henry Summerson, 'Responses to War: Carlisle and the West March in the Later Fourteenth Century', in Anthony Goodman and Anthony Tuck (eds), *War and Border Societies*, 155, 165. See also Jean-Philippe Genet, 'Scotland in the Later Middle Ages: A Province or a Foreign Kingdom for the English?' (n 855) 127, 134.

857 2 Ric II [Eng], st 1 c 6 (SR II 9–10).

858 Other famous fifteenth century major noble feuds in English history include the ones between Bonvilles and Courtenays, the Percies and Nevilles, and the Talbots and Berkeleys.

military confrontations against each other without the permission of their sovereigns.[859] Two private wars between them stand out in particular, during the 1380s before the eventual Percy Rebellion (1403) against Henry IV of England (1367–1413, King from 1399–1413). Despite earlier attempts by their respective monarchs to bind the two families to a truce,[860] particularly after the personal truce conducted between David II of Scotland and King Edward III (1312–1377, King of England from 1327–1377), violence flared again in 1384 when the Percies lost control of both Lochmaben and Berwick upon Tweed castles to the Scottish Earl of Douglas at a time when the two countries were not in conflict.[861] While the enforcement of any specific prohibition on private warfare was not feasible yet given the absence of direct Crown control, it is already evident by this point that innovations in customary law and royal pardons were beginning to curtail ancient rights to private warfare. Edward III, in particular, seemed quite passionate regarding this as seen by his ordinance in 1351 which encouraged nobles to resort to the common law to arbitrate disputes — specifically ordering that 'if strife [should] arise between English and English, being of the peace, neither of them [should] make distraint or take pledge or distress upon the other, nor take vengeance against the other'.[862]

According to Walsingham, the royal chronicler at the time, it was unfortunate for Sir Henry Percy (1364–1403, known to history as 'Hotspur') that he was in Westminster when news of his losses reached the English court;[863] soon after he was made to arrange another private treaty in 1385 between himself and Archibald Douglas, the Earl of Galloway, in exchange for a pardon from Richard II (1367–1400, King of England from 1377–99) 'for twice letting Berwick castle fall into the hands of the Scots since the king's coronation'.[864] The full letters patent issued by Richard II in February 17, 1385 regarding the matter

859 See, eg, Herbert Maxwell, *A History of the House of Douglas from the Earliest Times Down to the Legislative Union of England and Scotland* (Freemantle & Co, 1902) 130–1.

860 Cynthia J Neville, *Violence, Custom and Law: The Anglo-Scottish Border Lands in the Later Middle Ages* (n 855) 55; See also the compilation of English treaties in this period as compiled by Rymer: Thomas Rymer, *Foedera, Conventiones, Litterae* (1739) voliii, 158–9.

861 See HT Riley (ed), *Thomas Walsinham, Thomas Walsingham, Quondam Monachi S. Albani, Historia Anglicana* (Longman, Roberts and Green) vol ii, 118; See also FJ Amours (ed), *The Original Chronicle of Andrew of Wyntoun.* (William Blackwood and Sons, 1908) 288–90.

862 25 Edw III [Ire], c 16 (Statutes John–Hen V 388–91).

863 See HT Riley (ed), Thomas Walsinham, *Thomas Walsingham, Quondam Monachi S Albani, Historia Anglicana* (n 861) vol II, 118.

864 See Michael Brown, *The Black Douglases: War and Lordship in Medieval Scotland 1300–1455* (Barnes & Noble, 2004) 106–7.

goes on to restore his titles to the castles after recovering them from Douglas after the truce:

> Whereas the king's castle of Berwick-upon Tweed, now in the custody of the earl of Northumberland, has been twice in the hands of the Scots since the coronation, and at great expense to the said earl recovered for the king, the king in consideration of it having been so lost against the said earl's will pardons him therefor and for all forfeitures incurred thereby, and grants to him full restitution of his estate and all his possessions.[865]

The English and Scottish Crowns, who benefitted little from the private wars on their border — and the autonomy which this level of militarisation offered to local clans that would otherwise have been serving the wars of their liege lords — attempted to prohibit them by appointing 'Wardens of the Marches' to enforce regional security and settles dispute through arbitration by customary law.[866] As highlighted by Storey, following the *Treaty of Berwick* (1357) between Scotland and England,[867] the Kingdoms began empowering their wardens to maintain subsidised armies to then 'compel ... subjects to observe truces' by punishing parties who engaged in open hostilities and forcing them to 'restore their booty'.[868] Ultimately, the centuries-old position of warden was abolished in 1603 following the merger of the political integration of the two kingdoms through the *Union of England and Scotland Act 1603*.[869]

Moving away from the northern border, we can observe that private warfare remained a constant obstacle to internal peace in England and Wales through the late thirteenth and early fourteenth centuries. As noted previously, this was partly due to the quasi-independence that local barons retained over their own spheres of influence and estates; while perhaps not as independent as

865 *Calendar of the Patent Rolls Preserved in the Public Record Office: Prepared Under the Superintendence of the Deputy Keeper of the Records* (1381–1385, Richard II) vol II, at 526.

866 Ibid 133, 134.

867 It must be mentioned that this is different from the later *Treaty of Berwick* (1586) during the reign of Elizabeth I (1533–1603, Queen of England from 1558–1603).

868 RL Storey, 'The Wardens of the Marches of England towards Scotland, 1377–1489' (1957) 72(285) *The English Historical Review* 593, 594. See also his discussion of how the conditions of the officer position of Warden changed overtime: see RL Storey, 'The Wardens of the Marches of England towards Scotland, 1377–1489' (n 868) 598–9, 603, 607.

869 Bruce Webster, 'Anglo-Scottish Relations, 1296–1389: Some Recent Essays' (1995) 74(1) *The Scottish Historical Review* 99, 100. Scholars of northern English history and marsh law note the great power that the Wardens ended up wielding, sometimes to the distraught of the Crown that appointed them. See for instance the description in Richard Lomas, *A Power in the Land: The Percys* (Tuckwell Press, 1999) at page 78 of the eminent Henry

the lords on the Scottish marshes, the military capability of these landholding elites had not yet sharply diverged from the Crown, and many took advantage of this when not actively serving in royal wars. This was demonstrated in 1273, when the south English barons Hugh de Turberville and Reginald FitzPiers fought a private war against the Earl of Hereford without any strong reprimand from Edward Longshanks (1239–1307, King of England from 1272–1307).[870] The border between England and the Welsh marches would also be a recurring flashpoint for private warfare between feuding nobles throughout the thirteenth and fourteenth centuries. As per McKisack, this was especially apparent during the unstable reign of Longshanks' son Edward II (1284–1327) when centralised authority was weakened by rebellions against the Crown by leading barons such as Roger Mortimer (1287–1330).[871]

In Wales itself, where their blood payment custom of *galanas* had outlived its equivalent Anglo-Saxon *wergild* into the late twelfth-century, private warfare amongst the nobility was perceived as being so common that the Crown had to take active steps to begin its prohibition — most notably in 1284 when Longshanks enacted a statute banning Welsh criminal practices such as the *galanas*,[872] which had permitted the eventual resort to private warfare as a form of 'homicide arbitration' for the settlement of disputes.[873] Interestingly, this move was supported by the Church as per Davies. A surviving letter from the John Peckham (Archbishop of Canterbury from 1230–1292) to the Welsh Prince Llywelyn ap Gruffudd (1223–1282) condemned the latter's supposed tolerance for private warfare amongst his countrymen: 'In every way your customs ... seem to be a travesty of justice, as you fail to condemn homicides and many other crimes formally and specifically'.[874]

It is also worth considering the trends of private warfare in English-occupied Gascony and Ireland, being regions where lax royal authority was similarly reliant on the often 'turbulent' collaboration of powerful local lords.[875] In the

Percy, 1st Earl of Northumberland and Warden of the Marshes in 1362: '[T]he first earl of Northumberland and his son were men of almost boundless ambition. Like Icarus, however, they flew too close to the sun, their wings melted, and they crashed to earth'.

870 *Calendar of Close Rolls* (1272–79), vol i at 56.

871 May Kisack, *The Fourteenth Century, 1307–1399* (Clarendon Press, 1959) 58–61.

872 RR Davies, 'The Survival of the Bloodfeud in Medieval Wales' (1969) 54(182) History 338, 340. See also WH Waters, *The Edwardian Settlement of North Wales in its Administrative and Legal Aspects* (1284–1343) (University of Wales Press, 1935) 99.

873 RR Davies, 'The Survival of the Bloodfeud in Medieval Wales' (n 872) 354.

874 Ibid 339. See also CT Martin, *Registrum Epistolarum fratris Johannis Peckham* (Longman, Brown, Green, 1884) vol i, 357.

875 GH Orpen, *Ireland under the Normans* (1920) vol IV, 302–3.

former, the Edwardian Kings had to contend with the violent rivalry between the counts of Foix and Armagnac,[876] who constantly engaged in petty wars against one another and consequently hemorrhaged royal resources otherwise intended for war with France.[877]

Occupied Ireland was also a hotbed for noble intrigues and private wars,[878] with an added unique element of settler violence between English settlers following its conquest during the late twelfth century.[879] Not until the Cromwellian Conquest of Ireland (1649–53) however, was the prohibition on private warfare enforced effectively on the Irish frontier in conjunction with other wartime customs such as the prohibition on executing non-combatants.[880] Such was the Crown's reliance on its powerful Irish magnates that, in 1490, pardons were issued by Henry VII Tudor (1457–1509, King of England from 1457–1509) to the warring Butlers of Ormonde and FitzGeralds of Kildare for their 'infringements of statutes against badges and livery of cloths and caps and retinues'.[881] Half a decade earlier, a memorandum addressed to the Duke of York had noted the destruction that this feud had caused to the southeastern Irish counties when royal authority had been displaced by the Wars of the Roses (1455–87):

> hath caused more destruccionne in the said Counte of Kildare and liberte of Mith within shorte tyme now late passed, and dayly doth, then was done by Irish ennemys and English rebelles of long tyme befor.[882]

Another famous private war during this period was the four-day siege of Bothal Castle in 1410 by Sir Robert Ogle (1370–1436, later the MP and Sheriff for

876 See MGA. Vale, *English Gascony, 1399–1453: A Study of War, Government and Politics during the Later Stages of the Hundred Years' War* (Oxford 1970) 170–202.

877 David S Green, 'The Later Retinue of Edward the Black Prince' (2000) 44 *Nottingham Medieval Studies* 141, 144. See also G Templeman, 'Edward III and the Beginning of the Hundred Years War' in Clifford J Rogers, *The Wars of Edward III: Sources and Interpretations* (Boydell Press, 1999) 231, 242.

878 Peter Crooks, '"Divide and rule": Factionalism as Royal policy in the Lordship of Ireland, c. 1171–1265' (2005) 19 *Peritia* 263, 263.

879 James Lydon notes how some of the first surviving parliamentary records regarding the Irish colonial community included complaints regarding petty violence between settlers: James Lydon (ed), *Law and Disorder in Thirteenth- Century Ireland: the Dublin Parliament of 1297* (Dublin 1997). See also 25 Edw I [Ire] (Statutes John–Hen V 194–213).

880 See pt II ch I.

881 *Calendar of Patent Rolls* (1485–94), at 316.

882 Steven G Ellis, *Tudor Frontiers and Noble Power: The Making of the British* State (Oxford University Press, 1995) 111–2.

Northumberland) and his army of around two hundred Scottish and English knights.[883] Notably, Bothal was at this time occupied by his brother Sir John Bertram (also eventually an MP and Sheriff for Northumberland). While this matter ultimately went before both Parliament and King Henry V (1386–1422, King of England from 1413–22), who 'showed unaccustomed speed and firmness in dealing with the affair' in summoning Sir Robert,[884] the perpetrator was released after promising to end his war against Sir John — with the castle that had caused the dispute having already been 'virtually destroyed'.[885]

It is worth also considering how courts began interpreting English customs surrounding private wars, as the developing reach of royal justice and the common law were two of the primary death knells to the tradition of noble resorting to armed confrontations as arbitration method.[886] Most strikingly, by 1480 (towards the last decade of the Wars of the Roses (1455–87), we already start to see common law recognition of a nascent customary prohibition against private warfare. In that year, Chief Justice Brian determined the following when appraising an action of debt where the plea of an alien enemy had been raised:

> It seems to me you ought to show how the league was broken, for that is matter of record; for if at one time there was a league between the King of this country and the King of Denmark. notwithstanding that all persons in England wanted to make war with those in Denmark, if our Lord the King would not assent to it, it would not be called war; but if there be no hostilities in fact, but the peace is broken between the King of Denmark and our Lord the King, as by ambassadors or otherwise, in that case where the peace and the league are broken [there is war].[887]

883 Jean-Philippe Genet, 'Scotland in the Later Middle Ages: A Province or a Foreign Kingdom for the English?' (n 855) 127, 136, 137.

884 See the description of John Bertram in JS Roskell, L Clark, C Rawcliffe (eds), *The History of Parliament: The House of Commons, 1386–1421* (Boydell and Brewer, 1993).

885 Jean-Philippe Genet, 'Scotland in the Later Middle Ages: A Province or a Foreign Kingdom for the English?' (n 855) 136, 137.

886 Paul R Hyams, *Rancor and Reconciliation in Medieval England* (n 847). See also the 1351 ordinance of Edward III (1312–1377, King of England from 1327–1377) encouraging his nobles to use the common law to arbitrate disputes instead of taking private arms: 25 Edw III [Ire], c 16 (Statutes John–Hen V 388–91).

887 See Arnold D McNair, 'The Legal Meaning of War, and the Relation of War to Reprisals' (1925) 11 *Transactions of the Grotius Society* 29, 46, citing Y.B. Hil. 19 Edw. 4; f. 6. See also Arnold D McNair, *Essays and Lectures Upon Some Legal Effects of War* (Cambridge University Press, 1920) 19.

The dawn of the Tudor period following the Wars of the Roses, and the political consolidation processes under the reign of Henry VII Tudor (1457–1509, King of England from 1457–1509), hastened the enforcement of this prohibition further as nobles started to prefer settling their disputes directly before their monarch. For instance, when a private war was stirring up again in 1495 between the Geraldine and Butler clans of Ireland, they were summoned by the King to Hampton Palace as part of peace pact discussions and ordered to *'frely forgeve … alle maner of Rancore, malices, slaunders, evill willes, discordes, discencions, robbories, brennynges, Iniuries, mayms, manslaughters'*.[888]

These English movements seemed to align with the wider development of this prohibition internationally; as seen by the 1495 ordinances declared by the Holy Roman Imperial Diet of Worms which similarly prohibited private warfare and blood feud throughout the Empire in favour of binding courts to mediate disputes.[889]

Clearer differences between the concept of private wars and the public conflicts waged by sovereigns only began to take shape in the sixteenth to seventeenth centuries,[890] as a result of the influence of the Italian jurist Thomas Aquinas' (1225–74) 'just war' theory on English legal commentators.[891] Broadly, this was also part of the wider shift in this period towards the recognition of more universally humanitarian concepts including the safeguarding of civilians[892] particularly as natural reasoning and Christian thought remained the leading influences on legal development,[893] rather than positivist ideals.[894]

888 See Agnes Conway, *Henry VII's Relations with Scotland and Ireland, 1485–1498* (Cambridge University Press, 1932) app xl 226–9.

889 Ernest Nys, 'The Development and Formation of International Law' (1912) 6(2) *American Journal of International Law* 279, 302.

890 See Roger Manning, 'Explanations and Justifications of War in the British Kingdoms in the Seventeenth Century' (2020) 41(1) *Quidditas* 134, 136. See also Samuel White, 'The Late Middle Ages in Northern Europe' (n 9) 101, 103–4.

891 See Johnson's discussion of the influence of Aquinas: James Turner Johnson, *Just War Tradition and the Restraint of War: A Moral and Historical Inquiry* (Princeton University Press, 2014) 95, 106.

892 Beatrice Heuser, 'Ordinances and Articles of War before the Lieber Code, 866–1863' (n 75) vol 21, 139–64. See also: Christopher Duffy, *The Military Experience in the Age of Reason* (n 75) 10–13; John Collins, *Martial Law and English Laws, c1500–c1700* (n 64) 7–8.

893 See Antony Anghie, 'Francisco De Vitoria and the Colonial Origins of International Law' (n 76) 321, 323, citing Alfred Rubin, 'International Law in the Age of Columbus' (n 76) 5, 5–35.

894 See Alfred P Rubin, 'The Law of Piracy: British Practice in the Nineteenth-Century' (n 77) 201, 270–1.

While broad Christian principles had of course underpinned earlier developments such as Alfred of Wessex's codifications, the doctrine of just war and its more exact guidance was a product of the civilian jurisprudence of the twelfth to fifteenth centuries.

Aquinas would go on to discuss general wars (*bellum generale*) in part II-II of his magnum opus, the *Summa Thelogiae*, which he described as legitimate external conflicts between independent polities who both recognised that they were at war.[895] In contrast, Aquinas defined *bellum particular* or specific wars as narrower conflicts where private individuals resorted to use of force against other groups or individuals[896] — notably this was altogether a broader category which lacked the external element of general wars and could even include 'unjust' acts such as gang violence.[897]

According to the *Patriarcha, or the Natural Power of Kings* (1680), as written by the seventeenth century English political theorist Sir Robert Filmer, the unique authority to declare war was one of the essential attributes of the sovereignty of monarchs.[898] In their attempts to infuse Christian ideals on a wider scale, these 'just war' commentators sought to expel private motives of personal vengeance from how wars were declared by public authorities. Notably, this trend towards political consolidation was also combined with increasing '*asymmetry*' between the standing armies that would be fielded by the Crown and the private armies raised by local lords,[899] which accelerated the nascent prohibition on private warfare.

Perhaps the grandest example of this can be seen in the *Treaty of Universal Peace* (1518), which itself was the latest of many previous attempts by Church leaders of the millennial Peace of God movement to contain the violent urges of Europe's military leaders through treaties.[900] While notoriously only lasting less than five-years, it still represented a new pinnacle of the Crown's monopoly over the use of force and violence.

---

895 See Thomas Aquinas, *Summa Theologica* pt II-II. See also Gregory M Reichberg, 'The Moral Equality of Combatants — a Doctrine in Classical Just War Theory? A Response to Graham Parsons' (2013) 12(2) *Journal of Military Ethics* 181, 188.

896 Ibid.

897 Ibid, as discussed in Gregory M Reichberg, 'The Moral Equality of Combatants — a Doctrine in Classical Just War Theory? A Response to Graham Parsons' (n 895) 188.

898 See generally Robert Filmer, *Patriarcha, or the Natural Power of Kings* (1680) as discussed in Roger Manning, 'Explanations and Justifications of War in the British Kingdoms in the Seventeenth Century' (2020) 41(1) *Quidditas* 134, 137.

899 Justine Firnhaber-Baker, 'Techniques of Seigneurial War in the Fourteenth Century' (n 385) 90, 102.

900 See also Ibid 95.

Parallel to this, the use of private military companies during the thirteenth century also altered the trajectory of warfare by beginning to reduce the English Crown's dependency on the landholding elite.[901] Instead of waging their own private wars, members of the gentry became stalwarts and captains of highly profitable, professional mercenary companies where they were able to wield considerable influence on international affairs.[902] Their adventures, and the literature that they inspired, would go on to capture the imagination of public otherwise used to Late Elizabethan plays about warfare:

> May you live long, sir,
> The king of peace, so you deny not us
> The glory of war; let not our nerves
> Shrink up with sloth, nor want of employment
> Make younger brothers thieves; 'tis their swords, sir,
> Must sow and reap their harvest.[903]

This is particularly lionised in British history through the example of Prince Rupert of the Rhine (1619–82, later the Lord High Admiral of the English Royal Navy from 1668–1682), the nephew of King Charles I (1600–49) and mercurial commander of the Royalist cavalry during the early stage of the English Civil War (1642–51). A notable favourite of modern-day military historians for his colourful adventures while in exile from Cromwell's England,[904] Rupert was at different times employed as a mercenary commander by Prince Frederick Henry of Holland, and Louis XIV of France to serve against the Spanish during the Dutch Revolt (1566–1648) and Thirty Years' War (1618–1648) respectively.[905] As royal authority once again began to haemorrhage during the English Civil War

901 William Stubbs, The Constitutional History of England, in its Origin and Development (1875), vol ii, 307–8; see also War Office, *Manual of Military Law* (His Majesty's Stationery Office, 1899) 193, citing William Stubbs, Select Charters and Other Illustrations of English Constitutional History from the Earliest Times to the Reign of Edward the First (1913) 359.

902 See Sean McFate, *Mercenaries and War: Understanding Private Armies Today* (National Defense University Press, 2019) 9.

903 The Maid of Honour (1632), lines 202–206, 215–20, in Philip Edwards and Colin Gibson (eds), The Plays and Poems of Philip Massinger, i.127–8. See also Roger Manning, 'Explanations and Justifications of War in the British Kingdoms in the Seventeenth Century' (n 834) 134, 160–1.

904 See, eg, Geoffrey Smith, *Royalist Agents, Conspirators and Spies Their Role in the British Civil Wars, 1640–1660* (Routledge, 2016); RBB Manning, 'Styles of Command in Seventeenth-Century English Armies' (2007) 71(3) *The Journal of Military History* 671, 671–699.

905 See CR Boxer, 'Some Second Thoughts on the Third Anglo–Dutch War, 1672–1674' (1969) 19 *Transactions of the Royal Historical Society* 67, 67–94.

(1642–51), the Crown turned to private military actors such as Prince Rupert to advance its wartime goals. The Royalist defeat and subsequent Parliamentarian victory, however, oversaw the expansion of centralised, standing armies operated by the new Parliamentarian government and the continued reinforcement of the now crystallised prohibition on internal private warfare.[906]

As Read highlights, England's exploitation of private military actors continued into the seventeenth and eighteenth centuries — where their use in conduct such as privateer raids against foreign combatants could result in political reactions that were 'more sustainable compared to instances of outright state directed belligerency' such as open warfare.[907] While further commentary on their use had been covered in the separate chapter on brigandry[908] it must be noted that elites in this period were able to curry favour with the Crown to pursue private warfare against parties, outside of the nearly fully realised prohibition on internal private warfare between English military commanders.[909] This is evident through the Government's tolerance for the expeditions on the colonial frontier waged by adventurers such as Sir Francis Drake;[910] so long as their interests did not interfere with the English State's interests (eg by assisting enemies such as Spain), then they were outside the scope of the customary prohibition against private warfare.

In contrast to the historical dependency on powerful marsh lords on the Scottish, Welsh and Irish frontiers, however, and the difficulties in enforcing the prohibition against them, by this point the Crown had achieved asymmetry against local lords such that they had now monopolised the legitimate use of violence.[911] Even the famous Drake himself would have learned of this in 1589, when he was placed before a 'court of inquiry' by the Privy Council to answer charges related to his failed expedition against Spanish-occupied Lisbon to place the would-be usurper Don Antonio on the Portuguese throne.[912] As per

---

906 See, eg, Stephen Skinner, 'Blackstone's Support for the Militia' (2000) 44(1) *American Journal of Legal History* 1, 4–5.

907 Andrew Read, 'Pirates and Privateers in Elizabethan England' in Samuel White (ed), *The Laws of Yesterday's Wars: From Indigenous Australians to the American Civil War* (Brill, 2021) 171, 172. See also Peter Lehr, *Pirates: A New History, from Vikings to Somali Raiders* (Yale University Press, 2019) 86.

908 See Pt II Ch VIII.

909 Andrew Read, 'Pirates and Privateers in Elizabethan England' (n 777) 171, 182.

910 Ibid.

911 Charles Tilly, *Coercion, Capital, and European States, AD 990–1990* (Basil Blackwell, 1990) 69.

912 CS Goldingham, 'The Expedition to Portugal, 1589' (1918) 63 *Royal United Services Institution Journal* 469, 472.

Goldingham, Drake's audacious and expensive defeat inconveniently strained England's otherwise friendly relations with Portuguese nobles at a time when the latter's support was material during the Anglo-Spanish War (1585–1604);[913] as punishment Drake was disgraced and stripped of his official military commands for the next half decade,[914] with his contemporary William Monson writing that '[Drake] was much blamed by the common consent of all men, the overthrow of the action being imputed to him'.[915] Throughout the sixteenth century, this dynamic continued with the Crown continuing to enforce this customary prohibition albeit in ways that protected its own advantage and interests. Ultimately, by 1799, we have a clear statement from the High Court of Admiralty emphasising the existence of a customary prohibition against private warfare. Specifically, in the case of *The Hoop*,[916] Sir William Scott (later known as Lord Stowell) held that 'by the law and custom of this country the Sovereign alone has the power of declaring war and peace'.

The role of the BEIC and other trading companies founded by royal charter, is another fascinating case study which engages with how the British Crown exploited private military actors in return for categorising their foreign expeditions as outside the prohibition against private warfare. As described by the Baron Macaulay (Secretary at War from 1839–41), the BEIC was at its height 'a joint stock society of traders … entrusted with the sovereignty of a larger population, the disposal of a larger clear revenue, the command of a larger army, than are under the direct management of the Executive Government of the United Kingdom'.[917] Indeed the royal charter of the BEIC gave it a specific right to wage war on foreign entities,[918] which appeared to erode the established prohibition on private warfare. This was a right that the military commanders of the BEIC would go on to utilise extensively, from the Carnatic

913 Ibid, 474.

914 See John Sugden, *Sir Francis Drake* (Random House, 2012) 285.

915 M Oppenheim (ed), *The Naval Tracts of Sir William Monson* (1902), vol I, 178. See also RB Wernham, *Expedition of Sir John Norris and Sir Francis Drake to Spain and Portugal, 1589* (Routledge, 2020) lxiv.

916 *The Hoop* (1799) 1 C Rob 196, as discussed in Arnold D McNair, 'The Legal Meaning of War, and the Relation of War to Reprisals' (n 887) 29, 47.

917 Philip J Stern, *The Company-State: Corporate Sovereignty and the Early Modern Foundations of the British Empire in India* (Oxford University Press, 2012) 3.

918 Philip J Stern, 'The English East India Company and the Modern Corporation: Legacies, Lessons, and Limitations' (2015) 39(2) *Seattle University Law Review* 423, 433. See also: Michael Mulligan, 'The East India Company: Non-State Actor as Treaty Maker' in James Summers and Alex Gough, *Non-State Actors and International Obligations: Creation, Evolution and Enforcement* (Brill, 2018) 39, 39; DP O'Connell, 'International Law and Boundary Disputes' (n 349) 77, 81.

Wars (1744–1763) in central India to the conquest of Naning (1831–2) in Malaya among many others.[919] An observation of the conduct of Robert Fullerton, the BEIC Governor of the Straits Settlements (1826–30) indicates that he did not view initiating the Naning War as a contravention of the British custom against private warfare.[920]

The challenge to the customary prohibition is also evident when observing case law at the time such as the *Nabob of the Carnatic v East India Company* (1791),[921] where the Chancery held that the wars and treaties engaged by the BEIC were potentially beyond the jurisdiction of the courts.

> by the law and municipal constitution of this country the Company having a right to make war for the defence and melioration of their trade, are advised, that they being armed by the charters and municipal authority of this country with that power, stand in all respects relating to the exercise of it in the same condition as if sovereigns.[922]

Curiously this position had been previously supported by the international lawyer and just war proponent Hugo Grotius (1583–1645), whose views on the war-making capacity of corporations are important to note given his influence on the unwritten customs of war considered by pre-Modern English commanders and their later Imperial successors.[923] In particular, Grotius offered a compromise position that a corporation's ability to wage private wars and its jurisdictional fluidity was not a contravention of the Crown's sovereign authority as it was acting as an agent of said Crown:[924]

---

919 For more on the Carnatic Wars, see, eg: GJ Bryant, 'The War in the Carnatic' (Brill, 2012); Swati Srivastava, 'Corporate Sovereign Awakening and the Making of Modern State Sovereignty: New Archival Evidence from the English East India Company' (2022) 76(3) *International Organization* 690. For further scholarship on the Naning War, see, eg: Siti Maisarah Bakar and Zulkarnain Abdul Rahman, 'Pentadbiran Naning Sebelum 1832' (2017) 44(1) *Malaysian Journal of History, Politics & Strategic Studies* 89, 89–118; Shaun Adam, *Acts of Resistance: Dol Said and the Naning War* (Gerakbudaya Enterprise, 2022).

920 Emrys Chew, 'The Naning War, 1831–1832: Colonial Authority and Malay Resistance in the Early Period of British Expansion' (1998) 32(2) *Modern Asian Studies* 351, 354, citing Straits Settlements Records, A 33, 13 March 1827.

921 *Nabob of the Carnatic v East India Company* (1791) 30 Eng Rep 391.

922 Francis Vesey, *Reports of Cases Argued and Determined in the High Court Of Chancery from the Year MDCCLXXXIX To MDCCCXVII* (Little & Brown, 1844) 389, citing ibid. See also Philip J Stern, 'The English East India Company and the Modern Corporation: Legacies, Lessons, and Limitations' (n 918) 423, 434.

923 GR Rubin, 'Parliament, Prerogative and Military Law: Who had Legal Authority over the Army in the Later Nineteenth Century' (n 479) 45, 46.

924 Rotem Giladi, 'Corporate Belligerency and the Delegation Theory from Grotius to Westlake Grotius on the Use of Force: Perfect, Imperfect and Civil Wars' (2020) 41(2) *Grotiana* 349, 358.

> Nature — the mistress and sovereign authority in this matter — withholds from no human being the right to carry on private wars; and therefore, no one will maintain that the East India Company is excluded from the exercise of that privilege, since whatever is right for single individuals is likewise right for a number of individuals acting as a group.[925]

In doing so, Grotius pointed to how the Company's power to wage war was conferred by royal charter, as opposed to an independent, inheritable right to private warfare as historically enjoyed by English barons. Eventually, this confusing departure from the otherwise developed State-centric would be resolved by the official dissolution of the BEIC in 1858 and the complete integration of its territories into the wider British Empire. This new reality was illustrated by the view taken by the pioneering British international lawyer John Westlake in 1894, when he wrote in his *Chapters on the Principles of International Law* that the relations of the BEIC was in fact 'those of the parent state' and where 'the company is engaged in hostilities with a foreign state or a company created by a foreign state, there is war defacto between England and the state in question'.[926] Rather disappointedly for our purposes, as reflected on by Giladi, Westlake argued that this had always been the position and that the BEIC's nature had never actually challenged the Crown's exclusive prerogative to make war.[927]

As the colonial frontier expanded, and the overseas theatres of war were waged increasingly further away from the Colonial and Foreign Offices in the Imperial metropole,[928] the scope of this prohibition altered. By the time of British High Imperialism (from 1850 onwards)[929] and assertive military expansion, as opposed to the previous Age of Commerce[930] and its higher focus on trade, the main issues in this space are the treatment of settler violence against indigenous peoples and how the prohibition applied to the ability of colonial governors to declare war.

925 Hugo Grotius, *Commentary on the Law of Prize and Booty* (Martina Julia van Ittersum, 2006) 302. See also Philip J Stern, 'The English East India Company and the Modern Corporation: Legacies, Lessons, and Limitations' (n 918) 423, 437, 440.

926 John Westlake, *Chapters on the Principles of International Law* (n 164) 191–2.

927 Rotem Giladi, 'Corporate Belligerency and the Delegation Theory from Grotius to Westlake Grotius on the Use of Force: Perfect, Imperfect and Civil Wars' (n 924) 349, 351.

928 See generally Roger Long, *The Man on the Spot: Essays on British Empire History* (n 680).

929 See Anthony Reid, 'A New Phase of Commercial Expansion in Southeast Asia, 1760–1850' (n 442) 57, 57–82.

930 See, eg: Nordin Hussin, *Trade and Society in the Straits of Melaka: Dutch Melaka and English Penang, 1780–1830* (n 649); Ben Kiernan, 'Afterword: Settler Colonies, Ethno-Religious Violence and Historical Documentation: Comparative Reflections on Southeast Asia

As mentioned previously, settler violence (which had been a major issue in the Anglo occupation of Ireland since the twelfth century) always appeared to be outside the scope of the prohibition against private warfare. By the High Imperial period, martial law was often used to displace the application of international law and allow the exploitation of settlers as private actors who could indirectly expand British sovereignty through conflicts with indigenous peoples.[931] As reflected elsewhere in this book, this ties together to the broader notion that European customary laws of war did not automatically extend to non-Western peoples (such as the Naning Malays) in colonial conflicts.[932]

The wide reach of the late Empire, and associated logistical challenges that this created[933] resulted in a broad discretion to lead military expeditions had to be given to for colonial commanders or 'men on the spot' without explicit Parliamentary sanction.[934] This discretion was used regularly throughout the High Imperial period, as seen by the examples of Sir William Jervois in Perak (1875–7),[935] Lord Lytton in Afghanistan (1878), and Sir Henry Bartle Frere in Zululand (1879).[936] Again however, for the same reasons explained by Grotius with regards to the wars waged by companies under royal charter, these conflicts were not contraventions of the prohibition given that these commanders were not warmaking in their personal capacity; these were not mere private wars but instead public wars based on the powers transferred by the Crown to overseas Imperial agents such as Governors, Superintendents and Residents.[937]

---

and Ireland' in Micheál Ó Siochrú and Jane Ohlmeyer (eds), *Ireland: 1641* (Manchester University Press, 2013) 254, 255.

931 See, eg, Lyndall Ryan, 'Martial Law in the British Empire' in Philip Dwyer and Amanda Nettelbeck (eds), *Violence, Colonialism and Empire in the Modern World* (Palgrave Macmillan, 2018) 93, 101. See also Gareth Knapman, 'Settler Colonialism and Usurping Malay Sovereignty in Singapore' (2021) 52(3) *Journal of Southeast Asian Studies* 418, 420.

932 See, Frédéric Mégret, 'From "Savages" to "Unlawful Combatants": A Postcolonial Look at International Humanitarian Law's "Other"' (n 91) 265, 278–80.

933 Emrys Chew, 'The Naning War, 1831–1832: Colonial Authority and Malay Resistance in the Early Period of British Expansion' (n 681) 351, 381.

934 Frédéric Mégret, 'From "Savages" to "Unlawful Combatants": A Postcolonial Look at International Humanitarian Law's "Other"' (n 91) 265, 281–2.

935 See John S Galbraith, 'The "Turbulent Frontier" as a Factor in British Expansion' (n 92) 150, 161. See also C Northcote Parkinson, *British Intervention in Malaya 1867–1877* (n 90) 207–8, 230–1. See also Michelle Gordon, 'The Dynamics of British Colonial Violence' in Philip Dwyer and Amanda Nettelbeck (eds), *Violence, Colonialism and Empire in the Modern World* (Palgrave Macmillan, 2018) 153, 156.

936 See Damian O'Connor, 'Defending Australia: Imperial Expansion and Local Defence' (n 89) 5, 14.

937 See John Collins, *Martial Law and English Laws, c1500–c1700* (n 64) 282–3.

Surridge's description of the discretion afforded to the Governors of Gold coast and Nigerian colonies illustrates this well.[938]

However, despite the significant discretion provided to these men on the spot,[939] they still faced disgrace and censure by Parliament for complacency. Notably, in much the same way that Sir Francis Drake had been condemned by the Privy Council in 1589 for his Lisbon expedition, Sir William FD Jervois (Governor of the Straits Settlements from 1875–7)[940] was denounced in the House of Lords for 'having gone beyond [their] instructions'[941] during the Perak War (1875–6) in Malaya.

When we take a step back from our musings to look more deeply at how Imperial military commanders perceived of the prohibition against private warfare prior to the 1899 (first) *Hague Convention*, it seems clear that they would have taken the view that it was fully crystallised and binding on their conduct. By then, the era of subordinates to the British Crown waging wars in their own right had long ceased to be a reality; even the last gasp of private corporate war-making already being re-written to support the uneroded existence of the prohibition. Instead, the uncertainties lie in how the scope of the custom extended to settler violence and the treatment of non-Western peoples. Based on the information we have considered, and the general argument of this text that specific customary prohibitions on wartime conduct were not automatically extended to non-Western peoples and instead dependent on consistent application, it does seem that private wars against non-Western entities were prohibited — but that settler violence was conveniently viewed as outside the breadth of this custom.

938 Keith Surridge, 'The Politics of War: Lord Kitchener and the Settlement of the South African War, 1901–1902' (n 684) 213, 215. See also, T Lloyd, 'Africa and Hobson's Imperialism' (n 684) 130, 130–53.

939 See, eg, Frédéric Mégret, 'From "Savages" to "Unlawful Combatants": A Postcolonial Look at International Humanitarian Law's "Other"' (n 91) 265, 281–2.

940 John S Galbraith, 'The "Turbulent Frontier" as a Factor in British Expansion' (n 92), 150, 161.

941 See United Kingdom, *Parliamentary Debates*, House of Lords, 3 July 1876, vol 230, col 827 (Lord Stanley of Alderly). See also: United Kingdom, *Parliamentary Debates*, House of Lords, 3 July 1876, vol 230, col 839 (Earl of Carnarvon); United Kingdom, *Parliamentary Debates*, House of Lords, 3 July 1876, vol 230, col 844 (Earl of Kimberley).

Conclusion

The modern laws of war are the result of a centuries long process, which tacitly acknowledges the inevitably of conflict, while attempting to place limitations on battlefield conduct. They have evolved from customary norms and agreements between warring European actors to a universally accepted body of international law, underpinned by the 1949 *Geneva Conventions* and the three 1977 *Additional Protocols*. In this respect, the modern laws of war exist as an uneasy reconciliation between principles of distinction, proportionality and humanitarianism, on the one hand, and military necessity on the other. Yet it is clear that these did not just emerge, without historical precedence. This book has shown that these laws of war were grounded in a particular time period; a particular stratified society; and a particular backdrop of colonisation.

Part 1 of this book highlighted that the modern laws of war were also an integral foundation of nineteenth century efforts to establish and maintain order within the then emerging international society of states. Membership was conditional: only 'civilised' states were permitted entry into international society and even modern compliance seems built around these regional blocks and original membership.[942] Part 1 reinforced that these rules, whilst still pervasive but implicit within international law, were explicit and heavily relied upon. The shift only came (realistically) against the growing distaste for colonialism that the horrors of Nuremberg demonstrated.[943] Nazism was simply colonial practice in Europe. What Hitler had done, Césaire wrote, was to apply to Europe 'colonialist procedures which until then had been reserved exclusively for the Arabs of Algeria, the 'coolies' of India, and the 'niggers' of Africa'.[944]

Yet as this work has made clear, exceptions did arise in frontier conflicts due to the dictates of the principles of humanity. In Part 2 of this work, these customary prohibitions (on executions, sexual violence, perfidy, slavery and forced movement, unnecessary looting of cultural property, brigandry, deportation and private warfare) were found to be crystallised or developing in customary law during the era of colonisation. Customary law and identifying moments of crystallisation has no articulated, clear formula. Yet the legal history process

942 Tanisha M Fazal and Brooke C Greene, 'A Particular Difference: European Identity and Civilian Targeting' (n 192) 829, 830.

943 Even as late as the 1930s, European nations were using chemical weapons against the 'fantatics' of the Other; see Pascal Daudin, 'The Rif War: a forgotten war?' (2023) 105 *International Review of the Red Cross* 914–946.

944 Aimé Césaire, *Discourse on Colonialism*, tr Joan Pinkham (Monthly Review Press, 1972) 14.

 | DOI:10.1163/9789004515987_013

undertaken in Part 2 has shown seven clear trends, and further studies will likely identify more.

It is important, for some discussions around the othering of international humanitarian law are perfunctory in their analysis of how the 'other' was actually included.[945] Without a doubt, discussions around IHL still refer to the 'the standard of civilisation' — be it from operators on the ground bemoaning the application of IHL to those viewed as too 'backward to apply it' or in 'othering' those from different civilisation blocs. This fundamentally goes to the heart and original sin of IHL; but there is a different story to be told, read between the lines. The principles of humanity have always existed within the customs and laws of war; from the ordinances of medieval Europe through to the modern era. They are found in all the different legal systems as they have evolved over time, aiming to regulate warfare. Jean Pictet, one of the most famous scholars and practitioners of the laws of war addressed the universality of what he titled 'international humanitarian law'. He held that

> humanitarian principles are common to all human communities wherever they may be. When different customs, ethics and philosophies are gathered for comparison, and when they are melted down, their particularities eliminated and only what is general extracted, one is left with a pure substance which is the heritage of all mankind.[946]

What is this 'pure substance'? Some works have tried to engage with the question, in isolation. For the most part they have either been through the International Review of the Red Cross, or in association with the International Committee of the Red Cross. Publications outside the English language have impacted the accessibility of some other publications. *The Laws of Yesterday's Wars* is the first systematic approach to the question posed by Pictet. Every chapter, in every volume, is a 'dataset'. The secondary research questions emerge then from having wider 'datasets' to find patterns in. Whilst approaching a critical mass of comparative case studies, we can begin to use *The Laws of Yesterday's Wars* as a resource to try address some of the more difficult questions in international humanitarian law through a truly international lens: who should be considered directly participating in hostilities? Is there

945 Doreen Lustig, 'Governance Histories of International Law' (n 230) 859, 859–882.

946 Jean Pictet, 'Humanitarian Ideas Shared by Different Schools of Thought and Cultural Traditions' (n 100) 3, 4.

a historical argument for 'sharp war'? Have the laws of war sought to protect non-combatants, or empower combatants? When does the principle of military necessity find a limit?

These datasets highlight the folly of the 'straight line history of eternal progression',[947] where a Great White Man (Grotius, Vitoria, Augustine) discovered international law and it was developed progressively into the modern era. For many parts of *European* law, this is without a doubt correct — read the chapters spread across *The Laws of Yesterday's Wars* on the progression of Roman,[948] Medieval,[949] and Renaissance[950] laws of war and how they shaped the framework of the American Civil War.[951] This 'straight line' can be extrapolated, and explains many of the findings in the customary international humanitarian law database of the ICRC. The risk of this methodology was championed in 1795 by Robert War, when he wrote:

> We expected too much when we contended for the *universality* of the duties laid down by the Codes of the Laws of Nations ... however desirable such universality might be ... what is commonly called the Law of Nations ... is not the Law of *all* Nations but only of particular classes of them; and thus there may be a *different* Law of Nations for *different* parts of the globe.[952]

Ensuring respect for IHL — which Common Article 1 commands, and the ICRC obligates — does not mean we are exempt from critical judgment. Universality does not mean unanimity. Within North-Eastern America, as Professor Wayne E. Lee wrote:

> A prisoner, particularly an adult male, became the target for their captors' rage and grief at their other losses. Elaborate and extended rituals of torture unto death existed in many of the Eastern Woodland cultures. Scholars continue to struggle to understand their exact meaning, but it

947 Alonso Dunkelberg, 'It's a Trap! Re-Thinking Samuel Moyn's *Humane* Beyond the North Atlantic' (n 256) 345–360.

948 Samuel White, 'Roman Laws of War' (n 257).

949 Samuel White 'The Late Middle Ages' (n 258) 101–127.

950 Kyle Walker, 'The Renaissance' (n 259) 127–150.

951 Christopher Bailey, 'Code of Necessity — Lawfare During the United States Civil War' in Samuel White (ed.) *The Laws of Yesterday's Wars* (Brill Njihoff, 2021) 187–209.

952 *Enquiry into the Foundation and History of the Law of Nations in Europe* (London, 1795) 1, XIII, XIV and 169.

> is clear that at the center of the process was a tremendous outpouring of violent grief—an outpouring in which the whole town, men, women, and children—participated. Native prisoners were well aware of what awaited them, and sought to remain impassive in the face of excruciatingly inventive torture. Not crying out certified their personal bravery, and some captor tribes sought to partake of that bravery through a ritual cannibalism in which they imbibed the courage and spirit of their prisoner.[953]

The prohibition on the mutilation of dead bodies, then, would seem to have not been found within this cultural practice. It supports the wider academic discussion that it is too far to claim, as some have, that:

> the foundations of international humanitarian law, or at least their equivalents, are thus found in the major cultural systems on our planet: the right to life, the right to physical integrity, the prohibition on slavery, and the right to fair legal treatment.[954]

It is hard to argue that Mongol culture — one of the largest Empires in history — somehow guaranteed the right to life, physical integrity, freedom of body and fair legal treatment. It was characterised by pillaging, summary executions, denial of quarter, sexual violence, hostage taking, and environmental destruction. Yet it did not exist in a legal desert; as underpinning all Mongol conduct was a fundamental custom: the great principle (*yeke*).

The ICRC's *Roots of Restraint* found that the law can play a crucial standard-setting role, but 'that encouraging individuals to internalise the values the law represents through socialization is a more durable way of promoting restraint'.[955] A continuous cycle of violations of the law appears less likely if the legal norms of IHL are central to an individual's identity and honour. Against this background, identifying the historical and contemporary reference points for values equivalent to IHL can increase the influence of arguments for restraint.[956]

953 Wayne E Lee, 'Eastern Native American Laws of War' in Samuel White (ed) *The Laws of Yesterday's Wars: Volume II* (n 264) 146, 146–182.

954 Marco Sassòli, Antoine Bouvier and Anne Quintin, *How Does Law Protect in War?* (ICRC, 3rd ed) vol 1, 6.

955 Fiona Terry and Brian McQuinn, *Roots of Restraint in War* (ICRC, Report, 2018) 65.

956 Ibid.

Across nearly every culture, the fundamental & foundational custom of keeping one's word is apparent. It is the 'pure substance' Pictet was hinting at — the heritage of all mankind. Breaking rules resulted in payback within First Nation Australians; the concept legitimacy and justice —*junkarti* ('straight' in Lardil); *dalgi giban* ('to make even' in Wiradyuri); makaratta ('coming together after a struggle' in Yolngu); *yorrp-ba* ('to fall out and rejoin' in Wagiman); or *warnmala* ('to seek balance' in Pitjantjatjara). Payback provided an exact, tit-for-tat reciprocity for past actions,[957] ensuring equity and helping curb the violence and brutality of warfare. Within New Zealand, the *Treaty of Waitangi* provided a clear legal framework for humane treatment. The repeated breaches of it during the Maori Wars (1845–72) was recgonised both at the time, and in subsequent formal apologies from the Crown, as being 'unwarranted' and 'unjust'.[958] Maintaining honour upon capture was so fundamental to Mexica warriors that upon their release by Spanish *conquistadors,* the *maltin* (captured foes) 'indignantly rejected the offer of release and demanded to be sacrificed'.[959] For those Scandinavian raiders known to history as Vikings, trickery and deception added to, rather than subtracted from, honour.[960] Yet honour still was core to warfare. The poem *Hávamál,* containing Odin's wisdom, demonstrates this:

> Cattle die, | and kinsmen die,
> And so one dies one's self;
> But a noble name | will never die,
> If good renown one gets.
>
> Cattle die, | and kinsmen die,
> And so one dies one's self;
> One thing now | that never dies,
> The fame of a dead man's deeds.[961]

Good renown was fundamental to warfare in the *Mahābhārata,* and as Zuzana notes 'A just war, *dharmayuddha,* is more about the means of warfare than

957 Ray Kerkhove & Samuel White, 'Indigenous Australians' in Samuel White (ed), *The Laws of Yesterday's Wars* (n 90) 3–44.

958 *Ngai Tāmanuhiri Claims Settlement Act 2012*, s 7(2)(g).

959 Bernal Díaz, *The True History of the Conquest of New Spain* (Penguin, 2009) 15.

960 Andrew Butler, 'Viking Laws of War' in Samuel White (ed), *The Laws of Yesterday's Wars* (n 90) 150–171.

961 *Hávamál,* Verses 77–78 in Henry Adams Bellows, *The Poetic Edda: Translated from the Icelandic with an introduction and notes by Henry Adams Bellows* (The American-Scandinavian Foundation, 1923), 44.

about the causes of a battle. The most important underlying rule of ancient Indian warfare is the idea of fairness.'[962] So too did Carthaginian and Hellenic custom elevate honor in warfare. *Timē* is one manifestation of the fundamental custom. The idea signals a need to retain a certain reputation — for effectiveness, ruthlessness, vengefulness but above all trustworthiness.[963] *Timē* is the idea of credibility; it is the act of generating a reputation, through a strong record, of being credible. For the Romans, it is the concept of *fides publica*; the breach of which was the grievous crime that Julius Caesar was to be recalled and punished for.[964] Qur'anic revelations ensure that conduct in war is not unlimited; it must be fought with credibility and to protect *al-mustaḍʿafīn.*[965] Divine approval, and operating within a framework of rules, is fundamental to those of the Book. Although endemic within the North American continent, Professor Wayne Lee highlights that the blood revenge system (similar to First Nations Australians) curbed violence. This was done through structure (such as the divide between peace and war chiefs) as well as spiritual means.[966] Remaining spiritually pure required abiding by the great principle of honour, and acted as a check against sexual excesses.[967] *Bushido* — the all-encompassing code of conduct for a specific class of warriors in Japan — sought to induce compliance with the great principle across all areas of life.[968] Wider research into African customs of warfare, subsequent to the publication of Dr Mutuma's and Dr Massingham's chapter in *The Laws of Yesterday's Wars*, has focused on the principle of *Ubuntu* — polylinguistic term that can be roughly translated as 'the belief in a universal bond of sharing that connects all humanity', underlying African traditions.[969]

Within the Highlands of Papua New Guinea, proverbs governing conflict highlight the underlying humanity laws of war sought to achieve: 'you live long if you plan the death of a pig, but not if you plan the death of a man'.[970]

962 Zuzana Spicova, 'Ancient Indian Laws of War' (n 264) 5–45.

963 David Feeny, 'Carthaginian Laws of War' in Samuel White (ed), *The Laws of Yesterday's Wars: Volume II* (n 257) 45–110.

964 Samuel White, 'Roman Laws of War' (n 257) 110, 117.

965 *Qur'ān* 4:75–76.

966 Wayne E Lee, 'Eastern Native American Laws of War (n 953) 146–183.

967 Ibid 166.

968 Anna Kretowicz, 'Japanese Laws of War' in Samuel White (ed), *The Laws of Yesterday's Wars: Volume II* (n 257) 183–214.

969 Kenneth Mutuma and Eve Massingham, 'East African Laws of War' in Samuel White (ed), *The Laws of Yesterday's Wars: Volume II* (n 257) 214, 214–220.

970 Emily Defina, 'Highland Papua New Guinea Laws of War' in Samuel White (ed), *The Laws of Yesterday's Wars 3: From Highland New Guinea to the Island of Malta* (Brill, 2024) 12.

Humans are recognised for the thing that makes them special — their humanity. This is in stark contrast to the Abrahamic concept of de-humanising one's foe. As Jonathan Shay, classicist and combat trauma psychologist notes:

> Twentieth-century nationalism has taken over the biblical tendency to measure loyalty by how vehemently one dehumanizes the enemy. When American soldiers and their commanders in Vietnam debased the enemy, they echoed very ancient proofs of their faith in God and of their own religious merit. ... The Judeo-Christian (and Islamic) world view has triumphed ... that dishonouring the enemy now seems natural, virtuous, patriotic, pious.[971]

This was expanded upon in the conclusion to Volume 2; however, its Eurocentricity is reinforced through Volume 3. So too did Chenggis' *anda,* Jamugha compare his breach of faith as that of an anima:

> What good would I be as your ally?
> I'd only invade your thoughts,
> Like a louse on your collar,
> Like a thorn under your shirt
> I went wrong when I strove to be a better man than my anda,
> It is I whose reached the end of his days.

Honour underpinned the *ankam*, and respect for the 12 year cycle brought a unique form of conflict-resolution along the Malabar coast. Dr Angeline Lewis outlined expertly the concept of *adat,* the importance of which cannot be understanded. The Malay idiom '*biar mati anak, jangan mati* adat' [better your children die than your *adat*] shows the extent to which *adat* is important to Malay people.[972] To this end, Rule 144 of the ICRC CIHL study seems clearly based in custom:

> States may not encourage violations of international humanitarian law by parties to an armed conflict. They must exert their influence, to the degree possible, to stop violations of international humanitarian law.

---

971 Jonathan Shay, *Achilles in Vietnam* (Simon & Schuster, 1995) 115.

972 Salihahs Razak and Arba'ie Sujud, 'Penerapan Undang-Undang Adat Terhadap Kesalahan Sahsiah pada Zaman Kesultanan Melayu' [The Application of Customary Laws against Negative Personality Traits during the Malay Sultanate Era] (2016) 2 *EDUCATUM Journal of Social Science* 16, 17.

Such a customary principle is based upon Common Article 1. Modern international humanitarian law demonstrates a constant, consistent desire to regulate warfare in increasingly humane ways. There has been a fusion of the laws of Geneva (to protect wounded) and the laws of the Hague (to regulate weapons). History shows, both through individual case studies and clashes of cultures, that rules will always be created to regulate warfare. Fundamental to this is the idea of *pacta sunt servanda*: agreements must be kept. Yet as Stanley Baldwin captured, these conventions will often break down in the test of warfare:

> If a man has a potential weapon and has his back to the wall and is going to be killed, he will use that weapon whatever it is and whatever undertaking he has given about it. Experience has shown us that the stern test of war will break down all conventions.[973]

This philosophical underpinning is core to the idea of sharp war, discussed in Volume 2.[974] Yet what these additional chapters have demonstrated is that the existence of rules, seeking to regulate warfare, is a resilient concept. Whilst intended to challenge the laws of war, this work find itself legitimising their existence through a historical lens; indeed, the very *existence* of rules was core to the concept of warfare. It supports the final proposition then that man indeed 'is not a "wolf to his fellow men" — *homo homini lupus* — as the comedian [Plautus] says, but a fellow.'[975]

---

973 Prime Minister Stanley Baldwin, United Kingdom, House of Commons, *Debates* (November 10, 1932) Cols 631–38.

974 Samuel White, 'Conclusion' in Samuel White (ed), *The Laws of Yesterday's Wars: Volume II* (n 257) 242–255.

975 Francisco de Vitoria, *Political Writings* (n 300) 278.

Index

www.ingramcontent.com/pod-product-compliance
Lightning Source LLC
LaVergne TN
LVHW012051011026
849162LV00017B/144
9789004515970